EARLY SETTLERS

OF

BARBOUR COUNTY,

ALABAMA

VOLUMES I & II

I0093242

COMPILED BY:

MARIE H. GODFREY

Copyright 1979
    By: The Rev. Silas Emmett Lucas, Jr.

All rights reserved. No part of this publication may be reproduced,
stored in a retrieval system or transmitted in any form or by any means
without the prior permission of the publisher.

Please direct all correspondence and orders to:

SOUTHERN HISTORICAL PRESS, Inc.
PO BOX 1267
375 West Broad Street
Greenville, SC 29601
ISBN: 978-0-89308-160-7

FOREWORD

Barbour Co., Ala. was formed in 1832 from parts of Pike and
Henry Counties and from Creek Indian Lands. The Indian boundary
line ran from the Southeastern corner of the present Barbour Co.
near the Henry Co. line to the Northwestern corner of Barbour Co.
near the present Bullock Co. line. Most of the settlements and
all of the land patents before 1832 lay below this line. The
Creek Indian War of 1836 was the result of disputes over the land
that lay Northeast of the boundary line. After the Civil War,
part of Bullock Co. was formed from the Northwestern section of
Barbour Co., and part of Russell Co. was formed from the North-
eastern section of Barbour Co.

Land could be entered (patented) in fractional sections of
forty acres by paying a nominal price per acre at the U. S. Patent Office at Sparta, Ala.. Some families lived on their land
for many years before securing a patent, and for that reason,
some of the earliest settlers are not included in this book.
The families included here were issued a patent by 1829. In several instances, men became dissatisfied and moved shortly after
receiving their patent.

There were two men who speculated in land in Barbour Co. who
are not included in this book as they did not actually live here.
One was John B. Jones, who entered at least 26 quarter-sections
between 1827 and 1832. The other was Phillip J. Weaver of Dallas
Co., Ala., who entered at least 18 quarter-sections in 1829.

The purpose of this book is to give some family information
about the early settlers, gathered primarily from the Barbour Co.
probate records, census records, newspaper abstracts, cemetery
records and descendants of these families. All dates and places

are in Barbour Co. unless marked otherwise. There are errors, and for this, I apologize. Many families are incomplete, but the records on them could not be found in this area. My sincere appreciation goes to all the descendants who shared their information. Without their help, this book could not have been compiled.

TABLE OF CONTENTS

ADAMS

Samuel Good Brooke Adams, b. 22 Jan. 1797 N. C., d. 6 March 1860 Macon Co., Ala., m. Margaret Hobdy. She was born 27 April 1807 N. C., died 24 Nov. 1834 - daughter of Edmund and Nancy (Harrel) Hobdy. Known Issue:

1. Lydia Ann Adams, b. 15 May 1825, m. Angus McBryde. Probable issue:

   a. Margaret Jane McBryde

   b. John Adams McBryde

2. John Hobdy Adams, b. 13 Dec. 1827 Ala.

3. Nancy Adams, b. 11 Jan. 1830 Ala., m. Nelson Johnson, who died Aug. 1848. Probable issue:

   a. Nelson Hobdy Johnson

4. Synthia Jane Adams, b. 15 Sept. 1832 Ala., m. Calvin Waits.

Sources of information:

Barbour Co., Ala. Probate Records
Macon Co., Ala. Probate Records
Hobdy family Bible
Macon Co., Ala. Census Records

BALL

Hartwell Ball entered land near Louisville from 1829 through 1839. Wade Ball entered land South of Batesville in 1836. There is nothing in the records to indicate that they were related.

In 1838, the household of Hartwell Ball consisted of 1 male under 21, 2 males over 21, 1 female over 21 and 8 slaves. In 1840, it consisted of 1 male 10/15, 1 male 15/20, 1 male 30/40 and 8 slaves. On 30 Oct. 1840, Hartwell Ball m. Jincy McCall. The last record of Hartwell Ball is where he and his wife, Jincy, sold land to John Douglass on 3 Dec. 1840.

J. F. (John F.) Ball was enumerated in the 1840 Census with 1 male under 5, 1 male 20/30, 1 female under 5, 1 female 15/20 and 1 slave. He and Green Ball of Ga. (Stewart Co.?) were administrators of the estate of Wade H. Ball, who died in Barbour Co. by Sept. 1840. No heirs were named.

On 27 Dec. 1839, William R. Ball made a deed of trust to William B. Deloach, trustee for Edward, Louisa and Lavinia Ball, minor children of William R. Ball. On 1 May 1833, Jane Shield of Beaufort Dist., S. C. deeded her estate to Edward, Louisa and Lavinia Ball.

Edward Ball was born ca 1826 S. C., m. Harriet ----. In 1850, Lavinia Ball, b. ca 1830 S. C., was living in his home. Louisa Ball, b. ca 1827 S. C., m. John W. Johnson 18 Aug. 1844.

Sources of information:

Barbour Co., Ala. Probate Records
Barbour Co., Ala. Census Records

2

BEASLEY

There are fragmentary records of Beasley estates in Barbour Co. dating back to 1828, but they are too incomplete to give a clear family picture. They are included here in hopes that someone can make a family connection.

William Beasley died by 1828 (Barbour Co. not yet formed). His wife, Temperance, may have been Temperance Jackson (married 3 Dec. 1814 Baldwin Co., Ga.). Only the minor children are named as follows:

1. James Beasley, a minor in 1830, of age by 1833.
2. Randle J. Beasley, a minor in 1838.
3. Elizabeth Beasley, a minor in 1838.
4. Sarah Ann Beasley, a minor in 1838.
5. Susannah Beasley, died 8 Jan. 1833 while still a minor. Her administrators were Joshua Lister, Thomas Pugh and Robert Hobdy.
6. William Beasley, died or came of age between 1830 and 1833.
7. Charles Beasley (possibly).

Guardians of William Beasley's minor children were Jacinth Jackson (in 1828) - he had married Prudence Allums 26 May 1814 in Baldwin Co., Ga.; Randle Jackson (in 1830) and James Beasley (in 1834). Joshua Lister was administrator. For further data on JACKSON, see Vol. I, pages

Charity Beasley also died here by 1828. There is a bill of sale from her estate to Temperance Beasley and one to John Beasley for a slave each. There are also receipts from these two to the estate of William Beasley who died by 1828.

James Beasley died here ca 1836/7 - his wife may have been Elizabeth. Administrators were F. W. Pugh (in 1837), Elizabeth Beasley and Joshua Lister (in 1836) and John C. and William Beasley (in 1849). Heirs of this estate were:

3

1. John C. Beasley

2. Francis Green Beasley

3. Elefar Beasley

4. Jane Beasley

The last three were minors and half-brothers and sisters of John
C. Beasley. They and their mother moved to Texas, probably before 1840.

The 1830 Census of Pike Co., Ala. includes John, James, William, Charles and Mrs. Temperance Beasley as heads of households.
The 1832 Census of Barbour Co. includes only Joh, James, William
and Charles Beasley. Of these four, John (John G.), William
(William M.) and James are covered in this chapter. There is no
further record of Charles Beasley after 1840.

In 1831, John G. Beasley patented land between Clayton and
Louisville, near Pratts. In 1835, James and William Beasley
patented land nearby. John G. Beasley was born 11 May 1792,
probably in Anson Co., N. C., and died 24 July 1883 (?). He
married Martha Allums 9 March 1820 Baldwin Co., Ga. and they
migrated to Alabama in 1821. Martha Allums was born 4 Jan. 1802
Washington Co., Ga. and died 11 Aug. 1880. They are buried in
the Beasley family cemetery near Pratts. Issue:

1. James Tarplin Beasley, b. 22 Feb. 1821 Ala., d. 12 Aug. 1885
   Dale Co., Ala., m. Lucy Rebecca Efurd 12 Aug. 1844 (see
   EFURD, page 78).   She was born 11 Dec. 1826 Ala. and
   died 8 Oct. 1908 Dale Co., Ala.. They are buried in Center
   Ridge Cem., Dale Co., Ala.. Issue:

   a. Narcissa E. Beasley, b. 30 Nov. 1846 Ala., d. 24 Nov.
      1920, buried Center Ridge Cem.. She never married.

   b. Milton Columbus (?) Beasley, b. ca 1849 Ala., may have
      died young.

   c. Florence Beasley, b. 25 July 1855 Ala., d. 18 Oct. 1916,

4

buried Center Ridge Cem.. She never married.

d. James Tarplin Beasley, Jr., b. ca 1858 Ala., married
Frances Patterson.

e. John G. Beasley, b. 4 May 1861, d. 12 Aug. 1936, m.
(1) Cliffie Patterson (2) Emma (Ann?) Grice.

f. Martha Anna Beasley, b. 18 March 1866, d. 20 June 1947,
m. George Washington King 12 Jan. 1881, probably in
Dale Co., Ala.. He was born 29 Sept. 1858 Dale Co.,
Ala. and died 1 Oct. 1934 Geneva Co., Ala.. They are
buried in Providence Church Cem., Dale Co., Ala..

g. Francis Seymour Beasley, b. 27 Sept. 1868, d. 21 Oct.
1938, m. Martha Annie Metcalf.

h. Leona R. (Rebecca?) Beasley, b. 27 Feb. 1871, d. 28
Oct. 1960, m. John W. Powell. He was born 26 Oct. 1856
and died 1 Jan. 1933. They are buried in Center Ridge
Cem..

i. Thomas Ira Beasley, b. 23 May 1873, d. 7 Jan. 1950, m.
Mary Patience Grice. She was born 7 Feb. 1874 and died
28 Aug. 1966.

2. Daniel F. Beasley, b. 1 Nov. 1825 Pike Co., Ala., d. 30 April
1908, m. C. Jane Herring (daughter of West Herring) on 30
July 1850. She was born 22 Sept. 1833 and died 23 Jan. 1914.
They are buried in Balkum Cem. near Headland (Henry Co.),
Ala.. Issue:

a. Louisianna Beasley, b. ca 1852 Ala., may have married
Calvin L. McCall 15 Aug. 1869.

b. Mary Addie Beasley, b. ca 1843 Ala., may have married
Neill McGilvray 19 Jan. 1873 (see McGILVRAY,
page 183).

c. Eugenia T. Beasley, b. ca 1855 Ala.

d. Louis P. Beasley, b. ca 1859 Ala.

5

e. Alpheus W. Beasley, b. ca 1861 Ala.

f. Dora Beasley, b. ca 1865 Ala., may have married William
    Charles Floyd 31 Jan. 1882 (see FLOYD).

g. Thomas Osker Beasley, b. 16 Jan. 1868 Ala., d. 2 Jan.
    1934, buried Balkum Cem., Headland (Henry Co.), Ala.

3. Martha A. Beasley, b. ca 1825 Ala., m. Wiley Eidson 21 Jan.
    1849. He was born ca 1824 Ga.. In 1880, they were living
    in Panola Co., Texas - in 1883, they were living in Smith
    Co., Texas. Known issue:

    a. John Eidson, b. ca 1850 Ala.

    b. Harris Eidson, b. ca 1850 Ala.

    c. James L. Eidson, b. ca 1854 Ala.

    d. Mary Eidson, b. ca 1855 Ala.

    e. Rhoda Eidson, b. ca 1857 Ala.

    f. Martha Jane Eidson, b. ca 1860 Ala.

    g. Daniel Eidson, b. ca 1862 Ala.

4. Asa F. Beasley, b. ca 1826 Ala., d. before 1870, m. Sarah A.
    E. Anglin 8 July 1850. She was born ca 1833 Ala., died
    after 1880. Issue:

    a. Thomas Beasley, b. ca 1855 Ala.

    b. Effie (Martha?) Beasley, b. ca 1858 Ala., d. after 1884,
        m. J. B. Bynum 17 Jan. 1882.

    c. Zenobia Beasley, b. ca 1860 Ala., m. J. B. Standifer.

5. Nancy Beasley, b. ca 1830 Ala., d. by 1880, m. Daniel G.
    Beverly 25 Jan. 1849 - she was his second wife. Issue:
    By 1st wife:

    a. Mary Jane Beverly, b. ca 1838 N. C.

    b. Ann Eliza Beverly, b. ca 1840 N. C.

    c. Christian Newell Beverly, b. ca 1843 N. C.

    d. William Norman Beverly, b. ca 1846 Ala., may have mar-
        ried Mary C. Martin 26 Nov. 1874.

Mary Jane and Christian Newell Beverly were living with John
G. McLendon in 1860. Christian Newell Beverly married Angus McSwean 30 Aug. 1867 (see McSWEAN, **page 218**).

By 2nd wife:

e. Martha A. Beverly, b. ca 1850 Ala., probably died by
    1870.

f. John C. Beverly, b. ca 1852 Ala., died after 1880, pos-
    sibly married Nancy Ann Lee 20 Feb. 1884.

g. Elizabeth Beverly, b. ca 1853 Ala., not married 1880.

h. Barbara Ella Beverly, b. 13 Oct. 1854 Ala., d. 23 June
    1934, m. Daniel Norton 6 April 1871 (see NORTON).

i. Kate L. Beverly, b. 15 Apr. 1857, d. 23 Oct. 1927,
    never married. She is buried in Clayton Cem..

j. Callie M. Beverly, b. ca 1860, m. Robert Jimpsey Rich-
    ards 18 Jan. 1885 (see RICHARDS).

6. Mary A. Beasley, b. 24 Sept. 1831 Ala., d. 22 April 1910,
   m. Norman A. Norton 4 Nov. 1858 (see NORTON).

7. Barbara G. Beasley, b. ca 1834 Ala., d. ca 1905, m. John C.
   Beasley 12 May 1850. He was born 23 Oct. 1823 N. C., died
   8 Feb. 1864. They are buried in the Beasley family cemetery.
   John C. Beasley may have been a son of the James Beasley
   who died ca 1836/7. Issue:

a. Calhoun Beasley, b. ca 1851, d. ca 1940, not married in
    1880. He is buried in the family cemetery.

b. James Livingston Beasley, b. ca 1852, d. ca 1934, not
    married in 1880 - also buried in the family cemetery.

c. John G. Beasley, b. 10 April 1854, d. 24 July 1870,
    buried in the family cemetery.

d. Nancy J. Beasley, b. ca 1856, d. 22 Jan. 1921, never
    married. She is buried in the family cemetery.

e. Daniel F. J. Beasley, b. 26 Jan. 1855 Ala., d. 27

7

Nov. 1922, m. Vassie L. Bedsole (or Bledsoe) 26 Dec.
1889. She was born 13 Jan. 1870, died 4 Dec. 1959.
They are buried in Clayton Cem..

   f. Mary Ann Beasley, b. ca 1862, not married 1921.

   g. Joseph A. (or Josephine) Beasley, b. ca 1864 Ala., probably died young.

8. Ann Beasley, died by 1880, married ---- Shanks. In 1883,
her children were living in Texas. Known issue:

   a. Tiney T. Shanks, living in Milan Co., Texas 1883.

   b. DuBose Shanks

   c. Ella Shanks m. ---- Jones, living in Grimes Co.,
Texas in 1883.

   d. Fannie Shanks m. ---- Bracewell, living in Grimes Co.,
Texas in 1883.

   e. Jefferson J. Shanks, living in Grimes Co., Texas 1883.

   f. Missouri Shanks m. ---- Mulkey.

   g. Flournoy Shanks (possibly).

William M. Beasley was born 17 Nov. 1801 N. C., died 7 May
1877. He married Elizabeth Allums, who was born 29 Mar. 1814
Ga., died 6 Sept. 1902. They are buried in the family cemetery
near Pratts. Issue:

1. Martha Jane Beasley, b. ca 1832, d. after 1878, m. Simpson
S. Lindsey 8 Jan. 1846. He was born ca 1820 S. C.. Known
issue:

   a. William Lindsey, b. ca 1846 Ala.

   b. Elizabeth Lindsey, b. ca 1848 Ala., m. Anderson Allums
5 May 1869.

   c. Serepta Lindsey, b. ca 1850 Ala.

2. Daniel Beasley, b. ca 1833 Ala., d. by 1877, m. Malinda
M. Capel 14 May 1854. She was born ca 1835 Ga.. Issue:

   a. Catherine Beasley, b. ca 1855 Ala., not married 1880.

8

b. Ella Beasley, b. 13 Jan. 1857 Ala., m. Mack Rammage. They were living in Pike Co., Ala. in 1878.

c. James C. Beasley, b. ca 1859 Ala.

d. Mary A. Beasley, b. ca 1861 Ala.

3. Asa F. Beasley, b. ca 1834 Ala., probably died by 1878.

4. John W. Beasley, b. 2 Dec. 1836 Ala., d. 5 Sept. 1903, m. Martha Long in 1867. She was born 20 March 1844 Ala., died 16 July 1908. They are buried in the Beasley family cemetery. Issue:

a. Anna Beasley, b. ca 1867 Ala.

b. John Beasley, b. Oct. 1870 Ala.

c. Thomas Beasley, b. ca 1872 Ala.

d. James Beasley (?), b. ca 1874 Ala.

e. Willie Beasley, b. ca 1876 Ala.

f. Walter Beasley, b. ca 1877 Ala.

g. Henry Beasley (?), b. ca 1878 Ala.

5. William H. Beasley, b. ca 1838 Ala., m. Eliza A. McLean 20 Dec. 1865. She was born ca 1850 Ala.. Possible issue:

a. Charles Beasley, b. ca 1867 Ala.

b. George Beasley, b. ca 1870 Ala.

c. Mary Beasley, b. ca 1874 Ala.

d. Ellison Beasley, b. ca 1876 Ala.

6. James Beasley, b. ca 1842 Ala., probably died by 1878.

7. Mary Beasley, b. ca 1843 Ala., m. E. B. Beasley 18 Nov. 1869. They were living in Dale Co., Ala. in 1878.

8. Sarah Beasley, b. ca 1844 Ala., not married in 1878.

9. George W. Beasley, b. 16 May 1850 Ala., d. 3 Feb. 1921, m. Lavinia L. Brown 13 Nov. 1873. She was born 30 June 1858, died 3 June 1921. They are buried in Clayton Cem.. Issue:

a. Martin L. Beasley m. Julia Hurst 15 Nov. 1899.

b. Laura Beasley m. Philip Rosenburg 9 May 1901. In 1921,

they were living in Orlando, Fla..

10.   Arkansas Beasley, b. ca 1856.

Other sources:

Pea River Presbyterian Church Records
Henry Co., Ala. Cemetery Records
Baldwin Co., Ga. Marriage Records
Information from descendants

BEAUCHAMP

In 1829, William and Green Beauchamp (brothers) patented land just South of the Indian boundary line, in what was then Henry Co., Ala.. After the Indian land was opened for settlement, they both patented land North of the line, near old White Oak Station, by then Barbour Co., Ala..

The parents of Green and William Beauchamp were Littleton Beauchamp, a Revolutionary Soldier, and his wife, Nancy. He was born 25 May 1759 in Coventry Parish, Somerset Co., Maryland - son of Edmund Beauchamp, Jr. and his wife, Elizabeth; grandson of Edmund Beauchamp and Sarah Dixon; great-grandson of John Beauchamp of London, England.

Littleton Beauchamp and his family migrated to Baldwin Co., Ga. after the Revolution, later to Henry Co., Ala., where he died by 1822. Issue:

1. Rachael Beauchamp m. William Moore 12 April 1812 Baldwin Co., Ga..
2. Hetty Beauchamp m. Thomas Stubbs Kettler 11 July 1816 Baldwin Co., Ga..
3. William Beauchamp m. Nancy Perkins (see later).
4. Green Beauchamp m. Caroline Kennon (see later).
5. Labon Beauchamp m. Permelia Curry 18 Nov. 1819 Baldwin Co., Ga..
6. Sarah Beauchamp m. Hampton Ryan.

(From Beauchamp file, Ala. Department of Archives & History).
Note: 1850 Census of Barbour Co., Ala.

Ryan, Hampton, age 53, born Ga.

" , Rachael, age 54, born Ga.

" , Risdin B., age 28, born Ala.

On 4 Feb. 1852, Hampton Ryan m. Susannah Baker in Barbour Co.,

Ala.. He died 17 June 1869, at which time his wife was Susannah. Therefore, his marriage to Sarah Beauchamp should be investigated further before being accepted.

William Beauchamp, born 16 June 1792, d. 2 March 1845, buried in White Oak Station Cemetery, m. Nancy Perkins. (Note: Mrs. Nancy M. Beauchamp m. John C. Weaver 5 Feb. 1846 in Barbour Co., Ala., but there is nothing to prove she was the widow of William Beauchamp.) Issue:

1. Mary Ann C. Beauchamp, b. ca 1812, d. before 1883, m. (1) John W. Moore ca 1835 (2) Absolom T. Dawkins 18 Oct. 1849. Known issue: By 1st husband:

   a. William B. Moore

   b. Americus Moore

   c. James P. Moore, living in Pike Co., Ala. in 1884.

   d. Mary Ella Moore, living in Pike Co., Ala. in 1884.

   By 2nd husband:

   e. Frank Dawkins, living in Pike Co., Ala. in 1884.

   f. Augusta Dawkins, married and living in Texas in 1884.

2. Nancy Eliza Jane Beauchamp m. J. G. McKay and was living in Lafayette Co., Miss. in 1884.

3. Sarah Ann Amanda Beauchamp, b. 3 April 1822, d. 31 May 1890, buried Perote Cemetery, Bullock Co., Ala., m. Jesse Locke. Known issue:

   a. William H. Locke

   b. Michael B. Locke

   c. Andrew Locke.

4. Andrew Hammell Beauchamp, b. ca. 1827, d. between 1860 and 1883, m. (1) Sarah H. Lowman 28 May 1845. She was born 19 Dec. 1829, d. 2 May 1852, buried Wyecott Cemetery - daughter of John J. and Mary Lowman. He m. (2) Margaret E. Allen on 21 Feb. 1854. She was born 16 July 1836 in Kilbarchan, Scotland, died June 1886 at Eufaula, Ala. - daughter of

12

Dr. George L. and Janet Allen, who came to American in 1840. Known issue:

By 1st wife:

a. William H. Beauchamp, b. ca 1846, moved to Texas.

b. John L. Beauchamp, b. ca 1849, died before 1884.

By 2nd wife:

c. George A. Beauchamp

d. Florence M. Beauchamp

e. Clara Elizabeth Beauchamp m. William E. McCormick.

5. *Joseph S. Beauchamp, b. ca 1832 Ala., living in Freestone Co., Texas in 1884.

6. Henry M. Beauchamp, b. ca 1836 Ala., died before 1884, m. Rebecca R. Fenn 9 Nov. 1854. She was the daughter of Matthew Fenn. Known issue:

a. Mary M. Beauchamp m. Thomas J. Sheffield, living in Corsicana, Texas in 1884.

b. Lula F. Beauchamp, living in Miss. in 1884.

c. Matthew A. Beauchamp, b. ca 1864.

d. Sarah A. Beauchamp, b. ca 1864.

e. Calvin Beauchamp, b. ca 1870.

f. Henry Beauchamp, b. ca 1873.

g. Green Beauchamp, b. ca 1876.

7. *Thomas Beauchamp, b. ca 1837 Ala., living in Waynesville, Ga. in 1884.

8. Richard K. Beauchamp, b. ca 1838 Ala., living in Bluffton, Ga. in 1884.

Also buried in the cemetery at White Oak Station are:

William L. Beauchamp, b. 3 Feb. 1825, d. 18 Sept. 1843.

Asbury G. Beauchamp, b. 7 Feb. 1830, d. 21 Jan. 1838.

They were probably children of William and Nancy Beauchamp.

Green Beauchamp, b. Baldwin Co., Ga. ca 1801, died Barbour Co., Ala. 17 Dec. 1883, buried at White Oak Station Cemetery,

13

m. Caroline H. Kennon, probably at Ft. Gaines, Ga.. She was
born ca 1810 in Ga., died after 1884. They had no children, but
raised the orphans of his brother, William.

Note: In the 1850 Census of Barbour Co., Ala., Jane Kennon
(age 65, born Ga.) was living in the Green Beauchamp household.

Sources of information:

Probate records of Barbour and Henry Cos., Ala..
Cemetery records of Barbour and Bullock Co., Ala.
1850, 1860 and 1880 Census of Barbour Co., Ala.
"Alabama Series", Vol. II, by Helen S. Foley

*ADDITIONS & CORRECTIONS AS OF JUNE 1, 1979:

Joseph Sears Beauchamp, b. 26 March 1832, d. 13 Jan. 1912,
buried Midway Cem., Navarro Co., Texas, m. Sarah P. Blount 4
Sept. 1851 Macon Co., Ala.. She died 29 July 1913 and is buried
in Oak Dale Ce., Stephensville, Erath Co., Texas.

Thomas H. Beauchamp, age 63, died at his home in Montgomery
(Ala.) - formerly of Eufaula - buried in Troy (Pike Co., Ala.).
He leaves a wife and five children (Miss Susie Beauchamp and
Tom Beauchamp of Montgomery, Mrs. Drake of Atlanta, Mrs. Mabry
of Dothan and Mrs. Wood of Pronto.

BENNETT

Elizabeth Bennett, b. ca 1770 N. C., d. after 1850, was probably the wife of Luke Bennett, who was born ca 1760/70, died after 1840. Their children were Redmond Bennett (see later), Harriett Bennett (b. ca 1808, d. after Aug. 1859, m. Robert Mann, son of Gilbert Mann - no known issue), Ryan Bennett (see later), Siney Bennett (see later), Orren Bennett (b. ca 1824 Ala., not married in 1860 - no record after 1867 when he was admr. of the estate of his sister, Elizabeth Bennett) and Elizabeth Bennett (b. ca 1826/30 Ala., d. by Jan. 1859, never married).

Redmond Bennett, b. ca 1797 N. C., d. by June 1855, m. (1) unknown (2) Maryann E. Grant 7 May 1843. She was born ca 1815 S. C., died after 1855. Issue (by 1st wife):

1. George W. Bennett, b. ca 1832 Ala., d. after 1880, m. Susannah (Coston?). She was born ca 1835 S. C., died after 1880. Issue:

   a. Green J. Bennett, b. ca 1855 Ala.

   b. Ira Monroe Bennett, b. ca 1858 Ala., m. Eudoxia M. Hinson 11 Dec. 1870. In 1883, they were living in Arkadelphia, Arkansas.

   c. Worthy Bennett, b. ca 1860 Ala., not in 1870 or 1880 Census of Barbour Co..

   d. Willie A. Bennett, b. ca 1863 Ala., probably married Mary Hinson 18 Oct. 1883.

   e. Millie Ann Bennett, b. ca 1866 Ala.

   f. George Allen Bennett, b. ca 1868 Ala.

   g. Alice Bennett, b. ca 1871 Ala.

   h. Ryan Bennett, b. ca 1874 Ala.

   i. George (?) Bennett, b. ca 1878 Ala.

15

2. Elizabeth Bennett, b. ca 1834 Ala., d. after 1880, m. James Carr, Jr. 8 July 1852. He was born ca 1827 Fla., died Oct. 1882. Issue:

   a. Sarah C. Carr, b. ca 1853 Ala.

   b. Frances L. Carr, b. ca 1856 Ala., not married 1880.

   c. Michael W. Carr, b. ca 1859 Ala.

   d. William E. Carr, b. ca 1862 Ala.

   e. Martha E. J. Carr, b. ca 1864 Ala.

   f. James D. Carr, b. ca 1866 Ala.

   g. Emily M. Carr, b. ca 1868 Ala.

   h. Adelah V. Carr, b. ca 1871 Ala.

   i. Sophronia N. Carr, b. ca 1873 Ga.

   j. Mary R. M. Carr, b. ca 1876 Ga.

3. Wellborn Green Bennett, b. ca 1837 Ala., died by Feb. 1862, probably never married.

4. Sarah Bennett m. Allen Hutto 14 Oct. 1850. They were living in Florida in 1859 and in Coffee Co., Ala. in 1867.

5. Matilda (Henrietta?) Bennett, b. ca 1839 Ala..

6. Augustus Bennett, b. ca 1841 Ala., not in any Barbour Co. Census after 1860.

7. Elvira Bennett, b. ca 1843 Ala., m. R. B. Coleman 25 Nov. 1860. Known issue (from 1880 Census):

   a. Mattie E. L. Coleman, b. ca 1869 Ala.

   b. Eugenia Coleman, b. ca 1871 Ala.

   c. George W. Coleman, b. ca 1880 Ala..

Issue (by 2nd wife):

8. Amanda Bennett, b. ca 1845 Ala..

9. Joanna Bennett, b. ca 1847 Ala.

10. Zachariah Taylor Bennett, b. 1849 Ala., d. 1937, buried Union Baptist Church Cem..

11. Orren Bennett - minor in 1859.

16

Ryan Bennett, b. 1809 N. C., d. 12 Sept. 1883, buried Clayton Cem.. He m. (1) Emily Bishop 23 Dec. 1835 Henry Co., Ala., daughter of William and Nancy Bishop. She was born ca 1815 Ga., died between 1850 and 1854. He married (2) Margaret Daniel 7 Nov. 1854, who died by 1860. Issue:

1. Wesley G. Bennett, b. ca 1836 Ala.
2. William L. Bennett, b. ca 1838 Ala., d. after 1880, m. Henrietta Laseter 10 Jan. 1867. She was born ca 1847 Ga., died after 1880. They are buried in Union Baptist Church Cem., but no dates are given. Known issue (from 1880 Census):
   a. William J. Bennett, b. ca 1868 Ala., buried Union Baptist Church Cem. but no dates are given.
   b. Ryan Bennett, b. ca 1870 Ala.
   c. Elisha M. Bennett, b. ca 1872 Ala.
   d. Mary A. Bennett, b. ca 1876 Ala.
   e. Tommie Lou Bennett (female), b. ca 1879 Ala.
3. Elizabeth Bennett, b. ca 1840 Ala., d. after 1880, m. William T. I. C. Efurd 14 Aug. 1856 (maybe his second wife). He was born 27 Nov. 1826, d. 9 May 1894, buried Union Baptist Church Cem.. Known issue:
   a. Thomas R. Efurd, b. ca 1855 Ala.
   b. Martha S. Efurd, b. ca 1860 Ala.
   c. William Monroe Efurd, b. ca 1862 Ala., d. 1944, m. Jamie B. ----. She was born 1887 (?), died 1949. They are buried in Union Baptist Ch. Cem..
   d. Mary Emma Efurd, b. ca 1864 Ala.
   e. Sallie Efurd, b. ca 1866 Ala.
   f. Nancy Efurd, b. ca 1868 Ala.
   g. Joseph Efurd, b. Jan. 1870, probably died young.
   h. Jesse W. Efurd, b. 9 Sept. 1872 Ala., d. 17 Nov. 1949, m. N. Ann Blakey 3 Jan. 1901. She was born 10 Aug.

1872, died 3 Aug. 1924. Both are buried in Union Baptist Church Cem..

i. Annie Efurd, b. ca 1875 Ala.

j. Susan Efurd, b. ca 1877 Ala.

k. Hattie Efurd, b. 29 Oct. 1879 Ala., d. 23 Aug. 1914, m. George W. Blakey 16 Nov. 1898. He was born 29 Oct. 1871, died 12 Dec. 1913. Both are buried in Union Baptist Church Cem..

(Also see EFURD, page 78).

4. Martha Bennett, b. ca 1842 Ala., may have married J. E. Thomas 23 Oct. 1864.

5. Josiah (Joel?) Bennett, b. ca 1846 Ala., no record after 1860 Census.

6. Nancy Bennett, b. ca 1852 Ala., no record after 1860 Census.

7. Lucinda Bennett, b. 1853 Ala., d. 1941, m. John B. Laseter 24 Dec. 1879. He was born 1854 Ala., d. 1933. They are buried in Clayton Cem.. Issue:

a. W. Ray Laseter - living Jackson, Miss. ca 1939.

b. James Laseter (Rev.) m. Ina Neilson

c. John Foy Laseter m. Lola Millborn.

8. Jesse Bennett, b. ca 1857 Ala., not married in 1880.

Siney Bennett, b. ca 1815, m. Elisha Davis, who was born ca 1803 Ga.. Issue:

1. John Davis, b. ca 1834 Ala., m. Nancy Lott 15 Jan. 1856. She may have been nee Nancy Butts, widow of E. G. Lott (m. 2 March 1851).

2. Mason L. Davis, b. ca 1837 Ala., m. Martha C. Dunn 13 Dec. 1860.

3. Pleasant Davis (male), b. ca 1839 Ala.

4. Elizabeth Davis, b. ca 1841 Ala., not married 1870.

5. Vasti Davis, b. ca 1846 Ala., not married 1870.

18

6. Orren Davis, b. 1849 Ala., d. 1922, m. Carrie Crew 21 Nov. 1872. She was born 1856, died 1939. They are buried in Pea River Cem..

7. Sarah Ann Davis, b. ca 1849 Ala.

8. Adeline Davis, b. ca 1852 Ala.

There was also a James Bennett who came to Barbour Co. about 1847. His will was written 22 July 1849 in Macon Co., Ala. but was probated in 1852 in Barbour Co.. At the time of his death, his wife was Nancy Humphrey (m. 20 Aug. 1816 Jackson Co., Ga.?) She was his second wife. Issue (by 1st wife):

1. Nevel Bennett - living Hall Co., Ga. in 1852. He probably married Nancy Smith 26 Aug. 1830 in Hall Co., Ga.

2. Thomas B. Bennett, b. ca 1811 S. C., d. after 1857, m. Elizabeth ----.

3. Silas A. Bennett, b. ca 1812 Ga., d. after 1857, m. (1) unknown (2) Matilda ----.

4. Frances Ann Bennett m. John Owens - living in Ga. in 1857.

Issue (by 2nd wife):

5. Sarah M. Bennett, d. by 1857, m. Charles Floyd. In 1852, they were living in Chambers Co., Ala..

6. Louisa E. Bennett m. James Jones. They were living in Chambers Co., Ala. in 1852.

7. Rachael J. Bennett m. William S. Webb. They were living in Macon Co., Ala. in 1857.

8. James Alexander Bennett - he was living in Macon Co., Ala. in 1852 and in Pike Co., Ala. in 1857.

9. Nancy Catherine Bennett m. James Flournoy. They were living in Russell Co., Ala. in 1852.

10. Eli F. Bennett, b. 5 April 1828, d. 12 Sept. 1898, m. Flora C. ----. She was born 15 Nov. 1837, died 22 April 1900. They are buried in Williams Cem. in Pike Co., Ala.

19

11. William A. Bennett - living in Pike Co., Ala. in 1857.

12. Harriett Emeline Bennett m. John W. Robinson (or Robertson).
     They married in Macon Co., Ala. in 1851 and were living in
     Tallapoosa Co., Ala. in 1857. She was born 6 April 1833
     Anson Co., N. C., died 25 July 1884, buried China Grove Cem.,
     Pike Co., Ala.. He was born 20 May 1824, died 5 Dec. 1899
     and is buried in Brundidge Cem., Pike Co., Ala..

Other sources:

"History of Barbour Co., Ala." by Thompson
Troy (Pike Co., Ala.) Messenger
Pike Co., Ala. Cem. Records.

BIZZELL

Bennett Bizzell was born ca 1775 N. C., died by June 1851, married Mary ----, who was born ca 1785 S. C., also died by June 1851. They may have been living in Darlington Co., S. C. in 1810. Known issue:

1. Henry N. Bizzell, b. ca 1810 S. C., d. by May 1856, m. (1) Cassandra Faulk ca 1832 (see FAULK, **page 86**). He m. (2) Mary ---- ca 1845. She was born ca 1827 Ala., died after July 1856. Issue:

   By 1st wife:

   a. Henry B. H. Bizzell, b. ca 1834 Ala., m. Sarah ---- ca 1852.

   b. James Curtis Bizzell, b. ca 1835 Ala., m. Mahala W. Bizzell 16 Feb. 1865, daughter of Harrison F. Bizzell.

   c. Mary Jenette Bizzell, b. ca 1840 Ala., may have married James W. Danner 15 Oct. 1857.

   By 2nd wife:

   d. Sarah Elizabeth Bizzell, b. ca 1847 Ala..

   e. Zachariah W. Bizzell, b. ca 1849 Ala.

   f. J. N. Bizzell

   g. William W. Bizzell

2. Harrison F. Bizzell, b. ca 1812 S. C., m. (1) Mary (or Nancy) Whitehurst, daughter of John Whitehurst. He m. (2) Mrs. Amanda N. McRae 26 July 1856 Henry Co., Ala.. He was living in Barbour Co. in 1840 and in Henry Co. in 1850. Known issue:

   a. Mary A. Bizzell, b. ca 1832 Ala.. This is probably the Mary Bizzell, b. 12 June 1832, d. 1 Dec. 1912, buried Pea River Presbyterian Cem., m. Hanson Lewis 11 Dec. 1860.

b. Dellana Bizzell, b. ca 1834 Ala..

c. Martha J. Bizzell, b. ca 1836 Ala., probably married Jesse Norwood 5 Aug. 1855.

d. E. E. Bizzell (female), b. ca 1837 Ala..

e. Seaborn B. Bizzell, b. ca 1838 Ala., d. 1875 Atlanta, Ga..

f. J. A. J. Bizzell (male), b. ca 1839 Ala..

g. Mahala W. Bizzell, b. ca 1842 Ala., m. James Curtis Bizzell 16 Feb. 1865, son of Henry N. Bizzell.

h. Minerva Bizzell, b. ca 1847 Ala., may have married Hursel Glenn 30 July 1868.

i. John W. Bizzell, b. ca 1850 Ala.

3. Curtis Bizzell, b. ca 1800/10, died between 1840/51, possibly in Arkansas, married Sarah Sowell 13 Sept. 1825 Henry Co., Ala.. Issue:

a. William H. Bizzell, a minor living in Arkansas 1851.

4. Charlotte Bizzell, b. 26 Aug. 1817 S. C., d. 28 Nov. 1891, m. Alfred Wright Faulk (see FAULK, page 85). He was born 30 June 1809 Ga., died 25 June 1888. They are buried in Faulk Cem.. Issue:

a. Nancy Ann Faulk, b. 15 April 1835, d. 21 Sept. 1876, never married. She is buried in Faulk Cem..

b. Charlotte T. Faulk, b. ca 1836 Ala., m. John Faulk 13 Feb. 1858, son of William Kendrick Faulk.

c. Mary Jane Faulk, b. 11 Feb. 1837 Ala., d. 16 Jan. 1843, buried in Faulk Cem..

d. Henry B. Faulk, M. D., b. ca 1839 Ala., m. Parthena ----. They were living in Navarro Co., Texas 1880.

e. James K. P. Faulk, b. ca 1842 Ala., m. Mary Jane Reynolds 6 Aug. 1865.

f. Mark Washington Faulk, b. 17 Oct. 1845 Ala., d. 15 April

1907, buried in Faulk Cem..

g. Daniel Winston Faulk, b. 1846 Ala., d. 1914, m. Texana
----. She was born 1866, died 1904. They are buried in
Faulk Cem..

h. Alfred Wright Faulk, Jr., b. ca 1848 Ala., m. L. E.
Herndon 27 Nov. 1881.

i. William Curtis Faulk, b. 15 Feb. 1850 Ala., d. 19 June
1854, buried Faulk Cem..

j. John Faulk, b. ca 1850 Ala..

k. Zenobia A. Faulk, b. 22 Nov. 1854 Ala., d. 7 Nov. 1933,
m. John B. Reynolds. He was born 1 Aug. 1851, died 10
April 1902. They are buried in Faulk Cem..

5. Sarah Jane Bizzell, b. 14 Jan. 1823 S. C., d. 24 April 1864,
m. Henry Lawson Faulk, Jr. 29 June 1845 (see FAULK, page 86).
He was born in Faulk Cem.. He m. (2) Nancy L. Faulk, daughter of Andrew S. Faulk, on 18 Aug. 1865. Issue (by 1st
wife):

a. William Wright Faulk, b. 26 Aug. 1846 Ala., d. 1 Mar.
1908, m. Sarah Jane Faulk 28 Nov. 1876. She was born
22 June 1854, died 9 Aug. 1886. Both buried Faulk Cem..

b. Henry Bennett Faulk, b. 29 Nov. 1848, d. Dec. 1907, m.
Mae Waddell.

c. James Harrison Faulk, b. 18 Nov. 1850 Ala., d. 15 Jan.
1885, buried in Faulk Cem..

d. Mary J. Faulk, b. 1 Feb. 1853 Ala., d. 15 May 1930, m.
W. Henry Faulk 23 Dec. 1875. He was born 22 Aug. 1848,
died 25 Nov. 1953. They are buried in Faulk Cem..

e. Leonora A. Faulk, b. 27 March 1855 Ala., d. 2 May 1879,
buried in Faulk Cem..

f. Nancy E. Faulk, b. 16 May 1857, d. 25 June 1862, buried
in Faulk Cem..

g. Charlotte A. J. Faulk, b. ca 1858 Ala., m. ---- Norwood.

h. Jefferson Davis Faulk, b. 13 June 1861, d. 9 Aug. 1883, buried Faulk Cem..

6. William A. Bizzell, b. ca 1825 Ala., m. Jemima ----. Issue:

a. Mary J. Bizzell, b. ca 1848 Ala.

b. George McD. Bizzell, b. ca 1849 Ala.

c. John Caldwell Bizzell, b. 25 Oct. 1850, d. 18 July 1856, buried in Faulk Cem..

d. Adonrum Judson Bizzell, b. 17 June 1854, d. 23 Sept. 1855, buried in Faulk Cem..

e. Martha Hasstletine Bizzell, b. 13 Aug. 1855, d. 5 July 1856, buried in Faulk Cem..

7. Mary Elizabeth Bizzell, b. 8 Feb. 1828 Ala., d. 24 June 1881, m. John Boswell James 8 May 1845. He was born 16 July 1819, died 13 April 1892. They are buried in Faulk Cem.. Probable issue:

a. Carlton A. James, b. ca 1846 Ala., living Texas 1892.

b. Roxanna A. E. James, b. ca 1848 Ala., m. J. W. Barr 3 Sept. 1869, living Barr's Mill (Pike Co.?), Ala. in 1892.

c. Claudia A. B. James, b. ca 1850 Ala., m. Deril J. Heron 14 Aug. 1873 (son of Dr. E. M. Heron). In 1892, they were living in Mt. Andrew.

d. Edwin Bennett James, b. ca 1851 Ala., living Texas 1892.

e. Bascom B. James m. ---- Turner, living in Clio 1892.

f. Mary A. James, b. ca 1854 Ala., m. ---- McNab. In 1892, they were living in Louisville.

g. Stella A. James, b. 28 Nov. 1855 Ala., d. 22 Sept. 1898, m. Timothy M. Redding. He was born 16 Sept. 1848, died 29 July 1908. They are buried in East Side Cem., Headland, Ala..

h. Charlotte J. James m. George Sangree 3 Nov. 1886. In 1892, they were living in Macon, Ga..

i. Ada A. (Lokey?) James m. ---- Griffin. In 1892, they were living in Brundidge (Pike Co.), Ala..

j. Fredonia (Donie) James m. Charles M. Abney of Macon, Ga. 10 Dec. 1890. In 1892, they were living in Macon, Ga..

8. Gabriella Bizzell, b. S. C., m. John S. Bizzell. He was also born S. C., died by 1851. He may have married (2) Mary Adams 12 Nov. 1844. Issue (by 1st wife):

a. Sophronia A. Bizzell, b. ca 1839 Ala., d. after 1880, m. Robert T. K. James by 1854. He was born ca 1831 S. C., died after 1880.

Other sources:

History of Henry Co., Ala. by Scott
Henry Co., Ala. Marriage records
Henry Co., Ala. Cemetery records.

BOSWELL

In 1827, William Boswell entered land in the South-western
part of Barbour Co. near the present Pike Co. line. He and Samuel Swilley entered one of the 1827 patents jointly. There are
no further records of William Boswell in Barbour Co., but on
20 Dec. 1850, Mary Boswell and D. A. Hall of Lowndes Co., Ala.
sold one of the original patents to Adam Grubbs.

Sources of information:
Barbour Co., Ala. Probate Records

BRADLEY

Salathiel Bradley patented land Southeast of-Clayton in 1829 and 1835. His brother, Robert Bradley, patented land just North of him in 1836. They were sons of Hobbs Bradley, b. Ireland, who migrated first to Delaware, then to Edgefield Dist., S. C., where he died. Known issue of Hobbs Bradley:

1. Salathiel Bradley, b. ca 1800 S. C., d. by Nov. 1872. According to the records of his estate, he left no widow or children. All of his estate was willed to Elizabeth Holmes. In the household of Salathiel Bradley in 1850 were:

    Delilah Bradley, age 50, born Ga..

    Yelverton J. Bradley, age 26, born Ga..

    Martha Bradley, age 18, born Fla..

    Louisa D. Bradley, age 12, born Ala..

    Their relation to Salathiel Bradley is not given.

    The 1860 Census of the household of Salathiel Bradley is as follows:

    Salathiel Bradley, age 58, b. S. C..

    Elizabeth Bradley, age 55, b. Ga..

    Jane Holmes, age 63, born Ga..

    Lucy Holmes, age 18, b. Ga..

2. Robert Bradley, b. ca 1809 S. C., d. 1881, m. Elizabeth Kemp, b. ca 1809 S. C., d. 1873. Known issue:

    a. Hobbs Bradley, b. ca 1828 Ala., living in Pensacola, Fla. in 1890.

    b. Ezekiel Bradley, b. ca 1830, living in Columbus, Ga. in 1890.

    c. Salathiel Bradley, b. 20 Feb. 1833, d. 15 July 1903, buried Pea River Cemetery, m. Mary E. ----.

    d. Henry Bradley, b. 25 April 1836, d. 27 Feb. 1887, m. Elvira ----, b. 19 Aug. 1849, d. 14 June 1891. Both are

27

buried in Clayton Cemetery.

 e. George Bradley, b. ca 1838. There is a George Bradley buried in Pea Creek Cemetery. No dates are given - the marker reads C. S. A.

 f. John Bradley, b. ca 1842 Ala..

 g. Abraham M. Bradley, b. ca 1844 Ala..

 h. James J. Bradley, b. ca 1846 Ala.. There is a James J. Bradley buried in Mt. Andrew Cemetery - the marker is C. S. A.. Mrs. J. J. Bradley d. March 1903 at Mt. Andrew.

 i. Martha Ann Bradley, b. ca 1848 Ala., not married in 1880.

 j. Taylor Bradley, b. ca 1862 Ala., m. Frances ----.

 k. Robert Bradley, living at Hurtsboro, Ala. in 1890.

3. John Bradley, died in Pickens Co., Ala. by 1872. Issue:

 a. John Bradley.

 b. Abram Bradley.

 c. Monroe Bradley.

 d. Polly Bradley.

 Also twelve more - names not known.

4. Abram Bradley, d. in Pickens Co., Ala. by 1872. Known issue:

 a. Wesley Bradley.

5. Mahala Bradley.

6. Ezekiel Bradley, living in Arkansas in 1872.

7. Harriet Bradley m. Henry Kemp, living in Mississippi in 1872.

8. Mary Bradley m. ----Shields. She died in Mississippi in 1872. Known issue:

 a. John Shields.

 b. William Shields.

 Also others, names not known.

9. Patsey Bradley m. ---- Jones. She died in Montgomery, Ala. by 1872.

There was a Hobes (Hobbs) Bradley listed in the 1838 Census of Barbour Co.; 1 male under 21, 1 male over 21, 1 slave.

Sources of information:

Memorial Record of Alabama
Barbour Co., Ala. Probate Records
Barbour Co., Ala. Census Records
Barbour Co., Ala. Cemetery Records

BRELAND

In 1829, Samuel Breland entered land West of Bakerhill. He
probably sold this land to Solomon Walker before 1832. There
are no further records of him in Barbour Co..

Sources of information:

Barbour Co., Ala. Probate Records

BROWN

Julana Brown entered land West of Clayton in 1829, at which time she was a widow. She is listed in the 1830 Census of Pike Co., Ala. six entries below John Brown. By 1834, she was living in Sumter Co., Ala., and died there ca 1837. Issue:

1. William W. Brown, d. by Nov. 1838.

2. John E. Brown.

3. Lewis S. J. Brown.

4. Julia A. E. Brown, a minor in 1838, m. Jesse Womack by Feb. 1838.

5. Sarah A. Brown, a minor in 1838, m. James Mitchell.

6. Jeremiah J. Brown, a minor in 1838.

7. Mary J. Brown, a minor in 1838.

8. Robert L. Brown, a minor in 1838.

9. Isaiah C. Brown, a minor in 1838.

There were several other Brown families in Barbour Co. before 1840, but none as early as Mrs. Julana Brown.

Stephen Brown died here by Dec. 1840, and Nancy Brown was his administratrix. In 1838, the Stephen Brown household consisted of 1 male under 21, 1 male over 21 and 1 female under 21.

One John Brown wrote his will 17 Nov. 1833, and it was probated 8 Sept. 1841. His wife was Dorothy ----, b. ca 1796 S.C., d. Sept. 1871 at the home of her daughter, Mrs. Hatch Cook, at Hamilton, Ga.. Known issue:

1. Mary Brown m. Abner Campbell (see Campbell family).

2. Samuel William Brown.

3. Eliza Brown m. ---- Crawford.

4. John James Brown.

5. Martha Brown m. Jacob Campbell (see Campbell family).

6. Lovett Harvey Brown, b. ca 1830 Ala., m. Mary J. Rouse 30 April 1854.

7. Elizabeth Brown, b. ca 1836 Ala., m. Hatch Cook 15 Dec. 1853.

Another John Brown* died by 30 March 1833. His wife, Elizabeth ----, was born ca 1790. About 1845, she and her children
migrated to Bienville Parish, La.. Issue:

1. Samuel Brown, b. ca 1820 Ala., m. Elizabeth Tilly 5 Oct.
   1840. She was born ca 1822 Ga.. Known issue:

   a. Amanda Brown, b. ca 1841 Ala..

   b. John Calhoun Brown, b. ca 1843 Ala..

   c. William H. Brown, b. ca 1845 Miss..

   d. Elizabeth Brown, b. ca 1848 La..

2. Jesse M. Brown, b. ca 1827 Ala..

3. David E. Brown, b. ca 1830 Ala..

4. John F. Brown, b. ca 1831 Ala..

Fielding R. Brown (a miller) entered land West of Clio from
1833 to 1836. He was born ca 1806 S. C., m. Mary McUlt 21 March
1844. This may have been a second marriage for both of them.
In the 1838 Census, F. R. Brown had 1 male over 21, 4 females
under 21 and 1 female over 21. Known issue of Fielding R. Brown
by his 1st wife:

1. Samantha Brown, b. ca 1837 Ala., m. Joseph F. Chambers 12
   March 1856.

2. Amanda Brown, b. ca 1843 Ala..

Sources of information:

Barbour Co., Ala. Probate Records
Barbour Co., Ala. Census Records
Sumter Co., Ala. Probate Records
Alabama Series, Vol. II by Helen S. Foley
Mrs. W. H. Bender, a descendant of John and Elizabeth Brown.

John Brown d. by 1833 - wife Elizabeth Moore Brown (b. 1788
N. C.) moved to Bienville Par., La. by 1850. Issue:

1. Samuel Brown, moved to Bienville Par., La. by 1850. In
    addition to the children listed, he had a son, Reuben Brown,
    b. 15 Nov. 1853 La., d. 24 Dec. 1897.

2. Jesse M. Brown, b. 20 May 1827, d. 7 July 1913, buried
    Arcadia, La.. He married the widow of his brother, John F.
    Brown.

3. David E. Brown, buried Arcadia, La. - no dates given,
    probably died about 1905.

4. John F. Brown, b. 28 July 1831 Barbour Co., Ala., d. 26 Jan.
    1858, buried Arcadia, La.

BURCH

Jesse Burch, b. ca 1790, d. by 1857 in Caddo Parish, La., m. Susan Dean before 1820. Owen's "History of Alabama", Vol. 4, page 1123 states that Jesse Burch was the son of William and Hattie (Blackwell) Burch, and his wife was Susan Dean. (Also see WARD family). *Jesse Burch was a Methodist minister, and came to what is now Barbour Co. possibly as early as 1822. The last record of him here is the 1838 Census, at which time he and his wife listed 4 males under 21 and 5 females under 21.

From 1829 to 1832, he patented land near Louisville, which he sold in 1834. He also patented land in 1836 in approximately the same area.

The succession of Jesse Burch was filed in Caddo Parish, La. on 23 Sept. 1857, naming the following heirs:

1. Jesse C. Burch, son.

2. Josephine E., wife of Thomas M. Penich, daughter.

3. Hetty S., wife of Richard T. Noel.

4. Hugh Currie, tutor of Edmund C. Currie.

5. Margaret E. (deceased), wife of J. B. Thompson.

6. Amanda (absent heir), wife of Daniel McKenzie. She was born ca 1821 Ga., d. 1869, m. Daniel McKenzie ca 1834, probably in Barbour Co.. He was born 25 Nov. 1805 N. C., d. 19 Jan. 1886 - both are buried in Bethlehem Cemetery, Barbour Co., Ala.. Known issue:

   a. James McKenzie, died 1836, buried Louisville Cemetery.

   b. Bethune B. McKenzie, b. ca 1837 Ala., m. C. E. Flournoy 14 Oct. 1858.

   c. Susan B. McKenzie, b. 21 April 1838, d. 6 Nov. 1889, buried Bethlehem Cemetery, m. Robert Flournoy 30 Sept. 1856.

d. Anna McKenzie, b. 4 March 1841, d. 21 Oct. 1872, buried
    Bethlehem Cemetery, m. Dr. W. U. Norton.

e. Louisianna McKenzie, b. ca 1843 Ala., m. James M. Hobdy
    ca 28 Nov. 1863. He was born 15 July 1839, died 13 May
    1900, is buried in Bethlehem Cemetery.

f. William McKenzie, died 1846, buried Bethlehem Cemetery.

g. Elizabeth E. McKenzie, b. ca 1849 Ala., d. by 1890, m.
    E. O. Petty 18 Nov. 1868.

h. Emma McKenzie m. William H. Norton; living in Warrenton,
    Ga. in 1886.

There were two other men by the name of Burch in Barbour Co.
as follows, but no relationship is shown to Jesse Burch:

1. A. J. Burch of Montgomery Co., Ala., who married Martha A.,
    daughter of John J. Slatter of Barbour Co., and is mentioned
    in the estate settlement of John J. Slatter in 1851.

2. Milton Burch, in the 1840 Census of Barbour Co. as follows:
    1 male 30/40, 1 female 20/30, 1 female under 5.

There was a Jesse Burch in Burke Co., Ga. in the 1820 Census.

Sources of information:

Owens "History of Alabama"
Records of Caddo Parish, La.
Barbour Co., Ala. Probate Records
Barbour Co., Ala. Census Records
Barbour Co., Ala. Cemetery Records

ADDITIONS & CORRECTIONS AS OF JUNE 1, 1979:*

Rev. Jesse Burch died 17 Sept. 1857 Caddo Par., La., age 66
years, 8 months and 3 days. His wife, Susan (Dean) Burch was
born 15 April 1798 Ga. and died 16 March 1861 Caddo Par., La..
Data given by Mr. Bickham Christian of Shreveport, La. who also
gives the following lineage:

I. Oliver Burch (d. 1729) emigrated to Maryland - descendants
    to Va., then Ga., Ala. and La..

II. Justinian Burch (1688-1758).

III. Edward Burch (1708-1765) m. Mary Crecoft (1710-1760).

IV. Rev. Jesse Burch (1728-1799) m. Ann Spink (1730-ca 1791).

V. Jesse Burch (1758-1818) m. Hettie Commander in 1785. She was born 1760, died 1807). He died Jefferson Co., Ga.

VI. Rev. Jesse Burch (1790 Ga. - 17 Sept. 1857 Caddo Par., La.) m. Susanna Dean in 1816, daughter of William Dean & Susanna Comston (or Compton). She was born 15 April 1798 Ga., died 16 March 1861 Caddo Par., La..

VII. Amanda Burch m. Daniel McKenzie.

BUSH

William R. Bush patented land West of Bakerhill from 1829 through 1836. In the 1840 Census, he was a single man, age 20/30. On 20 Dec. 1840, he married Eliza Jones. In 1841, William K. Jones gave them 11 acres of land, but his relationship to Eliza (Jones) Bush is not given in the deed.

Sarah Bush patented land adjoining William R. Bush in 1836. In Jan. 1836, she and William R. Bush were the administrators of William Bush, Sr.. In 1845, William R. Bush was the administrator of Bryant Bush.

Moses E. Bush entered land North of Bakerhill from 1829 through 1836. Scott's "History of Henry Co., Ala." states that Moses Eason Bush, b. 27 April 1797 Ga., d. 25 April 1847, married (1) Julia Ann Calhoun 9 April 1815 at Monticello, Jones Co., Ga. She was born 12 Oct. 1794 Laurens Co., Ga., died 18 April 1833 in Barbour Co., Ala.. They are buried in Rocky Mount Church Cemetery. He was the son of John Council Bush, b. 1 April 1781 Johnston Co., N. C., d. after Aug. 1814, and Edy (Tison?) of Trent River, N. C. and Laurens Co., Ga.. They are buried in Laurens Co., Ga.. William R. Bush and Zachariah Bush probably brothers of Moses E. Bush, also settled in Barbour Co..

Moses E. Bush m. (2) Nancy Jane Johnson by 1838. She was born ca 1815 N. C., died after 1880. She is also buried in Rocky Mount Church Cemetery. She was the daughter of Moses and Mary Johnson. Issue:

By 1st wife:

1. Mary Bush, b. ca 1812 Ga., died after 1870. She was living with James and Jane (Bush) Orr in 1850.
2. Council Vernon Bush, b. May 1817 Houston Co., Ga., d. Dec. 1893, m. Rebecca Bishop 20 Oct. 1843. She was born 8 May

1825 Ala., d. 28 May 1855, daughter of William and Nancy
(Pitts) Bishop. Council V. and Rebecca Bush are buried in
Clayton Cemetery. Known issue:

a. Louis Brown Bush, b. 4 Aug. 1843, d. 24 Oct. 1904 in
   Montgomery, Ala., m. Frances Johnson 16 Nov. 1869. He
   is buried in Clayton Cemetery.

b. William B. Bush, b. ca 1845 Ala., d. after 1870, m. Mary
   Antionette E. Goodson 29 Jan. 1867. She died in Corsicana, Texas in Feb. 1883.

c. Ryan Osley Bush, b. 10 May 1847 Ala., d. 14 Sept. 1906,
   m. Rebecca A. (Flowers?), b. 18 May 1848 Ala., d. 6 Feb.
   1898. Both are buried in County Line Cemetery, Henry
   Co., Ala..

d. Dixon H. Bush, b. ca 1849 Ala..

e. Rebecca R. Bush, b. 14 Nov. 1852 Ala., d. 7 July 1888,
   m. James B. Hooten 21 Dec. 1871. They are buried in
   Clayton Cemetery.

f. Emma Bush, b. 29 May 1855 Ala., d. 26 Jan. 1922, m.
   James LaFayette Columbus Martin 21 Dec. 1871. He was
   born 24 May 1859, died 26 Jan. 1922. Both are buried in
   Clayton Cemetery.

g. John C. Bush, b. ca 1858 Ala..

h. James Everett Bush, b. 29 June 1859 Ala., d. 8 May 1928,
   m. Fannie L. Cameron 7 Oct. 1896. She was born 11 Feb.
   1866, died 5 Sept. 1953. Both are buried in Clayton
   Cemetery.

i. Alpheus Sidney Bush, b. 1862 Ala., d. 1925, m. Ida Harrison 15 Jan. 1885. She was born 1868, died 1924. Both
   are buried in Clayton Cemetery.

j. Carden Luther Bush, b. 5 Sept. 1865 (?) Ala., died 16
   Sept. 1889, m. Willie D. Johnston 10 April 1884. He is

buried in Clayton Cemetery.

    k.   Lula Bush, b. ca 1867 Ala. - an adopted daughter.

3.   David Allen Bush, Sr., b. 10 May 1819 Ga., d. 4 June 1875, m. Julia Ann Flowers ca 1842, daughter of Abner and Rebecca Flowers. She was born 1821 Ga., died 29 May 1892. They are buried in a private cemetery on their old home place. Known issue:

    a.   Epsey Bush, b. 24 June 1844 Ala., d. 26 Dec. 1916, m. John H. McRae 6 Dec. 1866. He was born 1 Dec. 1844, died 1 June 1932. They are buried in Clayton Cemetery.

    b.   Americus Berrien Bush, b. 27 Dec. 1847 Ala., d. 31 July 1925, m. Martha Ann Crawford of Henry Co., Ala. on 4 March 1873, dau. of Nicholas and Loney Dana Crawford. She was born 30 Dec. 1851, died 10 Dec. 1919. They are buried in County Line Cemetery, Henry Co., Ala..

    c.   David Bush, b. ca 1849 Ala.. He is listed in the 1850 Census, but must have died young. In the 1860 Census, they have another child named David A. Bush (see later).

    d.   Ann Bush, b. 26 Aug. 1851, d. 23 May 1944, m. John V. Clark 18 June 1871, lived in Pike Co., Ala., later near Cuthbert, Ga..

    e.   Seth Bush, b. ca 1854 Ala., may have married Sing Tullis on 18 Dec. 1894.

    f.   Emma Bush, b. ca 1856 Ala., may have married ---- Clark.

    g.   David A. Bush, b. ca 1860 Ala..

4.   William J. Bush m. Mary Pugh 16 Nov. 1846.

5.   Martha (Matilda?) Bush, b. ca 1823 Ga., m. Harold F. Reeves 28 Jan. 1841. Known issue:

    a.   Columbus Reeves, b. ca 1842 Ala.

    b.   Walter Reeves, b. ca 1843 Ala.

    c.   Moses Reeves, b. ca 1844 Ala.

d.   Julia Reeves, b. ca 1845 Ala.

e.   Jane Reeves, b. ca 1847 Ala.

f.   Minerva Reeves, b. ca 1849 Ala.

6.   Elizabeth Bush, b. ca 1827 Ala., m. Joel D. Stokes 15 July
1841. Known issue:

a.   Amanda J. Stokes, b. ca 1843 Ala.

b.   Moses E. Stokes, b. ca 1845 Ala.

c.   Mary E. Stokes, b. ca 1848 Ala.

d.   Julia A. Stokes, b. ca 1853 Ala.

e.   James D. Stokes, b. ca 1856 Ala.

f.   Sarah A. Stokes, b. ca 1858 Ala.

7.   Nancy A. Bush, b. ca 1825 Ala., m. James Houston 9 Nov. 1843.
He was born ca 1818 N. C.. Known issue:

a.   Hannah Houston, b. ca 1844 Ala.

b.   Mosby (Mosley?) Houston, b. ca 1845 Ala.

c.   Edward Houston, b. ca 1847 Ala.

d.   Julia Houston, b. ca 1848 Ala..

8.   Moses E. Bush, Jr., b. ca 1831 Ala.. He was still a minor
in 1852 - at that time, his guardian was his brother-in-law,
James Orr.

9.   Julia Ann Bush, b. ca 1829 Ala., d. by 1861, m. *Harrell Flowers 8 July 1846, son of Abner and Rebecca Flowers. He married (2) Elizabeth Harrod 13 Aug. 1861. Known issue:
By 1st wife:

a.   Frances Jane Flowers, b. ca 1848 Ala.

b.   Cinthia Flowers, b. ca 1849 Ala.

c.   Harrel Flowers, b. ca 1850 Ala.

d.   Georgiann Flowers, b. ca 1853 Ala..

e.   John W. Flowers, b. ca 1855 Ala.

f.   Nina Amanda Flowers, b. ca 1857 Ala.

g.   Joseph Flowers, b. ac 1859 Ala.

By 2nd wife:

h. Lula Flowers, b. ca 1863 Ala.

i. Henry Flowers, b. ca 1867 Ala.

j. Mattie Flowers, b. ca 1869 Ala.

k. Thomas W. Flowers, b. ca 1872 Ala.

10. Jane C. (or E.) Bush, b. 4 April 1830 Ala., d. 27 Jan. 1907,
m. James Orr 20 Aug. 1846. He was born ca 1821 in Ireland,
died ca 1858. She married (2) Herbert Tiller 8 Jan. 1867.
She is buried in Rocky Mount Church Cemetery. Known issue:
By 1st Husband:

a. William M. Orr, b. 2 Aug. 1852, d. 16 Oct. 1922, m. Te-
resa J. ----. She was born 6 March 1857, died 17 March
1939. Both are buried in Rocky Mount Church Cemetery.

b. *James Orr, b. ca 1853 Ala., m. Callie Thomas.

c. Elizabeth Orr

Children of Moses E. Bush and his second wife, Nancy Jane Johnson:

1. Sarah Priscilla Bush, b. ca 1835 Ala., m. ---- Strayham.
They were living in La. by 1877.

2. Roxanna Johnson Bush, b. ca 1837 Ala., m. Joseph L. Parmer
2 Nov. 1854. Known issue:

a. Gordon Parmer, b. ca 1855 Ala.

b. Dora Parmer, b. ca 1862 Ala.

c. Edward Parmer, b. ca 1859 Ala.

d. Tyson Pitt Parmer, b. ca 1868 Ala.

3. Savannah Georgia Bush, b. 1841 Ala., d. 1892, m. George Lafayette Houston 26 Nov. 1867. He was born 1837, died 1906.
Both are buried in Rocky Mount Church Cemetery. He married
(2) Thessalonia ----. Known issue (by 1st wife):

a. William S. Houston, b. ca 1869 Ala.

b. Leona J. Houston, b. ca 1871 Ala., m. John Brown.

c. Dr. James Lafayette Houston, b. 6 Jan. 1872 Ala.,

d. 23 May 1937, m. Willie Bell McCarroll. She was born
10 Feb. 1880, died 3 May 1957. Both are buried in Fairview Cemetery at Eufaula, Ala..

d. Emma Houston, b. ca 1874 Ala., m. Dr. Wm. H. Harrison.

e. Lizzie Houston.

4. Johnston Dealware Bush, b. ca 1842 Ala., was living in Texas
by 1877, m. Alvina DuBose 13 Jan. 1868. Known issue:

a. Pauline Bush, b. ca 1869 Ala.

b. Josephine Bush, b. ca May 1870 Ala.

5. Tyson Bush, b. ca 1843 Ala.

6. Bethany (Paulina?) Bush, b. ca 1847 Ala..

The accepted DAR line of William Bush is as follows:

I.   William Bush, d. 1716 Albemarle Co., N. C., m. Martha Corlee.

II. John Bush m. Mary Bryan.

III. Hardy Bush m. Catherine Frank ca 1751. She m. (2) James
Blackshear.

IV. Lt. John Council Bush, Sr. (R.S.), b. 21 June 1752 Craven
Co., N. C., d. 1805 Wilkes Co., Ga., m. Susannah Bryan 16
March 1779. She was born 20 Nov. 1762 Johnston Co., N. C.,
died 27 June 1841 Talbot Co., Ga.. She married (2) Samuel
Alexander ca 1819 in Wilkes Co., Ga.

V.   John Council Bush, Jr., b. 1 April 1781 Johnston Co., N. C.,
d. after 1814 Laurens Co., Ga. m. Edy (Tison?) ca 1796.

Zachariah Bush patented land West of Bakerhill in 1835, next
to that of Sarah Bush and William R. Bush. Thompson's "History
of Barbour Co., Ala." states that his wife was Mary Dennis, m.
23 Sept. 1818 Laurens Co., Ga. He was born ca 1796 Ga., died by
March 1851. His estate was settled in Sept. 1852, at which time
his heirs were:

1. Mariah Jane Bush m. Jonathan Thomas (see Thomas family).

2. William Green Bush, b. ca 1823 Ga., d. by Aug. 1855, m. Mary

Ann Allen 25 June 1845. She m. (2) Neill Morrison 29 Dec. 1859. Known issue:

a. Hilliard Herbert Bush, b. ca 1848 Ala., d. Jan. 1886, m. Mahala Narcissa Thomas 6 Feb. 1867.

b. William M. Bush, b. ca 1852 Ala., not married in 1880.

3. Retencey Emeline Bush, died by 1852, m. Eli Thomas 31 Dec. 1840 (see Thomas family).

4. Charles Dennis Bush, b. ca 1829 Ala., d. by June 1853, m. Saleann B. DuBose 17 Feb. 1848, daughter of Seaborn J. Du-Bose. She m. (2) Edward E. Glover 5 Jan. 1862. Known issue: By 1st husband:

a. Frances Jane Bush, b. ca 1848 Ala., m. Wiley Beasley.

b. Zachariah Bush, b. ca 1850 Ala.

c. Charles Dennis Bush, Jr., b. ca 1852 Ala.

By 2nd husband:

d. Marcellus Glover, b. ca 1863 Ala.

e. Maximillian Glover, b. ca 1866 Ala.

5. Arrensa Bush, b. ca 1825, d. by 1852, m. William Williams. Issue:

a. Mary Amanda Williams, b. ca 1841 Ala.

b. Jane A. Williams, b. ca 1843 Ala.

c. Columbianna Williams, b. ca 1845 Ala.

d. Louisianna Williams

e. Sarah E. Williams, b. ca 1848 Ala.

6. Mary R. Bush, b. ca 1833 Ala., d. 15 April 1915, m. John Watson 10 Jan. 1850. He died 10 July 1910 - both are buried in Rocky Mount Church Cemetery. Known issue:

a. C. E. Watson (male), b. ca 1861 Ala.

b. D. C. Watson (male), b. ca 1867 Ala.

c. M. C. Watson (female), b. ca 1869 Ala.

7. Moses Eason Bush, b. 23 Nov. 1833 Ala., d. 26 Feb. 1905, m.

43

Elizabeth Jane Grubbs 15 Aug. 1849. She was born 20 Aug. 1831 Ala., died 28 Feb. 1905. Both are buried in New Hope Cemetery. Issue:

a. Mary J. Bush, b. ca 1850 Ala.

b. William Z. Bush, b. 8 Sept. 1852, d. 2 Dec. 1852.

c. Travis C. Bush, b. 31 Aug. 1853, d. 7 Nov. 1854.

d. Nancy E. Bush, b. 24 Aug. 1855, d. 15 Sept. 1856.

e. Moses E. Bush, Jr., b. ca 1857 Ala.

f. James A. Bush, b. ca 1859 Ala., d. 10 March 1935.

g. Rev. H. B. Bush, b. 24 April 1864, d. 7 Aug. 1886.

h. Jane E. Bush, b. 25 May 1870, d. 8 Sept. 1872.

All are buried at New Hope Cemetery. (Note: there were two men by the name of Moses E. Bush, so it is possible that this family is credited to the wrong man.)

8. Ruth C. Bush m. Elliott Thomas 16 Sept. 1852 (see Thomas family). She married (2) John O. Wise of Coffee Co., Ala..

9. Lucinda Bush, b. ca 1840 Ala., m. (1) Robert E. Ward 19 May 1857. She married (2) Barney Baldwin. She is buried in an unmarked grave in Epworth Church Cemetery. Known issue:

By 1st husband:

a. Ed Ward, b. ca 1860 Ala.

by 2nd husband:

b. Cornelia Baldwin, b. ca 1868 Ala.

c. Max Baldwin, b. ca 1871 Ala.

d. Barney Baldwin, b. ca 1874 Ala.

e. John Baldwin, b. ca 1876 Ala.

Bryant Bush died in Barbour Co. by Dec. 1840. His administrator was William R. Bush. There are no records of this estate after 1846, and no heirs are named. There was a John Bush, b. ca 1816 Ga., who named a son Bryant Bush, indicating a possible kinship.

Lewis Bush died in Barbour Co. by Nov. 1836. Moses E. Bush was guardian of his minor heirs, viz:

1. William Bush

2. John Bush

3. Allen Bush

4. Catherine Bush, b. ca 1826 Ga., m. James J. Sprowell 18 Nov. 1845.

5. Matilda Bush.

William Bush died in Barbour Co. by 1840. Moses E. Bush was guardian of his minor heirs, viz:

1. Greenberry Bush, b. ca 1823 Ala., m. Nancy Jane Walls 6 Jan. 1848.

2. Susan Bush, may have married Jefferson Smith 4 Feb. 1841.

3. William Bush

4. Matilda Bush m. George C. Jones 27 Dec. 1846.

Sources of information:

Barbour Co., Ala. Probate Records
Barbour Co., Ala. Census Records
Barbour Co., Ala. Cemetery Records
Bush family Bible
Henry Co., Ala. Cemetery Records
"History of Barbour Co., Ala." by Thompson
"History of Henry Co., Ala." by Scott
DAR National Number 519095

*ADDITIONS & CORRECTIONS AS OF JUNE 1, 1979:

Harrell Flowers died Feb. 1905, age 79, buried at White Oak.

James Orr, b. 24 Feb. 1854, d. 12 Nov. 1918, m. Charity Caroline Thomas, daughter of Jonathan Thomas and Mariah J. Bush. She was born 13 Nov. 1855 and died 22 Feb. 1900.

BYRD

According to the DAR records, George Byrd died in what is now Barbour Co., Ala. in 1817. He was a Revolutionary Soldier, born ca 1730 Tidewater, Va. and enlisted in the War from Middlesex Co., Va.. About 1752, he married Sarah Commander at Charles City, Va.. She was born about 1734 and died in 1818. Issue:

1. Sarah Byrd - no further record.

2. Janie Byrd - no further record.

3. Ellen Byrd - no further record.

4. Sherard Byrd - no further record.

5. Redden Byrd - see later.

6. John Byrd - no further record.

7. Sam Byrd - no further record.

8. William Byrd - no further record.

9. Thomas Byrd - no further record.

10. Elam Byrd - no further record.

Redden Byrd, b. 7 June 1786 Middlesex Co., Va., d. 19 July 1858 Darlington Co., S. C., m. Hannah Scott 5 Aug. 1819, daughter of Dr. Andrew Scott and Elizabeth Ritter. She was born 10 May 1802 Craven Co., N. C., died 4 Sept. 1862 or 1864 Darlington Co., S. C.. Issue:

1. Dr. Harvey L. Byrd, b. 8 Aug. 1820, m. Miss A. B. (P.?) Dozier 31 Oct. 1844.

2. Dr. James Ervin Byrd, b. 6 Feb. 1823 S. C., d. 20 March 1889 S. C., m. Mary L. Keith 20 Nov. 1845. She was born 20 Dec. 1831 Darlington Co., S. C., died 29 July 1888 in Timmonsville, S. C..

3. George Washington Byrd, b. 29 March 1826, d. 15 Dec. 1863 at Georgetown, S. C., m. Mary Stevenson 29 July 1852.

4. Andrew Jackson Byrd, b. 12 Nov. 1828, d. 8 July 1864 in the

Civil War, m. (1) Martha T. Baker 1 Oct. 1846. She died 3 March 1852 and he married (2) Miss A. J. Gaskins 5 Aug. 1852.

5. Sarah Elizabeth Byrd m. John K. McElveen 27 April 1847.

6. Mary L. Byrd m. Julius A. Mims 29 Dec. 1852.

7. Dr. S. D. M. Byrd m. Mary Elizabeth Graham 17 June 1863. She died 29 Aug. 1864.

8. Margaret Caroline Byrd, b. 8 Nov. 1837, m. James Morgan Carter 3 Jan. 1854.

9. Frances Caroline Byrd, b. 23 Sept. 1840, d. 13 Aug. 1914 in Homerville, Ga., m. (1) David Richard Carter 23 Oct. 1856 in Darlington Co., S. C.. He was born 29 April 1835 and died 1862. She married (2) Charles M. Stuckey 27 Oct. 1863 (b. 10 Jan. 1838, d. 31 Aug. 1868), then she married (3) R. Eatman in 1870.

After the death of his parents, Redden Byrd returned to South Carolina and died in Darlington Co. in 1858.

This Redden Byrd should not be confused with the Redden Byrd who settled first in Barbour Co., Ala., but later moved to Dale Co., Ala., although they may have been distantly related. The second Redden Byrd came to this area from North Carolina about 1828. None of the available records give the name of his wife. Known issue:

1. Isaac Byrd - no further record.

2. Curtis Byrd, b. 20 June 1809 N. C., d. 7 July 1905 in Dale Co., Ala., m. Elizabeth Harper 27 Sept. 1832 in Ala.. She was born 7 Nov. 1810 Ga., died 23 Oct. 1889. Known issue:

    a. Louise Byrd m. Sam Blackmon.

    b. Martha Byrd m. Henry Harris.

    c. Angus Burtis Byrd, b. 1856, d. 1938 Dale Co., Ala., m. Caledonia Chalker, buried Dale Co., Ala..

      d.   Benjamin G. Byrd, b. 4 March 1839, d. 29 Aug. 1864,
           buried in Dale Co., Ala..

      e.   Berry Byrd, b. 19 March 1853, d. 18 June 1855.

3. William Byrd - no further record.

4. Burtis Byrd, b. 24 June 1814 N. C., d. 30 Aug. 1854 in Dale
    Co., Ala., m. Mary Anderson ca 1833. She was born 17 June
    1815, died 4 March 1888 Dale Co., Ala.

5. Edward Byrd, b. 22 June 1815, d. 22 March 1895 Dale Co.,
    Ala., m. Louisa ----, b. 8 Nov. 1818, d. 14 June 1897.

6. Hansel Byrd - no further record.

7. Benjamin Byrd - no further record.

Other sources:

Scott-Byrd genealogy from "The Clinch Co. News" 17 Oct. 1930,
  published at Homerville, Ga.
DAR records
Byrd-Carter Bible
Redden Byrd Bible
"History of Southeast Ala." by Andrews
"Memorial Record of Ala.", Vol. 1, pages 803 & 804
Dale Co., Ala. Cemetery records

CADENHEAD
(Cattenhead)

Ivey Cadenhead patented land in Barbour Co. in 1827. The next record of him is in 1834, when he served on the jury. There is no further mention of him in the early records of Barbour Co. In Russell Co., Ala. on 7 Dec. 1840, William Cadenhead and Nancy Cadenhead posted bond as the administrators of an Ivey Cadenhead

Isham Cadenhead also patented land in Barbour Co. by 1834, and Levi P. Cadenhead and Francis M. Cadenhead patented land before 1850. All of this land lay between Louisville and Clio.

The 1830 Census of Pike Co., Ala. lists John, Isham, Joe and James Cadenhead as heads of households. The 1840 Census of Pike Co., Ala. includes James Cadenhead, Sr. as follows: 1 male 10/15, 1 male 60/70, 1 male 90/100, 1 female under 5, 1 female 20/30, 1 female 50/60. The Census of Pensioners, 1841 (page 149) lists James Cadenhead, Revolutionary Soldier, aged 98, a resident of Pike Co., Ala. on 1 June 1840.

In Perote Cemetery (now in Bullock Co., Ala.) is buried J. Cadenhead. The inscription reads "Soldier - 1776" - no other dates are given.

In Barbour Co., Ala. on 18 July 1855, Abner H. King, guardian of Ann Elizabeth Cadenhead, minor heir of Isaac and Sarah Ann Susannah Cadenhead, deceased, stated that on 4 Dec. 1854, he received $500.00 from the estate of James Cadenhead, deceased, of Macon Co., Ala. The heirs of this James Cadenhead were:

1. Alley Cadenhead, his widow. James Cadenhead married Alley Middlebrooks 18 Jan. 1818 in Jones Co., Ga.; she may have been his second wife.

2. James J. Cadenhead

3. John H. Cadenhead

4. Martha, wife of Samuel B. Harmon

5. Mary, wife of W. L. Flint

6. Samantha, deceased, wife of H. T. Crowder - her children were William T., Alley A. and Martha T. Crowder.

7. Isaac Cadenhead, deceased - his daughter, Elizabeth, a minor.

8. Sarah E. Cadenhead, a minor.

9. Walter Cadenhead, a minor.

10. Benjamin F. Cadenhead, a minor.

11. Robert H. Cadenhead, a minor.

12. Homer T. Cadenhead, a minor.

The 1840 Census of Barbour Co., Ala. lists John Cadenhead as follows: 2 males 15/20, 1 male 60/70, 2 females 5/10, 1 female 20/30 and 1 female 50/60. There is no estate settlement fo. him in Barbour Co., but on 23 Aug. 1843, he gave a slave to his son, Francis M. Cadenhead. On 16 Jan. 1849, Francis M. Cadenhead and wife, Rebecca, sold the land which they had patented in 1846 to William J. Faulk. This deed was headed Coffee Co., Ala.

Sources of information:

Barbour Co., Ala. Probate Records
Barbour Co., Ala. Census Records
Pike Co., Ala. Census Records
Bullock Co., Ala. Cemetery Records
Macon Co., Ala. Probate Records
Jones Co., Ga. Marriage Records
"Census of Pensioners, 1841"

CAMPBELL

William D. Campbell was born in South Carolina, probably
about 1790, and died by Dec. 1849 in Barbour Co., Ala.. He married Elizabeth ----, born ca 1797 S. C., d. ca Jan. 1869. In
1827 and 1836, he patented land near Pea River Church in Barbour
Co.. Issue:

1. Daniel Campbell, b. ca 1810 S. C., d. by Aug. 1853, m. Cor-
   nelia M. ---- ca 1834. She was born 19 July 1814, died 14
   Jan. 1900, is buried in Pine Level Baptist Church Cemetery.
   Known issue:

   a. Mary Ann, b. ca 1835 Ala., m. O. C. Doster 8 Aug. 1852.

   b. Cathy Ann, b. ca 1839 Ala..

   c. Nancy, b. ca 1843 Ala..

   d. Cynthia Ann, b. ca 1845 Ala..

   e. Duncan, b. ca 1849 Ala.

   f. Ann

   g. Daniel

2. Joshua Campbell, b. ca 1814 S. C., d. before 1849, m. Elizabeth ----. She was living in Ga. in 1849, and in Coffee
   Co., Ala. in 1869.

3. Wesley W. Campbell, b. ca 1818 S. C., m. Charlotte C. ----.
   Known issue:

   a. Elizabeth Ann, b. ca 1849 Ala.

   b. Analizer, b. ca 1852 Ala.

   c. John, b. ca 1854 Ala.

   d. Erastus, b. ca 1856 Ala.

   e. Java, b. ca 1858 Ala.

4. Abner Campbell, b. ca 1820 S. C., m. Mary Brown, daughter of
   John and Dorothy Brown. Known issue:

   a. Geraldine, b. ca 1836 Ala.

   b. Savannah, b. ca 1838 Ala., m. John G. Windham 30

Aug. 1858.

c. Elizabeth, b. ca 1840 Ala.

d. William, b. ca 1842 Ala.

e. Cornelius, b. ca 1846 Ala.

This family was living in Conecuh Co., Ala. in 1869.

5. Malinda Campbell, b. 1 Feb. 1822 S. C., d. 24 Sept. 1894, m.
Isaac H. Chambers, b. 1 April 1812 S. C., d. 29 Jan. 1882.
Both are buried in Pea River Cemetery. Probable issue:

a. Martha A., b. ca 1836 Ala.

b. Clarinda Jane, b. ca 1838 Ala.

c. Louise, b. ca 1840 Ala.

d. Amanda, b. ca 1842 Ala.

e. William, b. ca 1844 Ala.

f. James, b. ca 1846 Ala.

g. Isaac, b. ca 1849 Ala.

h. Cinderella, b. ca 1852 Ala.

i. Mary, b. ca 1854 Ala.

j. Catherine, b. ca 1856 Ala.

k. Arvenia, b. ca 1858 Ala.

l. George, b. ca 1861 Ala.

6. Jacob E. Campbell, b. ca 1824 S. C., m. Martha ----. She
may have been Martha Brown, daughter of John and Dorothy
Brown. Known issue:

a. Britton, b. ca 1846 Ala.

b. Jacob, b. ca 1847 Ala.

c. Robert, b. ca 1849 Ala.

d. Susannah, b. ca 1852 Ala.

e. William, b. ca 1854 Ala.

f. Q. A. (female), b. ca 1857 Ala.

g. F. W. (male), b. ca 1859 Ala.

7. Amanda Caroline E. Campbell, b. ca 1828 Ala., d. between

1850 and 1859, m. Needham B. Sutton on 12 March 1846 (see Sutton family).

8.   Joab Campbell, b. ca 1832 Ala..

Abner Campbell, b. ca 1778 S. C. and Susan Campbell, b. ca 1790 S. C., both living in 1850, were neighbors of William D. Campbell from 1836 through 1850, but the relationship cannot be found in the Barbour Co. records. In 1860, Susanna Campbell was living with Jacob Campbell. There were other Campbells in Barbour Co. before 1850, but none were so closely associated with William D. Campbell.

Sources of information:

Barbour Co., Ala. Probate Records
Barbour Co., Ala. Census Records
Barbour Co., Ala. Cemetery Records

CHILDS

Elisha Childs patented land East of Louisville in 1829. In 1853, he sold this land to William Cox. Although there were other families of this name in Barbour Co. before 1850, it is doubtful if Elisha Childs ever actually lived here. In 1850, he was a resident of Pike Co., Ala..

Elisha Childs was born ca 1800 Ga., m. Catharine ----, b. ca 1805 S. C.. Known issue:

1. Elijah Childs, b. ca 1829 Ala.
2. James Childs, b. ca 1831 Ala.
3. Thomas Childs, b. ca 1834 Ala.
4. Aaron Childs, b. ca 1837 Ala.
5. Sarah Childs, b. ca 1841 Ala.
6. Kezia Childs, b. ca 1842 Ala.
7. Mary Childs, b. ca 1848 Ala.

William G. Childs and John G. Childs were neighbors of Elisha Childs in Pike Co., Ala. in 1850. The household of John G. Childs was as follows:

Childs, John G.	age 26	born Ga.
" , Rebecca	age 21	born N. C.
" , Cynthia	age 5	born Ala.
" , Sarah	age 2	born Ala.
" , Mary	age 6/12	born Ala.
Rich, Anna	age 46	born S. C.

The household of William G. Childs was as follows:

Childs, William G.	age 26	born Ala.
" , Louisa	age 22	born N. C.
" , Sarah	age 4	born Ala.
" , Elisha	age 2	born Ala.
" , Sinthy	age 2/12	born Ala.

54

Childs, John L.	age 23	born Ga.
Childs, Gabriel	age 52	born S. C.
" , Margaret	age 37	born N. C.
" , Alfred	age 25	born Ga.
" , Sarah	age 15	born Ga.
" , William	age 6	born Ala.
" , Raburn	age 3	born Ala.
" , Jane	age 6/12	born Ala.

There are indications that Elisha Childs lived in Jones Co., Ga. before coming to Alabama, as follows:

1. On 9 Dec. 1819, Thomas Boswell m. Martha Childs (note: the will of Thomas C. Boswell in Pike Co., Ala. in 1849 names wife, Martha).

2. On 24 Dec. 1819, Gabriel Childs m. Susannah Thornton.

3. On 13 Jan. 1822, Elisha Childs m. Cynthia Thornton. (Note: in Pike Co., Ala. in 1844, Elisha Childs was guardian John Thornton, minor heir of Thomas Thornton, deceased).

These three marriages took place in Jones Co., Ga..

John Childs, Sr. died in Jones Co., Ga. by June 1825. His heirs were sons M. Satterwhite Childs, John Childs, Thomas M. Childs, William Childs, Elijah Childs and Elisha Childs; daughters Phanny, Lucy, Amy, Susaner and Patsey Childs.

Sources of information:

Barbour Co., Ala. Probate Records
Pike Co., Ala. Probate Records
Pike Co., Ala. Census Records
Jones Co., Ga. Records

COLE

Daniel Cole was born ca 1760, moved to Georgia by 1802 and
to Alabama by 1819 - he died in Pike Co., Ala. in 1831. His
wife, Mary DuBose, was born ca 1765 S. C. and died ca 1851 in
Pike Co., Ala.. She was a daughter of John DuBose who died ca
1800 Darlington Dist., S. C. and Lydia Carter. John DuBose was
a son of Stephen DuBose, who was a son of Isaac DuBose, the
emigrant from France. Issue of Daniel and Mary (DuBose) Cole:

1. John Mason Cole, b. ca 1792 S. C., came to Coffee Co., Ala.
    ca 1856 from Georgia.

2. Margaret Cole, b. 1794 S. C., d. 1875 Washington Co., Fla.,
    m. Rev. Isaac Hilliard Horne 14 Nov. 1816 Pulaski Co., Ga..

3. Noah B. Cole came to Barbour Co., Ala. (see later).

4. Elizabeth Cole, b. 1797 Cheraw Dist., S. C.

5. Thomas Delorum Cole, b. 1799 S. C., d. 1865 Coffee Co., Ala.,
    m. Elizabeth Horne.

6. Ransom Cole, b. 1800 Edgefield Dist., S. C., d. 1887 Bryon,
    Texas, m. Agatha Bostwick.

7. Jeanette Cole, b. 1804 Ga., m. James Wood and lived in
    Pike Co., Ala..

8. Daniel Cole, Jr., b. 13 Feb. 1806 Jefferson Co., Ga., m.
    (1) Nancy Wood (2) Mary Jane Dick 30 Dec. 1847. He died in
    1875 in Cass Co., Texas.

    Noah B. Cole, b. ca 1795 S. C., d. by 1853 Caddo Par., La.,
m. Wealtha Taylor 28 Jan. 1819 Conecuh Co., Ala.. She was born
1799 and died 1876. In 1822, they were living in Covington Co.,
Ala. - they were in Dale Co., Ala. in 1830 and in Barbour Co.,
Ala. in 1832. Issue (not in order):

1. Minerva W. Cole m. T. M. Bickham.

2. Mary Ann Cole m. Frederick Thomas.

3. Patience (Palestine?) Cole, b. 1830, d. 1918, m. Edward

Jacobs, who was born 1822, died 1896.

4. Jahazo J. Cole m. William Todd.

5. Ransom T. Cole was a minor in 1857 and living in La.. He married Virginia Noel.

6. Amazon Cole m. Benjamin Jacobs, lived Macon Co., Ala.

7. Calista A. Cole m. James B. McCain. They were living in Macon Co., Ala. in 1853.

8. Almira C. Cole, b. 11 Dec. 1822 Covington Co., Ala., d. 23 Sept. 1900 Bullock Co., Ala., m. James Madison Feagin in 1840. He was born 27 Feb. 1814 Jones Co., Ga., died 28 Nov. 1899 Bullock Co., Ala., son of Samuel T. Feagin of Carthage, N. C. and Nancy Wadsworth, who married 13 May 1813 Jones Co., Ga.. James M. Feagin and Almira C. Cole are buried in Fellowship Cem., Bullock Co., Ala.. Issue:

   a. Samuel Jefferson Feagin, b. 1841 Ala., d. 19 July 1862 (CSA), buried Fellowship Cem., Bullock Co., Ala..

   b. Noah Baxter Feagin, b. 7 July 1843 Midway, Ala.

   c. Martha Feagin, b. 2 April 1846 Ala., d. 9 Aug. 1937, m. Calvin W. Fenn 8 June 1868 Bullock Co., Ala.. He was born 25 April 1837, died 8 Nov. 1912, buried in Clayton Cem., (see FENN).

   d. Wealthy M. Feagin, b. ca 1847 Ala., m. Dr. W. U. Morton 26 June 1878 near Midway, Ala.. She was his second wife.

   e. Mary A. Feagin, b. 11 Jan. 1858, d. 11 May 1858, buried Fellowship Cem., Bullock Co., Ala..

   f. Missouri Amazon Feagin m. F. H. Tompkins.

   g. Almira C. Feagin m. A. G. Jordan.

   h. James Madison Feagin, Jr., b. 23 March 1854, d. 27 Dec. 1909, buried Fellowship Cem., Bullock Co., Ala..

   i. Beauregard Feagin, b. 16 March 1843, d. 11 Jan. 1847,

buried Fellowship Cem., Bullock Co., Ala.

j. Lavinia I. Feagin m. Rev. James M. Kelly of Jefferson, Ga..

k. Nancy Dixie Feagin m. Gus A. Orum of Union Springs, Ala.

l. George Wadsworth Feagin m. Nora Belle Baker 15 April 1896 at Midway, Ala.. He may have married (2) Mary N. Williams 14 Nov. 1905 Barbour Co., Ala.

9. Lucinda Cole m. Daniel M. Dansby. They were living in Cass Co., Texas in 1857 (see DANSBY).

Although there is nothing to show any relationship between Noah B. Cole and Edwin J. Cole, they were both living in Barbour Co. very early. Edwin J. Cole died here by Feb. 1841, leaving wife Sophia (daughter of D. Martin and Mary Efurd - see EFURD, page 78). She was born 31 Oct. 1812 and died after 1842. Issue:

1. Mary Ann Cole, b. ca 1828 Ala., m. John M. Hudspeth 12 Oct. 1850.

2. Sarah Ann Cole, b. ca 1830 Ala., m. (1) Amos Arrington 22 May 1851 (2) John O. Perry 29 Nov. 1859 Henry Co., Ala.. They lived in Baker Co., Ga.. Issue:

    a. Lula A. Perry m. ---- May, moved to Fla.

    b. Walter C. Perry.

    c. Edwin J. Perry.

    d. Willie Frank Perry, d. y.

3. D. J. Cole

4. James Cole

Other sources:
Georgia Pioneers, Vol. I, No. I, page 21
Pulaski Co., Ga. Marriage records
Dictionary of Ala. Biography, page 565
Pike Co., Ala. Cemetery records
Henry Co., Ala. Marriage records
"Transactions of the Huguenot Society of S. C.", No. 77,
    pages 46/69.

Between 1829 and 1837, Emanuel and Edward W. Cox patented
land between Clayton and Louisville.

Emanuel Cox was born 28 July 1795 near Newbern, Craven Co.,
N. C., d. 11 June 1872. He married Sarah McNeill 9 Feb. 1826
in what is now Barbour Co., Ala.. She was born 22 April 1806
Richmond Co., N. C. and died 21 Dec. 1889. They are buried in
Clayton Cemetery. She was the daughter of John McNeill, who
came to this area from Richmond Co., N. C. ca 1821, settled near
Pea River Presbyterian Church, and died about 1823.

Emanuel Cox volunteered for service in the War of 1812 from
Hancock Co., Ga. in 1814. He also served in the Creek Indian
War in Barbour Co. in 1836. The obituary of Mrs. Sarah (McNeill)
Cox states that she had eleven children, with only three sur-
viving in 1889. Known issue:

1. *Ann Cox, b. ca 1830 Ala., never married, died by 1891.

2. John Cox, b. 11 June 31 Ala., d. 28 Oct. 1862, buried in
   Clayton Cemetery. In 1860, he was not married.

3. Elizabeth Cox, b. ca 1834 Ala.. She was the first wife of
   Col. Whitfield Clark, who died in Clayton, Ala. in Feb. 1875.
   Issue:

   a. Sarah Whitfield Clark, died 11 Sept. 1887.

4. Charles M. Cox, b. 22 April 1836 Ala., d. 6 April 1915,
   buried in Clayton Cemetery. He was not married in 1860.

5. William Emanuel (?) Cox, twin brother of Charles M. Cox, b.
   22 April 1836 Ala., d. 23 Dec. 1875, m. Lydia Johnson,
   daughter of Jesse Johnson. She was born 25 Nov. 1842, died
   18 July 1939. Both are buried in Clayton Cemetery. Issue:

   a. Regie Cox, b. ca 1864 Ala.

   b. Montross Cox, b. ca 1866 Ala.

   c. Victor Cox, b. ca 1868 Ala.

d. Ophelia Cox, b. March 1870 Ala., probably died young.

e. Aubrey Cox

f. Sallie M. Cox - minor in 1891

g. William E. Cox - minor in 1891

6. Hamilton Cox, b. 11 Nov. 1842, d. 3 Nov. 1910, buried in
    Clayton Cemetery. He was living in Bullock Co., Ala. in
    1873.

7. James Lumley Cox, b. 9 Nov. 1844 Ala., killed at Battle of
    Chickamauga in the Civil War.

8. Columbus Cox, b. ca 1844 Ala. He was in the household of
    Emanuel Cox in 1860, but not in 1850, and is not in the
    estate settlement of Emanuel Cox. It is possible that he
    was not a child of Emanuel and Sarah Cox.

    John, Charles M., William E., Hamilton and James L. Cox,
sons of Emanuel and Sarah Cox, all served in the Civil War.

    Other early Cox families in Barbour Co. were:

    Jesse Cox, b. ca 1809 Ga., m. Sarah ----, b. ca 1809 Ga..
He entered land near Louisville by 1830. Known issue: Nancy,
Mary, Helen, William, John and Charles Cox.

    Jimpsey Cox, b. ca 1808 Ga., d. 15 July 1852, m. Rachael,
daughter of Stephen Johnson (see Johnson family).

Sources of information:

Barbour Co., Ala. Probate Records
Barbour Co., Ala. Census Records
Barbour Co., Ala. Cemetery Records
Pension Application of Emanuel Cox
"Alabama Series" Vol. II by Helen S. Foley

*ADDITIONS & CORRECTIONS AS OF JUNE 1, 1979:

Miss Ann Cox died 25 Oct. 1891. Her only sister, Elizabeth,
died before the (Civil) War and three brothers and her father
died a few years later.

David Creech (b. 1773, d. by 1840) married Jane (Cone?).
She was born ca 1785 S. C., living with Aaron Creech in Barbour
Co. in 1850. Their children must have been:

1. Joshua C. Creech, b. ca 1808, d. ca June 1849 Barbour Co.,
   m. Elizabeth (Pynes?), b. ca 1820 Ga.. She m. (2) Levi Glass 3 March 1850. Issue (by Joshua Creech):

   a. David Creech, b. ca 1840/3 Ala. - no record after 1855.

   b. Joel Wesley Creech, b. Sept. 1846 Ala. - no record
      after 1854.

   c. Franklin Creech, b. Dec. 1848 Ala. - no record after
      1854.

   Fair Pynes was administrator of this estate in 1853, and
   Jasper Pynes petitioned the court as a relative to have
   Wesley Creech apprenticed to him. This seems to bear out
   the theory that Elizabeth (wife of Joshua C. Creech) was
   nee Pynes.

2. William Carter Creech, b. 4 Jan. 1810 Ga., d. 23 Feb. 1892
   Butler Co., Ala., m. Amanda Elizabeth Daniels, b. 19 Sept.
   1820 Ga., d. 9 Sept. 1909 Butler Co., Ala.. Issue:

   a. Josephine Creech, b. 15 Nov. 1840 Ala., d. 22 Feb. 1920
      Butler Co., Ala., never married.

   b. Sidney Creech, b. ca 1842 Ala., d. 1 Feb. 1865.

   c. Henry Clay Creech, b. 22 Dec. 1843 Ala., d. 18 Oct.
      1921, m. (1) Dorothy Payne (2) Mary E. Phelps.

   d. Francis Lafayette Creech, b. 27 Nov. 1845 Ala., d. 24
      May 1926 Butler Co., Ala., m. Alabama Payne.

   e. Margaret Creech, b. 22 March 1848 Ala., d. 21 Jan. 1920,
      m. William Routen.

   f. Amanda Henrietta Creech, b. 22 March 1850, d. 30 Nov.
      1922.

g. Hulda Jane Creech, b. 17 Sept. 1853, died 12 Jan. 1934, m. M. E. Hawkins.

h. William Jasper Creech, b. 11 Jan. 1855, d. 2 May 1930, never married.

i. Laura Katherine Creech, b. 21 May 1857, d. 18 April 1951 Greenville, Ala., m. William W. Thagard.

j. Jerre Bolling Creech, b. 6 Oct. 1859, d. 27 June 1937, m. Mrs. Drew Thrower.

k. Eugenia Mehetabel Creech, b. 27 Nov. 1861, d. 16 Nov. 1949 Greenville, Ala., m. George Sherling.

The above family left Barbour Co. after 1850 and settled in Butler Co., Ala..

3. Maryanna Creech m. Fair Pynes (see PYNES).

4. Laura Creech, b. ca 1815 Ga., m. Benjamin Frank DeShazo 7 Feb. 1847. (see DeSHAZO, page). Known issue:

a. James L. DeShazo, b. ca 1848 Ala., m. Nancy E. Perkins 29 Aug. 1865.

b. E. J. DeShazo (female), b. ca 1851 Ala.

c. C. A. DeShazo (female), b. ca 1856 Ala.

5. Lydia Ann Creech, b. ca 1817 Ga., m. (1) Noel Register 18 Oct. 1837 Henry Co., Ala. (2) Jeptha Lindsey 5 Aug. 1846. Issue (by 1st husband):

a. Elizabeth Calista Register, b. ca 1840 Ala., m. William Stevens Johnson 25 Dec. 1853.

Issue (by 2nd husband):

b. Charity J. Lindsey, b. ca 1848 Ala.

c. William J. Lindsey, b. ca 1850 Ala.

6. Elizabeth Ann Creech, b. ca 1819, m. James P. Durham 17 Oct. 1838.

7. Aaron Creech, b. 4 June 1818, d. 9 Feb. 1910 Shelby, Tex., m. Charity Creech 27 Jan. 1848, daughter of Noah and Sarah

(Trammell) Creech. Known issue:

a. David B. Creech, b. ca 1849 Ala.

b. Mary J. Creech, b. ca 1850 Ala.

c. William J. Creech, b. ca 1853 Ala.

d. John Creech, b. ca 1855 Ala.

e. Jeptha Creech, b. 26 March 1858, d. 5 April 1928 Shelby,
    Texas.

8. Annie Jane Creech, m. Benjamin Lewis 8 Feb. 1833 Henry Co.,
    Ala.. She may have married (2) David Powell 7 Feb. 1847,
    in which case her children were:

    By 1st husband:

    a. Benjamin Lewis, b. ca 1833/4 Ala.

    b. John Lewis, b. ca 1835 Ala.

    c. Jackson Lewis, b. ca 1837 Ala.

    d. Harrison Lewis, b. ca 1840 Ala.

    By 2nd husband:

    e. Ann M. Powell, b. ca 1847 Ala.

    f. Caroline Powell, b. ca 1848 Ala.

    g. Elliphar Powell, b. ca 1850 Ala.

Noah Creech, Sr. was born ca 1798 S. C., died by 1866 in
Panola Co., Texas, probably a brother of David Creech. He married Sarah Trammell 15 Feb. 1817 Laurens Co., Ga.. She was born
ca 1802 Ga., died after 1860. They were living in Henry Co.,
Ala. in 1830, in Jackson Co., Fla. in 1840 and in La. in 1850
and in Panola Co., Texas in 1860. Issue:

1. Sion Creech, Sr., b. ca 1822, d. 3 April 1887 DeSoto Par.,
    La. (buried in the Creech family cemetery in DeSoto Par.,
    La.), m. (1) Nancy Spears 1 Jan. 1844 Barbour Co., Ala.,
    daughter of David and Sarah Spears (2) Tilitha Harris Bill-
    inglsey 26 July 1864 DeSoto Par., La.. She was the widow
    of Bright Billingley and daughter of Hudson Harris who died

in 1841 in Pickens Co., Ala.. She died 3 Feb. 1883 (buried Smyrna Cem.) and he married (3) Mrs. Emily Pate Story 13 Jan. 1885 DeSoto Par., La.. After the death of Sion Creech, Sr., she married Melvin Stephens 18 Sept. 1887. He had married (1) Mary Creech, her step-daughter. Issue (by 1st wife):

a. Emily Creech, b. ca 1849, m. James Billingsley 18 Feb. 1869 DeSoto Par., La..

b. Sion Creech, Jr., b. 8 Feb. 1852, d. 9 March 1926 (buried Bethel Cem., DeSoto Par., La.), m. (1) Emma Russell 20 Jan. 1871 DeSoto Par., La. (2) Emily Moseley 11 Nov. 1877 DeSoto Par., La..

c. Nancy Creech, b. ca 1854

d. William Creech, b. ca 1858, m. (1) Ella Moseley 3 Dec. 1884 DeSoto Par., La. (2) Viola Sims 23 June 1899 in DeSoto Par., La..

e. James Creech, b. ca 1860, m. Mollie Williams 4 Aug. 1884 DeSoto Par., La..

f. Mary (Molly) Creech, b. ca 1862, m. Melvin Stephens 17 March 1879 DeSoto Par., La..

Issue (by 2nd wife):

g. Carrie Elizabeth Creech, b. 14 Aug. 1865, d. 1 May 1919, m. Wiley Augusta Walker 3 Dec. 1884 DeSoto Par., La. He was born 14 July 1860 Crawford Co., Ga., died 20 Aug. 1935, buried Bethel Cem., DeSoto Par., La..

h. Annie Creech, b. 27 March 1869, d. 12 Sept. 1896, buried Logensport Cem., DeSoto Par., La., m. Robert Rhette Russell 9 Oct. 1884 DeSoto Par., La.. He was born 24 Dec. 1862 and died 3 Sept. 1941.

i. Nora Creech, b. 10 Dec. 1871, d. 14 July 1885, probably buried in Smyrna Church Cem., DeSoto Par., La..

Issue (by 3rd wife):

    j. Nettie Creech, b. ca 1885, m. Lonnie Moorman.

2. Paul J. Creech, b. ca 1823, m. Mary J. ----.

3. Daniel J. Creech, b. ca 1825 Ala., m. (1) Harriet Spears 11
Aug. 1852 DeSoto Par., La., (2) Mary Jane Johnson 5 Jan.
1854 Panola Co., Texas (3) Narcis (Narcissa?) J. Sinclair
16 Oct. 1865 Panola Co., Texas.

4. Nancy Creech, b. ca 1828 m. Thomas C. Pyle 12 Aug. 1848
DeSoto Par., La..

5. Charity Creech, b. 7 Sept. 1827, d. 9 Feb. 1910, m. Aaron
Creech 27 Jan. 1848 Barbour Co., Ala., daughter of David and
Jane (Cone?) Creech.

6. Thomas J. Creech, b. ca 1832, m. Rebecca Carter 6 June 1856
DeSoto Par., La..

7. Noah Creech, Jr., b. ca 1836, m. Missouri Hunt 18 March
1859 Panola Co., Texas.

8. Sarah Creech, b. ca 1838, m. Enoch M. Booker 21 Dec. 1854
Panola Co., Texas.

9. James J. Creech, b. ca 1842, m. Missouri Caroline Billingsley 13 Feb. 1867 DeSoto Par., La.

Other sources:

Henry Co., Ala. Probate Records
Data from descendants

CREWS

Arthur (Anderson?) Crews was born 28 Jan. 1792 Ga., d. 1 Feb. 1872, m. (1) Mary V. King. She was born 11 April 1796 S. C., died 29 May 1861. They are buried in New Hope Cem.. He m. (2) Maisy C. Walker 12 May 1863. She was born 21 Dec. 1832, died 17 Jan. 1889 and is buried in the Walker family cemetery (see WALKER).

Issue (by 1st wife):

1. William Berry Crews, b. 8 Dec. 1816 Ga., d. 20 July 1865, m. Catherine, daughter of Roderick and Mary McSwean, on 8 Dec. 1842 (see McSWEAN, page 218). She was born 25 Feb. 1822 N. C., died 25 Jan. 1902 and is buried in New Hope Cem.. She married (2) Rev. Wm. H. Chambers 7 Jan. 1868. Issue:
   a. Mary V. Crews, b. 1843 Ala., d. 1923, m. James J. Winn 9 June 1868. He was born 1841 and died 1924. They are buried in Clayton Cem..
   b. Nancy Jane Crews, b. 1849 Ala., d. 1923, never married. She is buried in Clayton Cem..

2. Dr. John E. Crews, b. 1 Jan. 1819 Jones Co., Ga., d. 2 June 1901, m. Margaret E. DuBose 25 March 1851 Early Co., Ga.. She was born 30 June 1831 S. C., died 15 May 1917. Issue:
   a. William Newton Crews, b. 21 April 1852 Ala., d. 3 Oct. 1865, buried New Hope Cem..

3. Cynthia Crews, b. 24 March 1829 Ala., d. 16 June 1851, m. Wesley Bishop 24 Feb. 1848. He was born 20 Oct. 1819 in Twiggs Co., Ga., died 24 March 1884, son of William and Nancy Bishop. They are buried in the Bishop-Blair Cem.. He married (2) Louisa M. M. Laura Weaver 11 Nov. 1862, b. ca 1839, d. 4 July 1879. Issue (by 1st wife):
   a. Nancy J. Bishop, b. 14 March 1849 Ala., d. 2 March 1914, m. James Harvey Long 14 Nov. 1867. He was born 16 Feb.

1840, died 27 Nov. 1923. They are buried in Spring Hill Methodist Cem..

    b. William A. Bishop, b. ca 1853 Ala., died after 1903, m. Mary L. Cowan 20 Oct. 1875.

(by 2nd wife):

    c. D. B. (Bolen?) Bishop, b. ca 1866 Ala., d. 1896 Alacia, Ark.

    d. Cynthia (Clifford?) E. Bishop, b. 1867, m. George A. Johnston (see JOHNSTON).

    e. Frederick Stephen Bishop, b. ca 1871.

    f. Edward B. Bishop, b. ca 1873.

    g. a son, born & died 6 June 1878.

4. Arthur Anderson Crews, b. 1 March 1831 Ala., d. 27 Jan. 1910, m. Sarah Jane Thomas 18 Jan. 1857 (see THOMAS, page   ). She was born 5 Feb. 1837 and died 21 March 1926. They are buried in Clayton Cem.. Issue:

    a. Cynthia Marshall Crews, b. 12 Nov. 1857 Butler Co., Ala., d. 30 Aug. 1885, m. Dr. George M. Bobbit 1 March 1881. He was born 7 Nov. 1851 and died 8 Aug. 1885. They are buried in Fairview Cem., Eufaula, Ala..

    b. Clifford Ann Crews, b. 20 April 1860 Ala., d. 1934, m. John Robert Ventress 26 Feb. 1879 (see VENTRESS).

    c. Jennie Crews, died young

    d. Dolly Crews, died young

5. Jane Crews, died by 1903, m. Rev. John D. Worrell 27 July 1847. In 1872, they were living in McCullough Co., Texas. Known issue (living in Texas in 1903):

    a. J. S. Worrell

    b. J. D. Worrell

    c. Francis Worrell

    d. Laura Worrell m. _____ Taylor

e. M. J. Worrell (female) m. _____ Reed.

6. Whittemore R. Crews, d. by 1903, living in Comanche Co.,
   Texas in 1872. Probable issue (all of Texas in 1903):

   a. John E. B. Crews

   b. Synthia S. Crews

   c. W. B. Crews

   d. Sophronia Crews m. _____ Jenkins

   e. Catherine Crews m. _____ Whitney

   f. Lottie P. Crews m. _____ Howard

7. Harriett A. Crews, b. ca 1825 Ala., d. by 1872, m. James
   Johnston 17 Dec. 1846 (see JOHNSTON).

By 2nd wife:

8. Mary V. Crews, b. 25 Aug. 1864 Ala., d. 21 July 1865, buried
   New Hope Cem..

9. Ella C. Crews, b. ca 1866 Fla., m. E. M. Glover 10 April
   1890.

10. Andrew Johnson Crews, b. ca 1870 Ala., living Cuba 1903.

DANSBY

Daniel M. Dansby first entered land in 1827 in the Southwestern edge of what is now Barbour Co., Ala.. In 1834, he and John Dansby entered 40 acres jointly near Palmyra Church, North of the Indian Boundary Line. In 1835 and 1838, John Dansby entered more land near Daniel M. Dansby's original patent. In 1835 and 1836, Isham M. Dansby also entered land nearby. Charles Dansby entered land in 1836 in what is now Bullock Co., Ala.

Winza Dansby, a widow, was born ca 1782. The name of her husband does not appear in the Barbour Co. records. She died after 1850, as she was enumerated that year in the household of Jesse Johns in Pike Co., Ala.. Probable issue:

1. Daniel M. Dansby, b. ca 1800/10, m. Lucinda, daughter of Noah B. Cole. They were living in Cass Co., Texas by 1857. Known issue:

   a. A son, name unknown, b. ca 1835/40.

2. *John Dansby, b. ca 1805 S. C., m. Sarah ---. She was born ca 1814-17 Ga.. Probable issue:

   a. Hiram Dansby, b. ca 1832 Ala., m. Mary A. Danner 23 Dec. 1850.

   b. Martha Dansby, b. ca 1834 Ala.

   c. Elizabeth Dansby, b. ca 1836 Ala., m. William M. Roundtree 23 Oct. 1860.

   d. Daniel Dansby, b. ca 1838 Ala.

   e. John Dansby, b. ca 1839 Ala., m. Melvina E. Scroggins 23 Dec. 1860.

   f. Winzey Dansby, b. ca 1840 Ala.

   g. George Dansby, b. ca 1841 Ala., may have married Clarisy A. D. Minshew 30 Aug. 1860.

   h. Catherine Dansby, b. ca 1843 Ala.

   i. Jane Dansby, b. ca 1844 Ala.

69

j. Mahala Dansby, b. ca 1846 Ala.

k. Isham Beal Dansby, b. 5 Sept. 1855 Ala., d. 28 Oct. 1915, may have married Mary Joiner 20 June 1872. He is buried in Elam Baptist Church Cemetery.

l. Monroe Dansby, b. ca 1860 Ala.

m. Mary Dansby, b. ca 1864 Ala.

3. Isham M. Dansby, b. ca 1810 S. C., m. Abigail J. McClure, b. ca 1823 S. C.. They moved to Choctaw Co., Ala. ca 1855. Known issue:

a. Mary Dansby, b. ca 1840 Ala.. A Mary Jane Dansby m. William P. Lester 28 Sept. 1854 at Isham Dansby's.

b. Martha Dansby, b. ca 1842 Ala., may have married William Utsey.

c. Lawrence Dansby, b. ca 1844 Ala.

d. Thomas B. Dansby, b. ca 1846 Ala.

e. James M. Dansby, b. ca 1851 Ala.

f. William J. Dansby, b. ca 1854 Ala.

g. Amanda O. Dansby, b. ca 1856 Ala.

h. Alice A. Dansby, b. ca 1858 Ala.

4. Catharine Dansby, b. ca 1814, m. Jesse Johns, b. ca 1805 S. C.. They were living in Pike Co., Ala. in 1850. Known issue:

a. Elijah Johns, b. ca 1837 Ala.

b. Hicks Johns, b. ca 1839 Ala.

c. Mary Johns, b. ca 1844 Ala.

d. Aenis Johns (female), b. ca 1846 Ala.

e. Lucinda Johns, b. ca 1849 Ala.

5. Mary Dansby, b. ca 1817 S. C., m. Jacob Minshew, b. ca 1808 N. C. Known issue:

a. Catherine Minshew, b. ca 1837 Ala.

b. Melissa Minshew, b. ca 1838 Ala.

c. Lorenzo Minshew, b. ca 1840 Ala.

d. Julia Minshew, b. ca 1841 Ala.

e. Alonzo Minshew, b. ca 1844 Ala.

If Charles Dansby, who entered land in 1836, is related to the other Dansby families of Barbour Co., it is not shown in the records. In 1836, he and his wife, Frances Elizabeth, gave the land they had entered to their daughter, Frances Elizabeth Dansby.

There are no estate settlements in the Barbour Co. records for these early Dansby families, and almost no cemetery records. There are a few deeds, and it is from them and the census records that the foregoing information was obtained.

Sources of information:

Barbour Co., Ala. Probate Records
Barbour Co., Ala. Census Records
Barbour Co., Ala. Cemetery Records
Pike Co., Ala. Census Records

*ADDITIONS & CORRECTIONS AS OF JUNE 1, 1979:

John Dansby died Jan. 1896 near Elamville (Ala.), age 102 (note: age doubtful). He was one of the oldest citizens of Barbour Co.

DESHAZO

Wilson Deshazo patented land from 1829 through 1849. His
earliest patent was just North of Clayton, but later ones were
further East on Cheneyhatchee Creek, where he and William Tate
owned a mill.

He was born ca 1804 in Edgefield Dist., S. C., died 27 Nov.
1892, m. (1) Delilah (Prescott?). She was born ca 1809 in Ga.,
died ca 1870. He m. (2) Mary H., widow of Edward Dillard, on
14 Nov. 1872. She died 5 Dec. 1905. Known issue (all by 1st
wife):

1. Paul Hamilton Deshazo, b. ca 1831 Ala., d. 1 Sept. 1864 New
    Orleans, La. (CSA), m. Sarah Ginwright 2 April 1851. She
    died in Lakeland, Fla.. Probable issue:

    a. Louisa Alabama Deshazo, b. ca 1852 Ala., m. Green Barry
        James 22 Dec. 1872.

    b. James Monroe Deshazo, b. ca 1854 Ala., m. Martha A. Coats
        24 Nov. 1872.

    c. John Calhoun Deshazo, b. ca 1856 Ala., lived in Milton,
        Fla..

    d. William Preston Deshazo, b. ca 1858 Ala., m. Lucy J.
        Lunsford 1 Dec. 1875. They lived in Panama City, Fla.

    e. Allen Deshazo, b. ca 1860 Ala.

    f. Jesse B. Deshazo, b. ca 1862 Ala., m.*Susan Bush 1 Dec.
        1881, lived in Lakeland, Fla..

    g. Wilson Deshazo, lived in Noma, Fla.

2. Moses Wilson Deshazo, b. 12 Jan. 1832 Ala., d. 28 Sept. 1915,
    m. (1) Amanda A. Brown 11 Feb. 1858 (2) Lydia K. Brown 14
    June 1865. She was born 9 March 1832 Fla., died 24 Oct.
    1915. Moses W. and Lydia K. Deshazo are buried in Mount
    Aerial Cemetery. Known issue:

By 1st wife:

a. Theodosia Deshazo, b. ca 1859 Ala.

b. Henry L. Deshazo, b. ca 1860 Ala., may have married
   Martha Redman 18 Jan. 1892.

By 2nd wife:

c. James H. Deshazo, b. ca 1868 Ala., may have married Emma
   Richards 5 Dec. 1897.

3. Hugh Deshazo, b. ca 1838 Ala.. Descendants of Wilson Deshazo say that Hugh Deshazo lived in Dothan, Ala..

4. Louisa M. Deshazo, b. ca 1840 Ala., m. James W. Brown 5 Jan.
   1860.

5. Annie Deshazo, b. ca 1849 Ala., m. James G. S. Baker 18 July
   1865.

6. Martha Deshazo (see Jernigan family). Descendants say she
   was the oldest daughter of Wilson and Delilah Deshazo, but
   there is no proof except that the 1838 Census shows Wilson
   Deshazo with a daughter under 21 years of age. William Jernigan and Martha Deshazo married 12 March 1845.

In the 1838 Census of Barbour Co., there was a John Deshazo.
He was also in the 1840 Census, age 30/40, wife age 30/40, 1
male under 5, 1 male 10/15, 2 females under 5, 1 female 5/10 and
1 female 10/15. He entered land in 1836 adjoining Wilson Deshazo (North of Clayton) as John Deshazo, Sr..

In the 1838 Census of Barbour Co., there was a J. E. Deshazo,
and in the 1840 Census, John E. Deshazo was age 20/30, wife age
15/20, and one female under 5. There was no John Deshazo in the
1850 Census of Barbour Co.. In a deed dated 15 March 1850, John
Deshazo of Union Co., Ark. sold his land in Barbour Co. to Thomas
Canady.

Robert Deshazo entered land East of Clayton on the Indian
Boundary Line in 1836. In 1835, he bought land near Wilson

73

Deshazo on Cheneyhatchee Creek. In the 1838 Census, there were Robert Deshazo, Sr. and Robert Deshazo. In the 1840 Census, Robert Deshazo was age 60/70, wife age 40/50, 1 male under 5, 1 male 5/10, 1 male 15/20, 1 female under 5, 1 female 10/15 and 2 females 20/30. In the 1840 Census, R. H. Deshazo was age 20/30, wife age 20/30, 1 male under 5 and 1 female under 5. Neither are in the 1850 Census.

There was a Gracy Deshazo, b. ca 1787 S. C., who was enumerated near Wilson Deshazo in the 1850 and 1860 Censuses. It is possible that she was the widow of Robert Deshazo, Sr.. In this household were:

1. Benjamin Franklin Deshazo, b. ca 1822 S. C., m. Laura A. Creech 7 Feb. 1847. She was born ca 1826 in Ga.. Known issue:

   a. James L. T. Deshazo, b. ca 1848 Ala., m. Nancy E. Perkins 29 Aug. 1865.

   b. E. J. Deshazo (female), b. ca 1851 Ala.

   c. C. A. Deshazo (female), b. ca 1856 Ala.

2. William Deshazo, b. ca 1833 S. C.. There was a William R. Deshazo who served in the Civil War (a resident of Clayton, Ala.). On 3 Aug. 1865, he married Mrs. T. C. Holley.

3. Thomas J. Deshazo, b. ca 1837 Ala., served in the Civil War.

4. Andrew E. Deshazo, b. ca 1843 Ala., m. Susan Ann Spencer 29 Sept. 1864. He also served in the Civil War.

Also in this household in 1860 was Milly McLeod, b. ca 1815 S.C., who may have been a widowed daughter of Gracy Deshazo.

Sarah Deshazo, b. ca 1811 Ga., was enumerated next to Wilson Deshazo in the 1850 Census. In her household were:

1. Thomas Deshazo, b. ca 1830 Ala.

2. James Deshazo, b. ca 1834 Ala.

3. Elizabeth Deshazo, b. ca 1840 Ala.

Sarah Deshazo may have been the widow of Robert H. Deshazo.

There was a Nancy Deshazo in the 1840 Census of Barbour Co., age 15/20, 2 males under 5 and 1 male 5/10. On 1 April 1840, James Black made a return as guardian of her minor children. She is not listed in the 1850 Census, but on 17 Sept. 1855, she married James Casey, Sr.. In 1860, she is enumerated as Nancy Casey, b. ca 1809 S. C..

Mrs. Louise Clark of Stuart, Fla., who is a Deshazo descendant, gives the following line:

I.   Jean de Chazeaux (John Deshazo) - from France to King & Queen Co., Va. 1695.

II.   Richard Deshazo, b. 1699 Va.

III. Peter Deshazo, b. 1730 King & Queen Co., Va., had sons Louis (to Putnam Co., Ga.), Robert and Richard.

IV. William Robert Deshazo, b. 1758, had sons Richard, Robert, Wilson and probably John.

V.   Wilson Deshazo, b. ca 1804 S. C., migrated to Barbour Co., Ala.

Sources of information:

Barbour Co., Ala. Probate Records
Barbour Co., Ala. Census Records
Barbour Co., Ala. Cemetery Records
Deshazo descendants

*ADDITIONS & CORRECTIONS AS OF JUNE 1, 1979:

Susie A., wife of Rev. J. B. DeShazo, died 9 Oct. 1901, buried near Eufaula. She leaves a husband (m. 1 Dec. 1881) and eight children.

EADES

Thomas Eades patented land North of Louisville in 1829.
There is no further record of him in Barbour Co..

Source of information:

Barbour Co., Ala. Probate Records

EFURD
(Eaford, Euford, Efort)

The Efurd family came to this area between 1823 and 1828 from Edgefield Co., S. C. and settled in an area West and Northwest of Clayton. Their neighbors in South Carolina were James McCarty, James W. Corlee, Benjamin Adkins, Isaac Gosset, Watts Mann, William Morris, William Loveless, William Grubbs, John DeShazo, William Deloach and Burris Warren (from deeds of Edgefield Co., S. C.). Many of these men were in Barbour Co. very early, which lends credulity to the legend of the large caravan of settlers that arrived here from South Carolina while this part of the country was a wilderness.

Thomas C. Efurd was the first of the family to patent land here (1829), and his mother, Lucy Efurd, entered her first patent in 1830.

Lucy Efurd was a widow when she arrived in Alabama; her husband, John Adam Efurd, died in Edgefield Co., S. C. by June 1822. There is much variation in the dates given for her birth. The 1830 Census of Pike Co., Ala. reads age 40/50, the 1850 Census of Barbour Co., Ala. reads age 79, and the inscription on her grave in the Warren Cemetery says she died in 1857, age 95 years. She gave her birthplace in 1850 as South Carolina. In 1830, Mrs. Lucy Efurd had in her household (besides herself) one female, age 90/100. Tradition says that she brought her mother-in-law with her when she came to Alabama, but her name is not on the records of this area.

In 1850, Enoch Fowler (age 76, born S. C.) was living with Lucy Efurd. It is generally assumed that he was her brother, but there is no proof of this. He died by Jan. 1852, and Thomas C. Efurd was his administrator.

Issue of John Adam and Lucy Efurd:

77

1. Mary Efurd, b. 27 Dec. 1792, d. by Sept. 1834, m. D. Martin, who died in S. C. before 1832. Issue:

   a. Sophia Martin, b. 31 Oct. 1812, d. after 1842, m. Edwin J. Cole by 1829.

   b. John T. Martin, b. ca 1815 S. C., m. Hepsey Worthington 11 May 1845. She was born 24 Sept. 1825, died 27 July 1866, daughter of Robert and Holland Worthington. She is buried in the Warren Cemetery.

   c. Cornelius O. Martin, b. 9 Nov. 1819 S. C., d. by Oct. 1865, n.m.

   d. William O. Martin, b. 28 Jan. 1822. He must have died young, as he is not mentioned in his mother's estate in 1834.

2. Giles C. Efurd, b. between 1790/1800, d. by Jan. 1840, m. ---- Warren, a daughter of Thomas and Rebecca Warren. She probably died before 1840, as she is not mentioned in the estate records of Giles C. Efurd. Issue:

   a. Rebecca Lucy Efurd, b. ca 1828 Ala., m. James T. Beasley 12 Aug. 1844.

   b. Thomas A. Efurd, b. ca 1830 Ala..

   c. Giles C. Efurd, b. ca 1832 Ala., m. Martha Collins 19 Dec. 1852.

3. Thomas C. Efurd, b. 14 Jan. 1800 S. C., d. by Nov. 1856, m. Mary Johnson 30 Nov. 1820 in S. C.. She was born 24 May 1805 S. C., d. after 1860 in Texas. Issue:

   a. John Adam Efurd, b. 18 Feb. 1822 S. C., d. Upshur Co., Texas, m. Mary Cope 12 Sept. 1844.

   b. Lucy Ann Efurd, b. 3 Feb. 1824 Ala., d. before 1890, m. Daniel G. Lewis 5 Oct. 1843.

   c. William T. I. C. Efurd, b. 27 Nov. 1826, d. 9 May 1894 (buried Union Baptist Cemetery), m. Elizabeth Bennett

14 Aug. 1856.

d. Sarah Ann Efurd, b. 1 June 1828, probably died young, as she is not named in the estate of Thos. C. Efurd.

e. Thomas C. Efurd, b. 27 Dec. 1830 Ala., d. after 1880, m. Elizabeth C. Herring 27 Dec. 1855.

f. Mary Ann Louisa Efurd, b. 27 Nov. 1833 Ala., m. Tandy W. King 31 Jan. 1854. She was his second wife.

g. Giles C. Efurd, b. 18 Nov. 1836 Ala., died in Texas, m. Nancy E. H. Johns 25 Oct. 1860 in Pike Co., Ala..

h. Julyann Efurd, b. 28 June 1839. She is not named in the estate of Thos. C. Efurd, nor is she in the 1850 Census, so she must have died before this date.

4. Lucinda Efurd, b. 28 Feb. 1811 S. C., d. 10 March 1888, m. Burris Warren in S. C. (see Warren family).

Sources of information:

Barbour Co., Ala. Census Records
Barbour Co., Ala. Probate Records
Barbour Co., Ala. Cemetery Records
Thomas C. Efurd Bible

FAULK
(Falk, Folk)

There were two Faulk families that settled South of Clio in 1827. If they were related, it was very far back.

James K. (or R.) Faulk (called "Red" James) settled first near the Pike Co., line, but in 1829 he patented land East of Louisville. He was born 27 Dec. 1786 in N. C., died 3 May 1851. His first wife was Rhoda Sellers, born 11 Nov. 1784 S. C., died 8 Nov. 1847, daughter of Benjamin and Leticia Sellers of N. C./ S. C.. They are buried in a family cemetery East of Louisville. James K. Faulk may have married (2) Mary ----. James K. and Rhoda Faulk came to Alabama from Marion Co., S. C. by 1822. Issue (all by 1st wife):

1. Sarah Faulk, b. ca 1805 S. C., never married.

2. Jason Faulk, may not have been a son of James Faulk. May have lived in Georgia.

3. Lorenzo Faulk, b. 12 Sept. 1811 S. C., d. 26 April 1861, m. Mary L. Willis in 1835. She was born 4 April 1818, died 1 March 1870, daughter of Joel and Elizabeth (Head) Willis. Lorenzo and Mary are buried in a family cemetery near Midway (now Bullock Co.) Ala.. Issue:

   a. Mary E. Clementine Faulk, b. 28 July 1837 Ala., d. 9 Jan. 1877 in Texas, m. Wiley Stripling 27 July 1855.

   b. Martha Emma Caroline Faulk, b. 8 July 1838, d. 24 Oct. 1881, m. Thomas C. Parker, b. 1832 Johnston Co., N. C., d. 1868, son of Pleasant L. Parker and Elizabeth Lee.

   c. William Benjamin Faulk, b. 6 July 1840, d. 27 Nov. 1907 Bullock Co., Ala.. He never married and is buried in the family cemetery.

   d. Richard Joel Faulk, b. 14 May 1843 Midway, Ala., d. 9 Aug. 1862 in Civil War at Mobile, Ala..

80

e. James Madison Faulk, b. 29 May 1845, d. 15 July 1881
    Harrisonburg, La., m. Frances E. Sherwood 24 March 1870
    in Harrisonburg, La.. She was born 11 June 1852, died
    6 July 1930 - both are buried in Harrisonburg, La..

f. John Fletcher Faulk, b. 5 March 1847, Ala., d. 29 Dec.
    1938 in a Confederate Soldiers' Home in Oklahoma, m.
    Martha Caroline Reeves, b. 1 Feb. 1849 Ala., died 8
    Jan. 1895, buried Bowman's Point Cem., Wilson Co., Okla.
    They were living in Navarro Co., Texas in 1880.

g. Daniel Henderson Faulk, b. 16 March 1849 Ala., d. 1935
    Ellis Co., Texas, m. (1) Anna E. Faulk 3 Dec. 1869, b.
    10 April 1853 (?), died 11 Oct. 1876, buried Fincastle
    Cem., Henderson Co., Texas (2) Catherine Warren in Tex.

h. Elizabeth Lanora Faulk, b. 2 Jan. 1851 Ala., d. 23
    April 1870, m. James E. Speller 24 May 1869.

i. Rhoda A. Faulk, b. 30 Dec. 1852, d. 2 March 1853, buried
    in the family cemetery in Bullock Co., Ala..

j. Sarah Viola Faulk, b. 27 April 1854 Midway, Ala., d.
    27 July 1917 Kaufman, Texas, m. Joel B. Willis 15 Dec.
    1880 in Bullock Co., Ala..

k. George Harvey Faulk, b. 2 June 1856 Ala., d. 18 Jan.
    1940 in Montgomery Co., Ala., m. Sarah Catherine King,
    b. 1858 Union Springs, Ala., d. 1928 Montgomery, Ala..
    They are buried in Greenwood Cem., Montgomery, Ala..

l. Jessie D. Faulk, b. 21 Oct. 1858, d. 13 April 1859,
    buried in the family cemetery in Bullock Co., Ala..

m. Fletcher Comer Faulk, b. ca 1860, died young.

n. Lorenzo Kendrick Faulk, b. 21 Nov. 1861, d. 15 Oct.
    1886 at Ft. Worth, Texas, buried in Oakwood Cemetery
    Montgomery, Ala.. He married Lillian G. Robson 7 Sept.
    1882, b. 14 Nov. 1863 near Cuthbert, Ga., d. 20 Jan.

1956 in Rock Hill, Mo.. She was daughter of Jesse Robson and Susan Marie Worthington. She married (3) Benjamin D. Lydick and is buried in Valhalla Cem., St. Louis, Mo..

4. William Kendrick Faulk, b. 28 Oct. 1817 Ala., d. 24 April 1872, buried Fincastle Cem., Henderson Co., Texas, m. Lucretia Faulk, b. 24 April 1808 Ga., daughter of "Black" James Faulk (see later). Known issue:

    a. John Faulk, b. 6 Dec. 1839, d. 2 March 1922 at Corsicana, Texas, m. Charlotte Terence Faulk 13 Feb. 1868, b. 20 Dec. 1838 Barbour Co., Ala., d. 11 March 1907, Corsicana, Texas. She was a daughter of Alfred Wright Faulk (see later). (Note: According to updated information from Mrs. C. E. Berkman, Austin, Texas given to Mrs. Foley, the first wife of John Faulk was Sallie Jane Stewart, born 30 May 1842, died 28 May 1862, buried Fincastle Cem., Henderson Co., Texas.)

    b. William L. Faulk, b. ca 1846 Ala., d. 1924 in Texas, m. Talula P. Coleman 1870 in Henderson Co., Texas. Still living there in 1880.

    c. James E. Faulk, b. 1849 La., died Trinidad, Texas, m. ---- Murray.

    d. Anna Faulk, died in Ellis Co., Texas, may have married her cousin, Daniel Henderson Faulk.

5. Jesse Faulk, b. 9 Nov. 1822 Ala., d. 26 May 1854 - he is buried in the family cemetery East of Louisville. He married Nancy Head on 25 July 1843. She m. (2) John Sloan 17 March 1857. He died 21 Sept. 1857. Issue:

    a. Sarah Elizabeth Faulk, b. ca 1843 Ala., m. Andrew J. Anglin on 13 Feb. 1862.

    b. Mary L. Faulk, b. ca 1844, m. Jefferson Lee 27 Sept.

1860.

   c.   James E. Faulk, b. ca 1847 Ala.

   d.   Martha A. E. Faulk, b. ca 1852.

6. Levi (or Levin) B. Faulk, b. 15 May 1827, d. 8 Nov. 1862
    Canton, Texas, m. Savannah Sloan, b. 20 June 1820 Ga.; d.
    2 Oct. 1895 Canton, Texas, a sister of John Sloan. Both
    buried in Cox Cem. near Canton, Texas. Known issue:

   a.   Jasper N. Faulk, b. 10 Feb. 1845 Ala., d. 1 April 1906
      Canton, Texas, m. Hannah ----. She was born 8 July
      1849, d. 2 Oct. 1895 Canton, Texas. Both are buried in
      Prairie Springs Cem., Canton, Texas.

   b.   Rhoda K. Faulk, b. 1846 Ala.

   c.   Sophronia Faulk, b. 1847, d. 1849 Ala.

   d.   Jane Elvina Faulk, b. 1851 Ala.

   e.   Zelpha Faulk, b. 1853 Ala.

   f.   Nancy Faulk, b. 1856 Ala.

"Black" James Faulk was born ca 1775, d. 1849 Marshall,
Texas and is buried there. He is believed to have come to what
is now Barbour Co. about 1819, and had migrated to Marshall Co.,
Texas by 1847. His descendants say he married Nellie (Elender)
Sheppard, b. 3 Nov. 1783, d. 27 Dec. 1870. They married in
Twiggs Co., Ga. about 1803. She is buried in Fincastle Cem.
near Frankston, Texas. Known issue:

1. Nancy Faulk, b. 1 Aug. 1805 Ga., d. 3 Oct. 1883, m. Francis
    Johns 15 June 1843. He was born 12 Dec. 1800 and died 2
    Nov. 1881. Both are buried in the Johns family cemetery
    near the Pike Co. line. No issue.

2. Lucretia Faulk, b. 24 April 1808 Twiggs Co., Ga., m. William
    Kendrick Faulk, son of "Red" James Faulk. In 1883, they
    were living in Athens, Texas. (See William Kendrick Faulk).

3. Andrew Sheppard Faulk, b. ca 1812 Ga., d. by 1860, m.

Lourana Faulk, b. ca 1812 N. C. There is very little docu-
mented record of this family. Most of the following has
been pieced together from census records and information
furnished by descendants. It appears that Andrew Sheppard
Faulk and his wife, Lourana, went to Texas, then returned
to Barbour Co., Ala.. Probable issue:

a. Mark Faulk, b. 15 March, died young when he fell off a
    river or gulf steamer while returning from Texas.

b. Jane Lucretia Faulk, b. 15 May 1839, m. (1) Frances An-
    drew Miles 1 Aug. 1855 (2) Robert Thompson 7 Feb. 1867.

c. Julianna V. Faulk, b. 11 Feb. 1841, m. (1) William A.
    Liptrot 2 Feb. 1857 (2) ---- Jordan. In 1850, Julianna
    V. Faulk and her sister, Nancy L. Faulk, were living
    with Francis and Nancy Johns.

d. Nancy L. Faulk, b. 17 Sept. 1840 (1842?), m. Henry L.
    Faulk, Jr. on 18 Aug. 1865. She was his second wife.

e. Alabama Faulk, b. 14 Dec. 1843, died young.

f. James Faulk, b. 2 Jan. 1845, d. 20 April 1845.

g. Jefferson Pruett Faulk, b. 22 May 1846, m. Elizabeth
    Cox. In 1883, they were living in Pike Co., Ala.

h. Rhoda K. Faulk, b. 11 May 1849, m. John Newberry 7 April
    1867. They were living in Pike Co., Ala. in 1883.

4. Kisiah Faulk, b. 25 Dec. 1814, d. 5 Oct. 1886 in Texas, m.
    (1) ---- Vickers, (2) Francis Howard 23 May 1844, (3) John
    Tillman Faulk 1 Jan. 1849 Monroe, La.. She was living in
    Henderson Co., Texas in 1870. He was born 26 Dec. 1784, d.
    5 Nov. 1871 Fondah, La., son of Jonathan and Phoebe Faulk of
    Bladen Co., N. C. and Monroe, La.. He was her third husband
    and she was his fourth wife. They are buried in a family
    cemetery in Logtown, La.. Known issue:

    a. J. J. Faulk, b. ca 1851 La.

b. Alfred A. Faulk, b. ca 1853 La.

c. Nancy J. Faulk, b. ca 1854 La.

5. William H. Faulk, b. ca 1818, d. ca 1860 in Texas, buried in Fincastle Cem. near Frankston, Texas.

6. Jane Faulk, b. ca 1820, d. 1874 Navarro, Texas, m. Thomas B. Herndon. Known issue:

   a. Lucretia E. Herndon, b. ca 1861 in Texas, m. A. W. Faulk 27 Nov. 1881. In 1880, she was living with Francis and Nancy (Faulk) Johns in Barbour Co..

7. Gaines Faulk, b. ca 1822, d. 1850 Lavaca, Texas, never married.

Henry Lawson Faulk, Sr. came to this area in 1827 and settled West of Clio near the present Pike Co. line. It is generally believed that he came from Twiggs Co., Ga., and was a brother of "Black" James Faulk. He is buried in an unmarked grave in the Faulk Cemetery, as is his wife, Nancy (Kelly?). He died by July 1847; she was born ca 1790, died after 1870. Issue:

1. Alfred Wright Faulk, b. 30 June 1809 Ga., d. 25 June 1888, m. Charlotte Bizzell. She was born 26 Aug. 1817 S. C., died 28 Nov. 1891. Both are buried in Faulk Cemetery. Issue:

   a. Nancy Ann Faulk, b. 15 April 1835, d. 21 Sept. 1876. She never married, and is buried in Faulk Cemetery.

   b. Charlotte T. Faulk, b. ca 1836 Ala., m. John Faulk 13 Feb. 1858. He was a son of William Kendrick Faulk.

   c. Mary Jane Faulk, b. 11 Feb. 1837 Ala., d. 16 Jan. 1843. She is buried in Faulk Cemetery.

   d. Henry B. Faulk, M.D., b. ca 1839 Ala., m. Parthenia ---. They were living in Navarro Co., Texas in 1880.

   e. James Knox Faulk, b. 21 May 1843 Ala., d. 24 July 1901, m. Mary Jane Reynolds 6 Aug. 1865. She was born 25

July 1846 and died 16 May 1917. Both buried in Faulk
Cem. near Clio, Ala.

f. Mark Washington Faulk, b. 17 Oct. 1845 Ala., d. 15 April
    1907, and is buried in Faulk Cemetery.

g. Daniel Winston Faulk, b. 1846 Ala., d. 1914, m. Texana
    ----. She was born 1866, died 1904. They are buried
    in Faulk Cemetery.

h. Alfred Wright Faulk, Jr., b. ca 1848 Ala., m. L. E.
    Herndon on 27 Nov. 1881. She was a daughter of Thomas
    B. and Jane (Faulk) Herndon.

i. William Curtis Faulk, b. 15 Feb. 1850 Ala., d. 19 June
    1854, buried in Faulk Cemetery.

j. John Faulk, b. ca 1850 Ala.

k. Zenobia A. Faulk, b. 22 Nov. 1854 Ala., d. 7 Nov. 1933,
    m. John B. Reynolds. He was born 1 Aug. 1851, died 10
    April 1902. They are buried in Faulk Cemetery.

2. Cassender Faulk, died ca 1845, m. Henry Nathaniel Bizzell.
    He was born 1810, died 1856, son of Bennett Bizzell and
    Mary Fields. He m. (2) Mary ----. Issue (by 1st wife):

    a. Henry Bartemus Horatio Bizzell, b. 1833 Dale Co., Ala.,
        d. 1903 Jacksonville, Texas, m. Sarah Thorne, b. 1830
        S. C.

    b. James Curtis Bizzell, b. 1834 Barbour Co., Ala., d.
        before 1880, Fincastle, Texas, believed to have married
        his first cousin, Mahala W. Bizzell.

    c. Mary Jeanette Bizzell, b. 1840 Ala., d. Frankton, Texas,
        m. James W. Danner 15 Oct. 1857.

3. Henry Lawson Faulk, Jr., b. 14 Nov. 1813 Ga., d. 27 July
    1870, m. Sarah J. Bizzell 29 June 1845. She was born 14
    Jan. 1823, died 24 April 1864. Both are buried in Faulk
    Cemetery. He m. (2) Nancy L. Faulk, daughter of Andrew S.

Faulk, on 18 Aug. 1865. Issue (by 1st wife):

a. William Wright Faulk, b. 26 Aug. 1846 Ala., d. 1 March 1908, m. Sarah Jane Faulk 28 Nov. 1876. She was born 22 June 1854, died 9 Aug. 1886. They are buried in Faulk Cemetery.

b. Henry Bennett Faulk, b. 29 Nov. 1848, d. Dec. 1907, m. Mae Waddell.

c. James Harrison Faulk, b. 18 Nov. 1850 Ala., d. 15 Jan. 1885, buried in Faulk Cemetery.

d. Mary J. Faulk, b. 1 Feb. 1853 Ala., d. 15 May 1930, m. W. Henry Faulk 23 Dec. 1875. He was born 22 Aug. 1848, died 25 Nov. 1953. Both are buried in Faulk Cemetery.

e. Leonora A. Faulk, b. 27 March 1855 Ala., d. 2 May 1879, buried in Faulk Cemetery.

f. Nancy E. Faulk, b. 16 May 1857, d. 25 June 1862, buried in Faulk Cemetery.

g. Charlotte Ann Faulk, born and died 1858 Ala..

h. Jefferson Davis Faulk, b. 13 June 1861 Ala., d. 9 Aug. 1883, buried in Faulk Cemetery.

4. Ellena Jane Faulk, b. ca 1820 Ala., m. John D. Seals. Known issue:

a. Ann Seals, b. ca 1839 Ala., m. Henry Day 13 Feb. 1859.

b. Warren Seals, b. ca 1841 Ala.

c. Laura Seals, b. ca 1843 Ala., m. Thos. F. Ellington 7 Aug. 1864.

d. Mary Seals, b. ca 1846 Ala.

e. Martha Seals, b. ca 1849 Ala., m. R. P. Tombelin 21 Nov. 1861.

f. Amanda Seals, b. ca 1850 Ala.

g. Ella Seals, b. ca 1852 Ala.

h. William Seals, b. 9 March 1860 Ala., d. 30 May 1935, m.

Nita Sims. They are buried in Bethlehem Church Cemetery.

    i. Frances Seals, b. ca 1862 Ala.

    j. John Seals, b. 1864 Ala., d. 1943, buried in Bethlehem Cemetery.

5. Elizabeth Ann Faulk, b. ca 1822 Ala., m. Jackson Miller, b. ca 1817 N. C.. Known issue:

    a. Nancy V. Miller, b. ca 1845 Ala.

    b. John W. Miller, b. ca 1846 Ala.

    c. Lucretia J. Miller, b. ca 1849 Ala.

6. Louie Faulk (possibly).

7. Nancy Faulk, died by 1847, married Everett Loveless. Issue:

    a. Everett Loveless, Jr.

8. James K. Faulk, b. 14 May 1823 Ala., d. 24 July 1901, m. Mary Phillips 9 Sept. 1847. He is buried in Faulk Cemetery. Known issue:

    a. Lucretia Faulk, b. ca 1849 Ala., m. Frank M. Williamson on 11 Jan. 1869.

    b. William Faulk, b. ca 1851 Ala.

    c. Henry R. Faulk, b. ca 1856 Ala.

    d. Martha Faulk, b. ca 1861 Ala.

9. Mark Washington Faulk, b. ca 1827 Ala., d. ca 1863 (CSA), m. Marinah Joiner 6 June 1850. She was born ca 1831 Ala., must have died by 1860. Issue:

    a. Nancy M. Faulk, b. ca 1851 Ala.

    b. Henry N. Faulk, b. ca 1853 Ala., died 5 March 1901, buried in Faulk Cemetery.

    c. Cynthia J. Faulk, b. 1 Oct. 1857 Ala., d. 14 Jan. 1904, m. William E. Wilkinson. He was born 5 March 1859 and died 7 Oct. 1917. Both are buried in the Faulk Cem. near Clio, Ala.

10. John William Faulk, b. 14 April 1828 Ala., d. 18 Dec. 1912,

m. (1) Mary Caroline Ketcham 23 Nov. 1848, daughter of David and Mary Ann Ketcham, (2) Mary Jane Faulk 31 July 1860, daughter of Henry and Sarah (Pryor) Faulk. She was born 7 May 1838, died 5 Feb. 1917. They are buried in Faulk Cemetery. Known issue:

By 1st wife:

a. Henry William Faulk, b. ca 1850 Ala.

b. Mark W. Faulk, b. ca 1851 Ala.

c. Sarah J. Faulk, b. ca 1854 Ala.

d. John Calhoun Faulk, b. ca 1856 Ala.

e. Francis M. Faulk, b. 1859 Ala., d. 21 Jan. 1901, buried in Faulk Cemetery.

By 2nd wife:

f. Albert Jackson Faulk, b. 18 April 1862 Ala., d. 11 April 1948, buried in Faulk Cemetery.

g. Everett L. Faulk, b. 18 Oct. 1864 Ala., d. 6 Feb. 1938, buried in Faulk Cemetery.

h. Willie L. Faulk (female), b. ca 1870 Ala.

i. Lee Ola Faulk, b. 28 April 1870, d. 1 March 1951, buried in Faulk Cemetery.

j. George W. Faulk, b. 15 May 1871 Ala., d. 11 Oct. 1925, m. Lula ----. She was born 23 Sept. 1878, died 1 Dec. 1946. They are buried in Faulk Cemetery.

Henry Faulk, b. ca 1798 Ga., came to Barbour Co. and settled near Henry Lawson Faulk, Sr.. He is believed to be a son of John Faulk of Twiggs Co., Ga. - this John Faulk may have been a brother of Henry Lawson Faulk, Sr. and "Black" James Faulk. Henry Faulk married Sarah (Pryor?), b. ca 1801 S. C.. He died before 1870 - she died after 1870. Known issue:

1. John F. Faulk, b. 18 July 1821, lived Dale Co., Ala.

2. Amanda Faulk, died young.

3. William Faulk, b. ca 1827 Ala.

4. Emaline Faulk, b. ca 1830 Ala., not married in 1880.

5. Sarah Ann Faulk, b. ca 1832, not married in 1880.

6. Martha Faulk, b. ca 1833 Ala., not married in 1880.

7. Mary Jane Faulk, b. ca 1835 Ala., m. John William Faulk, son of Henry Lawson Faulk, Sr.. She was his second wife.

8. Elizabeth A. Faulk, b. ca 1837 Ala., m. Leroy E. Stafford on 17 Oct. 1858. Known issue:

   a. Sarah J. Stafford, b. ca 1860 Ala.

9. Henry Lafayette Faulk, b. 21 April 1838, d. 2 June 1910 Austin, Texas, m. Lucy Card 26 Dec. 1867. In 1860, he was living with Francis and Nancy (Faulk) Johns.

10. James Andrew Faulk, b. ca 1841 Ala. (called "Uncle Babe"). In 1880, he was not married and was head of a household consisting of himself and his sisters, Emaline, Sarah Ann and Martha Faulk.

11. Laura Faulk

There were other Faulk families in Barbour Co., but the records do not give any clue as to their connection with the ones discussed previously.

In 1839, Nancy Faulk made her annual return as administratrix of John Faulk, deceased. He was born 27 March 1806, died 13 Aug. 1839, and is buried in Louisville Cemetery.

There was a Thomas Faulk, b. ca 1799 N. C., died after 1860. His wife was Emily (Penny) M. ----, b. ca 1815 Ga.. Known issue:

1. Jane Faulk, b. ca 1835 Ga.

2. Emily Martha Faulk, b. ca 1842 Ala.

3. Jeremiah Faulk, b. ca 1844 Ala.

4. Rachael Faulk, b. ca 1846 Ala.

5. James Faulk, b. ca 1848 Ala.

6. Sarah J. Faulk, b. ca 1849 Ala., m. James M. Danford.

7. Elizabeth Faulk, b. ca 1851 Ala.

8. Eliza Faulk, b. ca 1852 Ala.

9. Thomas Faulk, b. ca 1857 Ala.

10. John Faulk, b. ca 1860 Ala.

There was also a John Faulk who lived in Dale Co., Ala. near the Barbour Co. line. He was born 12 June 1811 Ga., d. 16 May 1898, and is buried in Shilo Baptist Church Cemetery, Geneva Co., Ala.. His wife, Mary (Gilmore?) was born 15 Sept. 1815 Ga., died 7 April 1885, is buried in Salem Cemetery, Dale Co., Ala.. Probable issue:

1. George G. B. Faulk, b. ca 1836 Ala., d. after 1880, m. Martha Sheppard 4 Aug. 1852 in Barbour Co., Ala.

2. John Marvin Faulk, b. ca 1840 Ala.

3. Henry Thomas Faulk, b. 1 June 1842 Ala., d. 1 March 1908, m. Ruth Elizabeth Fountain 12 Dec. 1865.

4. Catherine Faulk, b. 18 March 1844 Ala. (Coosa Co.?), d. 2 Aug. 1910 Geneva Co., Ala., m. Ruben H. Whitfield 8 Jan. 1869.

5. Daniel Ross Faulk, b. 3 Feb. 1848, d. ca 1903 Fannin Co., Texas, m. Emily J. Woods 5 Sept. 1867. She was born 29 Jan. 1851 Dale Co., Ala., d. 8 Aug. 1932 Fannin Co., Texas. She is buried in Forest Grove Cem. in Telephone, Texas.

6. Mary J. Faulk, b. ca 1850 Ala., m. John Arnold.

7. Lee Faulk, b. ca 1852 Ala., m. (1) Mollie ----, (2) Laura ----.

8. Rachael Faulk, b. 1855 Dale Co., Ala., m. Luke Smith.

Sources of information:
Barbour Co., Ala. Probate Records
Barbour Co., Ala. Census Records
Barbour Co., Ala. Cemetery Records
Dale Co., Ala. Census Records
Dale Co., Ala. Cemetery Records
Henderson Co., Texas Census Records
Navarro Co., Texas Census Records
"Two Centuries With a Willis Family" by D. M. Willis

FENN

Matthew Fenn entered land South and East of Clayton from
1829 through 1840. He was born ca 1798 Ga., died 8 Sept. 1885.
In his will, he requested that he be buried on his plantation 2
miles East of Clayton, but the Fenn family cemetery has since
been destroyed. He married (1) Matilda Williams, b. ca 1807 Ga.,
d. by Jan. 1852, (2) Martha Cordelia Weston on 11 Jan. 1852.
She was born ca 1834 S. C., died after 1880. Issue:
By 1st wife:

1. Lucinda Fenn, b. 13 Jan. 1828 Ala., d. 25 April 1897, m. (1)
   Richard Holland Fryer, M.D. on 25 July 1848. He was born
   17 Aug. 1819 in Laurens Dist., S. C., died 24 May 1864. She
   m. (2) Seaborn Jones by 1866. They are buried in Clayton
   Cemetery. Issue (by 1st husband):

   a. Margaret Caroline Fryer, may have married ---- Jennings.
   b. Paul Fryer, b. 4 Oct. 1854, d. 3 Dec. 1854, buried in
      Clayton Cemetery.
   c. Richard Dawdell Fryer, b. after 1860.

2. John Travis Fenn, b. ca 1835 Ala., d. July 1860, m. Rachel
   Ann Fryer 23 Dec. 1856. She was born ca 1838 S. C., died
   after 1880. Issue:

   a. Sallie T. Fenn, b. ca 1860 Ala.

3. Calvin William Fenn, b. 25 April 1837 Ala., d. 8 Nov. 1912,
   m. Martha E. Feagin, b. 2 April 1846 Ala., d. 9 Aug. 1937.
   In 1912, she was living in Richland Co., Ga.. Both are
   buried in Clayton Cemetery. Issue:

   a. Tina Fenn, b. ca 1872 Ala., m. ---- Wilkerson, living
      in Troy, Ala. in 1912.
   b. Edgar J. Fenn, b. ca 1874 Ala., living in Union Springs,
      Ala. in 1912.
   c. Hugh M. Fenn, b. ca 1872 Ala., living in Clayton in 1912.

d. Weltha Fenn, b. ca 1879 Ala., m. ---- Perry, living in Illinois in 1912.

e. Calvin William Fenn, Jr., living in Union Springs, Ala. in 1912.

f. Eula Cole Fenn, m. ---- Coffin, living in Richland, Ga. in 1912.

g. Harry Fenn, living in Youngstown, Fla. in 1912.

4. Rebecca R. Fenn, b. ca 1838 Ala., d. before 1885, m. Henry M. Beauchamp 9 Nov. 1854 (see Beauchamp family).

5. *Matthew Cullers Fenn, b. 22 Oct. 1842 Ala., d. 4 Sept. 1898, m. Mary Emerson 10 Oct. 1867. She was born 1849, died 1873. He m. (2) Nancy Emerson. They are buried in Mt. Zion Cemetery. Known issue:

a. Otto Fenn, m. Monnie Laster

b. Emme E. Fenn, b. ca 1870 Ala., m. Wallace McRae.

c. James M. Fenn, b. ca 1872 Ala., m. Effie Veal.

d. Mary A. Fenn, b. ca 1874 Ala., m. Gene Smith.

e. Calvin E. Fenn, b. ca 1876 Ala., m. Addie Lou Sanders.

f. William B. Fenn, b. ca 1878 Ala., m. Annie Evans.

g. Nancy Fenn, b. ca 1879 Ala.

6. Matilda Fenn, b. ca 1843 Ala., may have died young.

7. Sarah A. Fenn, b. ca 1845 Ala., d. after 1885, m. Benjamin Jones - living in Montgomery, Ala. in 1885.

8. James E. Fenn, b. 1848 Ala., d. 1920, m. Josephine Glover. She was born 1856 Ala., d. 1928. Both are buried in Clayton Cemetery. Known issue:

a. Matthew Homer Fenn, b. ca 1875

b. Ava M. Fenn

(other brothers and sisters living out of Barbour Co. in 1924)

9. Mary Emma Fenn, b. ca 1849 Ala., m. John A. Turner, living

in Jackson, Miss. in 1885.

10. (probably) Madison B. Fenn, b. 17 Dec. 1830, d. 6 April
    1850, buried in Clayton Cemetery.

By 2nd wife:

11. Eugenia Caroline Fenn, b. ca 1854 Ala., not married in 1885.

12. Martha Z. Fenn, b. ca 1855 Ala., not married in 1885.

13. Lillie A. Fenn, b. ca 1857 Ala., m. L. L. Cochran before
    1880.

14. Anna R. Fenn, b. ca 1859 Ala., m. Jno. W. Coggins before
    1880. He is buried in Mt. Zion Cemetery, but no dates are
    given.

15. Charles Robert Fenn, b. ca 1865, d. after 1885.

16. Lula W. Fenn, b. 28 Sept. 1864, d. 11 Dec. 1899, m. William
    J. Miles after 1880.

17. Ida W. Fenn, b. ca 1866 Ala.

There was a Zacheus (Zachariah) Fenn who died in Barbour Co.
by 1835. His widow, Susan, married (2) Edward Williams by 1842,
and was living in Macon Co., Ala. in 1850. Issue:
By 1st husband:

1. Allen T. Fenn, b. ca 1820 Ga., d. by 1860, m. Jane E. ----.
   In 1850, they were living in Macon Co., Ala. later moved to
   Lowndes Co., Ala.

2. John T. Fenn, b. ca 1826 Ala., was living in Macon Co., Ala.
   in 1850.

3. Matilda Jane Fenn m. Hugh Caffey and lived in Montgomery Co.
   Ala.. She died by 1882.

4. Mahala Fenn m. Alfred J. Sistrunk, lived in Macon Co., Ala.
   She died by 1860.

5. Madison B. Fenn, b. ca 1832 Ala., d. by 1860, m. Mary E.
   Winn. They were living in Macon Co., Ala. in 1850. She
   m. (2) Benjamin Franklin Caffey, b. 14 May 1824 Montgomery,

Ala.. He had m. (1) Mary Ann E. Fenn (2) Carolyn Baker.

6. Mary Ann E. Fenn, b. ca 1834 Ala., d. by 1860, m. Frank Caffey of Montgomery Co., Ala.

By 2nd husband:

7. Pinckney Williams, b. ca 1836 Ala., living in Macon Co., Ala. 1850.

8. Edward Clay Williams, b. ca 1842 Ala., living in Macon Co., Ala. in 1850.

9. Alice E. Williams, b. ca 1844 Ala., living in Macon Co., Ala. in 1850.

The last three were living with Hugh Caffey in Montgomery Co., Ala. in 1882.

Sources of information:

Barbour Co., Ala. Probate Records
Barbour Co., Ala. Census Records
Barbour Co., Ala. Cemetery Records
Macon Co., Ala. Census Records

*ADDITIONS & CORRECTIONS AS OF JUNE 1, 1979:

The obit. of Matthew Cullers Fenn says he was survived by a wife and twelve children but other records indicate there were fourteen. However, we do not know whether some died young or prior to his death. "The Fenn Family Reunion" listed:

1. Emma Fenn
2. Jim Fenn
3. Mary Fenn
4. Calvin Fenn
5. Will Fenn
6. Lessie Fenn m. Honer Sanders
7. Richard Fenn m. Eula Bennett
8. Ed Fenn m. Virginia Russum, a widow
9. Bart Fenn m. Gertrude Norton
10. Otto Fenn m. Monnie Laster
11. Bob Fenn m. Mary Ventress
12. Katie Lou Fenn m. Clyde Caraway
13. Sam Fenn m. (1) Edith Willie (2) Loyce Grant
14. Sallie Fenn - never married.

FLOYD

Theophilus Floyd was born 12 March 1787, probably in Horry Co., S. C., died 19 May 1842, m. Delilah Page. She was born 2 Dec. 1790, died 7 Nov. 1935. They are buried in Pleasant Plains Baptist Church Cem.. Issue:

1. Francis Floyd, b. ca 1810/20, probably moved to Texas after 1840.

2. Page Floyd, b. 22 Sept. 1816, d. 16 April 1907, m. Elizabeth M. Bowden. She was born 22 Oct. 1822 N. C., died 2 July 1903 (daughter of William Bowden and Louie Price). They are buried in Pleasant Plains Baptist Church Cem.. Issue:

    a. William P. Floyd, b. 5 April 1839 Ala., d. 5 June 1863 in the Civil War.

    b. Lucinda Floyd, b. 12 Oct. 1840, d. 3 Oct. 1841, buried Pleasant Plains Baptist Church Cem..

    c. John J. Floyd, b. 1 Nov. 1843 Ala., d. 26 July 1881, (buried Bethlehem Cem.), m. Julia A. Cox 14 Oct. 1869 at Jimpsey Cox's. She married (2) Daniel A. McGilvray 22 June 1885.

    d. Molsey J. Floyd, b. ca 1845 Ala., d. after 1891, m. John T. Watkins 12 Oct. 1865. He is buried in Pleasant Plains Baptist Church Cem. but no dates.

    e. Louisa Floyd, b. 10 Oct. 1846 Ala., d. 3 March 1910 m. Mirabeau L. Blakey 7 Nov. 1867. He was born 27 June 1845, died 10 Nov. 1910. They are buried in Pleasant Plains Baptist Church Cem..

    f. Mary Catherine Floyd, b. 8 March 1849 Ala., d. 28 Sept. 1849, buried Pleasant Plains Baptist Ch. Cem..

    g. Ann Elizabeth Floyd, b. 1 Jan. 1851 Ala., d. 20 Oct. 1937, m. David K. Thomas 25 Nov. 1869 (see THOMAS, page 289). He was born 13 April 1849, died 26 May 1899.

96

They are buried in Clayton Cem..

h. Colon Page Floyd, b. 5 May 1854 Ala., d. 31 Jan. 1864,
buried Pleasant Plains Baptist Church Cem..

i. Henry Lang Floyd, b. 19 Sept. 1856, d. 14 Jan. 1915
Houston Co., Ala., m. S. Ann Greene 4 Jan. 1877. She
was born 19 Jan. 1857, died 22 Jan. 1922.

j. Monroe Floyd, b. 22 Jan. 1859 Ala., d. 13 Nov. 1913, m.
Anne Bowden 27 Jan. 1881. She was born 1862, died 1938.
Both buried Pleasant Plains Baptist Ch. Cem..

k. Calvin Church Floyd, b. 18 Oct. 1862, d. 19 Nov. 1863,
buried Pleasant Plains Baptist Church Cem..

l. Nancy Emma Floyd, b. 29 June 1864 Ala., d. 4 Aug. 1947,
m. Thomas Jefferson Green. He was born 18 Feb. 1859,
died 31 Oct. 1935.

3. Isabella Floyd m. William V. Norton (see NORTON).

4. Elizabeth Ann Floyd, b. ca 1806, d. between 1850 and 1860,
Rusk Co., Texas, m. James H. Graham. He was born 1811 in
S. C., died 1869 Rusk Co., Texas. He m. (2) Mary Jane Wasson
28 March 1868 in Texas. Issue:

a. William L. Graham, b. ca 1835 Ala., m. (1) Ann E. Alley
28 June 1857 Rusk Co., Texas (2) Sarah Simmons.

b. Prudence Ann Graham, b. ca 1842 Ala., m. Sharp E. Whit-
ley 30 May 1860 Rusk Co., Texas.

c. E. Matilda Graham, b. ca 1845 Ala., m. Joseph A. Galloway 1 Dec. 1870 Rusk Co., Texas.

d. Lucinda C. Graham, b. ca 1847 Texas, m. S. L. Rogers 5
Sept. 1869 Rusk Co., Texas.

e. Elizabeth A. Graham, b. ca 1850 Texas, m. Daniel J.
Haney 19 Feb. 1873 Rusk Co., Texas.

f. James H. Graham, Jr., b. ca 1850 Texas, m. A. E. Williams
18 Aug. 1874 Collins Co., Texas.

97

5. Delilah Floyd, b. ca 1820, d. after 1860, m. Mathew C. Graham, who probably died by 1860. They also moved to Rusk Co., Texas. Known issue:

   a. Josephine Graham, b. ca 1842 Ala.

   b. Elizabeth Graham, b. ca 1850 Ala.

   c. Margaret Graham, b. ca 1852 Ala.

6. Nancy Ann (Jane?) Floyd, b. 31 July 1823, d. 5 June 1879, m. John Johnston Norton 29 July 1841. He was born 2 Nov. 1824, died 9 Aug. 1887. They are buried in Pleasant Plains Baptist Church Cem.. Known issue:

   a. Elbert T. Norton, b. ca 1843 Ala.

   b. Amy A. (or Laura) Norton, b. ca 1844 Ala.[1]

   c. Mary A. Norton, b. ca 1846 Ala.[4]

   d. Erasmus H. Norton, b. ca 1848 Ala.

   e. Henry T. Norton, b. ca 1850 Ala.

   f. Emeline Norton, b. ca 1852 Ala., not married 1880.

   g. Martha J. Norton, b. ca 1853 Ala.[2]

   h. James R. Norton, b. ca 1855 Ala., not married 1880.[3]

   i. John Norton, b. 1860 Ala., not married 1880.

   j. Adolphus Norton, b. ca 1866 Ala.

7. Theophilus Floyd, Jr., b. ca 1832 Ala., d. by 1880, m. Elizabeth Bonds 26 Aug. 1852. She was born ca 1832 Ala., probably died by 1880. Known issue:

   a. Benjamin N. Floyd, b. ca 1853 Ala.

   b. Angelina Floyd, b. ca 1855 Ala.

   c. William H. Floyd, b. ca 1858 Ala., may have married Mary E. Ethridge 17 Dec. 1878.

   d. Green W. Floyd, b. ca 1862, living with William H. Floyd in 1880.

   e. John F. (?) Floyd, b. ca 1866 Ala., living with William H. Floyd in 1880.

8. Joseph Floyd, b. ca 1836 Ala., d. by 1864, m. Sarah A. Butts 17 Dec. 1856 at Charles Butts'. She was born 15 Jan. 1840 Ala., died 24 Sept. 1924, buried Louisville Cem.. She married (2) Richard Abner Pickett 29 April 1864. He was born 18 March 1845 Ala., died 16 Feb. 1926, buried Louisville Cem.. Issue (by Joseph Floyd):

a. William Charles Floyd, b. ca 1858 Ala., may have married Dora Beasley 31 Jan. 1882 (see BEASLEY).

b. Thomas (or Joseph) George W. Floyd, b. 18 July 1860 Ala., d. 29 Dec. 1929, buried Christian Grove Cem..

By her second husband, Sarah A. Butts Floyd Pickett had:

c. Sarah A. (Alabama?) Pickett, b. ca 1865 Ala., d. 14 Oct. 1935, m. W. M. Passmore 30 Dec. 1883.

d. Minnie Vela Pickett, b. 8 Nov. 1866 Ala., d. 26 May 1950 Bland Lake, Texas, m. William Henry Richards 27 Nov. 1887.

e. Lydia Jane Pickett, b. 10 Nov. 1868 Ala., d. 29 Sept. 1955 Barbour Co., Ala., m. James Henry Caraway 20 Dec. 1893. He was born 12 Nov. 1871, died 25 March 1956. They are buried in Louisville Cem..

f. Thomas M. Pickett, b. 23 June 1871 Ala., d. 20 Nov. 1929, m. Emma Beaty. He is buried in Louisville Cem..

g. Tandy B. Pickett, b. 2 July 1873 Ala..

h. A. Alexander Pickett, b. 28 Feb. 1876 Ala..

i. Strawda E. Pickett, b. 2 Jan. 1879 Ala., d. 26 Nov. 1950, m. Thomas Hagler 1 Sept. 1928 (second wife?). He was born 26 March 1876, died 9 June 1955. They are buried in Louisville Cem..

j. Edgar (Edgie) Pickett, b. 10 Oct. 1882.

k. Johnie Pickett m. L. C. Mullins 22 May 1897.

9. Polly Ann Floyd m. Gideon Bowden 5 Nov. 1844.

99

10. Rosa Ann Floyd, lived in Rusk Co., Texas with James H. Graham and his family.

Other sources:

1850 Census Rusk Co., Texas
Marriage Records, Rusk Co., Texas
Floyd Bible
Pickett Bible
"Early Floyds of Pike Co., Ala." by Floyd & Taylor

1. Amy A. Norton m. Nathan W. Boyd (alias Loftin) 15 Oct. 1865.
2. Martha J. Norton m. James Allen Green 31 Dec. 1874.
3. James R. Norton m. E. C. Andrews 27 Jan. 1881.
4. Mary A. Norton m. John W. McGilvray 6 Jan. 1867.

GILLIS

The Gillis families of Barbour Co. must be included in this
book because they were some of the earliest in this area. However, the very fact that they were here so soon means that they
left very few records. Maybe this chapter will be read by someone who can connect the family groups.

As a general rule, those born before 1800 were born in Scotland. The next generation was born in N. C. and by 1820, they
were in S. C.. By the mid-1820's, some were already in Alabama,
with others joining them through the years.

The following outline was made from the family record of
Calvin Gillis that was printed in the Shreveport (La.) Journal:

Donald Gillis married Catharine McLeod in Scotland. They
came to Fayetteville, N. C. in 1803, then moved to Moore Co.,
N. C.. They were in Sparta (Conecuh Co.), Ala. about 1823, lived
for a short time in Barbour Co. then moved back to Sparta near
their son, John. Catharine (McLeod) Gillis died there ca 1837/8.
Donald Gillis went to Miss. with his son, John, and died there.
All their children were born in Scotland before 1803 - only the
following three lived to maturity:

1. John Gillis, b. Scotland, moved to Sparta, Ala. ca 1821/2,
    then he and his family moved to Miss..

2. Malcolm Gillis, b. Scotland, also moved to Sparta where he
    soon died.. His wife and children returned to N. C.

3. Margaret Gillis, b. 1800 Kingsdale (?), Scotland, d. 23 June
    1888 in Texas (buried in Plum Creek Academy), m. Alexander
    Gillis. He was born ca 1786, died 15 Sept. 1854 near Elba,
    Ala., son of Donald and Dora (McLeod) Gillis who both died
    in Richmond Co., N. C.. Margaret and Alexander Gillis lived
    in Barbour Co., Ala. in the Pea River Settlement from about
    1824 to 1836 when they moved to Elba. They returned to

Barbour Co. by 1840. Issue:

a. Calvin Gillis, b. 30 April 1820 Moore Co., N. C., d. af-
    ter 1890 in Abilene, Texas.

b. Malcolm Gillis, b. 12 July 1823 Sparta, Ala. - he moved
    to Hernando Co., Fla. while a young man, then to San
    Antonio, Texas.

c. John Quincy Gillis, b. 7 Dec. 1825 Barbour Co.. He mar-
    ried in Coffee Co., Ala., then moved to Texas after the
    Civil War.

d. Alexander Hamilton Gillis m. Nancy Elizabeth Watson 28
    Dec. 1854 in Coffee Co., Ala., then moved to Texas ca
    1867.

e. Diana Catharine Gillis, b. 26 Sept. 1830 Barbour Co.,
    d. 22 Sept. 1870, m. Jesse O'Neal.

f. Cyrus Washington Gillis, b. 22 Feb. 1833 Barbour Co.,
    moved to San Antonio, Texas before the Civil War.

g. Donald (also called Daniel) Gillis, b. 13 Nov. 1835 Dale
    Co., Ala., d. 7 May 1878, m. Mary Elizabeth Johnson 14
    April 1867. They moved to Palatka (Fla.?), then back to
    Elba (see page 149).

h. Angus Gillis, b. 10 June 1838 Dale Co., Ala..

This family record mentions "Uncle Hugh Gillis" of Barbour
Co.. He was probably the Hugh Gillis who died here by July 1833.
His estate was divided into nine shares. All were equal except
the one received by Mary Gillis - she got an equal share plus a
bed and bedding. His heirs were:

1. Mary Gillis, probably the wife of Hugh - no record after
    1833.

2. Archibald McIntosh, b. ca 1790 Scotland, no record after
    1850. He married Mary (Gillis?), b. ca 1795 Scotland. In
    their household in 1850 were:

102

a. John McIntosh, b. ca 1826 S. C.

b. Angus McIntosh, b. ca 1832 S. C.

c. John McIntosh, b. ca 1837 Ala.

3. Margaret McIntosh, b. ca 1800 Scotland. In her household in 1850 were:

a. Norman McIntosh, b. ca 1820 S. C.

b. John G. McIntosh, b. ca 1822 S. C.

c. Mary McIntosh, b. ca 1831 S. C.

4. Donald (also called Daniel) Gillis, b. ca 1800/10.

5. Christian Gillis, b. ca 1810 Scotland, not married in 1850.

6. Sarah Gillis, b. ca 1815 Scotland, not married in 1880.

7. Margaret (Gillis) McGilvray, b. ca 1813 Scotland, d. 20 Jan. 1885, wife of John McGilvray (see page 182). In 1850, Christian and Sarah Gillis (above) were living with her - in 1880, only Sarah Gillis was there. Margaret (Gillis) McGilvray is buried in Old Scotch Cem. - her inscription states that she was a daughter of Hugh and Mary Gillis.

8. John Gillis, died by 1835 leaving a wife and minor children, names unknown. Archibald McIntosh was his administrator.

9. Norman Gillis, d. by 1835, Archibald McIntosh was admr.

John Gillis (Sr.), b. 23 July 1801 N. C., d. 30 Oct. 1884, came to Alabama between 1835 and 1838 from S. C.. He could have been a son of John C. Gillis who died by Feb. 1847 (Roderick McSwean, admr.) but there are no records to prove it. He married Catharine (McLeod?), probably in S. C.. She was born 7 Oct. 1802, died 3 Dec. 1879 - they are buried in Louisville Cem.. Christian McLeod (b. ca 1788/90 N. C.) was living with them in 1850 and 1860. The following children are found in the 1850/1880 census records but there may have been more older ones:

1. John Gillis, Jr., b. 24 Nov. 1835 S. C., d. 6 April 1908 (or 1909), m. Catherine McLean 28 Jan. 1857. She was born

ca 1840 in N. C., died 6 July 1912. They are buried in Louisville Cem.. Issue (from 1860/80 Census):

a. Daniel A. Gillis, b. ca 1858 Ala., not married in 1880.

b. Mary Gillis, b. ca 1860 Ala.

c. Eddie Gillis, b. ca 1867 Ala.

d. Leila (Lonie) Gillis, b. 21 July 1870 Ala., d. 27 Oct. 1879, buried Louisville Cem..

e. Charlie Gillis, b. 1875 Ala., d. 1941, m. Belle Tomberlin 1 Dec. 1897. She was born 1879, died 1948. They are buried in Louisville Cem..

f. (female) Gillis, b. ca 1877 Ala.. She may have been Minnie Gillis, b. 27 Sept. 1876, d. 8 Oct. 1924, buried Louisville Cem..

2. Nancy Gillis, b. ca 1835/8 S. C..

3. Sarah Gillis, b. 7 April 1838 Ala., d. 7 Jan. 1873 (or 1878) never married. She is buried in Louisville Cem..

4. Malcolm Gillis, b. 27 Jan. 1839 Ala., d. 2 Feb. 1917, m. Narcissa Victoria Lee 29 Jan. 1868 (see LEE). She was born 25 Oct. 1847 Ala., died 26 March 1899. They are buried in Louisville Cem.. Issue (from 1880 Census):

a. Naomi (Nancy?) Gillis, b. ca 1869 Ala.

b. William H. Gillis, b. ca 1870 Ala.

c. Christian Gillis, b. ca 1872 Ala.

d. Maggie Gillis, b. 1874 Ala., buried Louisville Cem..

e. Fannie Gillis, b. ca 1876 Ala.

f. Cora Gillis, b. ca 1879 Ala.

g. Laurence Gillis, b. 27 July 1890, d. 9 Jan. 1891, buried Louisville Cem..

5. Effie Gillis, b. ca 1844 Ala., not married in 1880.

The following Gillis families were enumerated in the 1850 Census in the same neighborhood as follows:

Household #324 - Neill Gillis, b. ca 1816/20 S. C., d. 25 March 1883, m. Nancy Herring 11 Nov. 1847. She was born ca 1830 N. C., died 1897, buried Mt. Mariah Cem., Shady Grove, Texas. Issue (from 1850/80 Census and descendants):

1. Alexander West (Westley?) Gillis, b. ca 1849 Ala.

2. Ichabod Gillis, b. 9 March 1850, d. 21 May 1921, buried Mt. Mariah Cem., Shady Grove, Texas. He married Tabitha Ann Moreland 8 Dec. 1870 in Barbour Co., Ala..

3. Malcolm Columbus Gillis, b. ca 1852 Ala., not married 1880.

4. Mary A. (or E.) Gillis, b. ca 1853 Ala., m. William A. Barr 27 Dec. 1874.

5. Charity Gillis, b. ca 1856 Ala.

6. Virginia Augusta Gillis, b. 6 March 1858 Ala., d. 5 April 1926, buried Mt. Mariah Cem., Shady Grove, Texas. She never married.

7. James (also called William and Jefferson) D. Gillis, b. 1860.

8. Lewis G. Gillis, b. 10 April 1862 Ala., d. 21 July 1936, buried Mt. Mariah Cem., Shady Grove, Texas.

9. Stephen D. Gillis, b. ca 1865 Ala.

10. Eliza Gillis, b. ca 1866 Ala. (in 1870 Census only).

11. Flora Gillis, b. 30 Aug. 1866 Ala., d. 18 July 1903, never married. She is buried in Mt. Mariah Cem., Shady Grove, Texas.

12. Americus W. Gillis, b. 6 Jan. 1868 Ala., d. 31 May 1936, m. Anzania Strand, b. 5 March 1883, d. 13 Sept. 1936. Both are buried in Mt. Mariah Cem., Shady Grove, Texas.

13. Henrietta Gillis, b. 1 Sept. 1870 Ala., d. 22 March 1950, never married - buried Mt. Mariah Cem., Shady Grove, Texas.

14. Thomas Neal Gillis, b. 15 Nov. 1872 Ala., d. 24 July 1929, buried Mt. Mariah Cem., Shady Grove, Texas.

15. Jackson Gillis, b. ca 1875 Ala.

Household #325 - Flora Gillis, b. ca 1788 Scotland, not in any Census after 1850. She may have been the widow of Alexander C. Gillis who died after 1840. In her household in 1850 were:

1. Charles Gillis, b. ca 1820 S. C., may have married Harriett Baxley 15 Sept. 1864.

2. Hugh Gillis, b. ca 1822 S. C., probably married Jane Norton 16 May 1850.

3. Jane Gillis, b. ca 1830 Ala.. She may have been the wife of Hugh Gillis (above) and not a child of Flora Gillis.

4. Nancy Gillis, b. ca 1825 S. C.

5. John Gillis, b. ca 1848 Ala., probably a grandchild.

Flora Gillis may also have been the mother of Neill Gillis (household #324) and Daniel Gillis (household #336).

Household #327 - Christian Gillis, b. ca 1784 Scotland, not in any census after 1850. In her household in 1850 were:

1. Margaret Gillis, b. ca 1810 N. C.

2. Mary Gillis, b. ca 1812 N. C.

3. Christian Gillis, b. ca 1818 S. C.

4. John W. Gillis, b. ca 1838 S. C.

Household #334 - Roderick C. McSwean, b. ca 1791 Scotland. His wife, Mary, is thought to have been a Gillis, but there is no proof. She was born 1795 Richmond Co., N. C., died 16 Dec. 1861 (see page 218). In this household in 1850 was Christian Gillis, born 7 July 1831 N. C., died 2 Jan. 1894. She married John Murdock Cunningham 22 Feb. 1854. He was born 5 June 1831 N. C. and died 13 Oct. 1888. They are buried in Pea River Presbyterian Church Cem..

Household #336 - Daniel Gillis, b. ca 1820 S. C., m. Catherine McKenzie 22 Feb. 1849. In his household in 1850 were Sarah McLeod, b. ca 1790 Scotland. In 1880, they were in Bullock Co., Ala..

One more Gillis family that must be included is that of Catharine Gillis (a widow by 1850). She was born ca 1807 in N. C., possibly the daughter of Angus McLeod and widow of Daniel (Donald) Gillis who was born ca 1800/10 and died by 1850. In her household in 1850 were the following:

1. Neill Gillis, b. ca 1830 S. C.. According to "History of Methodism" by Lazenby, he was born 17 Sept. 1830, died 7 March 1907 (buried in Clayton Cem.). He m. (1) Margaret Josephine Miles in 1863 (2) Ella Nora Rebecca Farish 1870.

2. Roderick Gillis, b. ca 1831 Ala.

3. John Gillis, b. ca 1836 Ala.

4. Norman Gillis, b. ca 1838 Ala.

5. Hugh Gillis, b. ca 1840 Ala.. "History of Methodism" syas he was Hugh McLeod Gillis, b. 9 March 1843 Barbour Co., Ala., d. 18 Nov. 1913, buried Snow Hill, Ala..

6. Mary Gillis, b. ca 1843 Ala.

Neill and Hugh Gillis were heirs in the estate of Angus McLeod who died by 1868 (see McLEOD).

Another book that deals with these Gillis and McLeod families is "Your Inheritance", Vol. II, by Mrs. Grady Ross, 2138 Sherwood Ave., Charlotte, N. C. 28207.

Other sources:

"Shreveport Journal", Shreveport, La.
"History of Methodism" by Lazenby
Information from descendants

GRIGGS

Asberry Griggs entered land in 1829 near Louisville, and in 1836, he entered more land, this time near the Pike-Bullock Co. line. It is possible that he never actually lived in Barbour Co..

In 1839, Thomas Griggs patented land a little North of the 1836 patents of Asberry Griggs. On 17 Feb. 1840, Thomas Griggs married Mahala Hosenback. He died by 1854, leaving one child, Isabel Griggs. Mahala (Hosenback) Griggs married (2) Elbert Jordon by 1854.

In 1839, Robert Griggs patented land in the Northern part of Barbour Co. near the present Russell Co. line. He probably made his home in Russell Co..

James Griggs settled near Glennville in what is now Russell Co., Ala. by 1860. He was born 12 Feb. 1795, died 8 Aug. 1866. His wife, Martha Matilda Cox, was born 26 Feb. 1811, died 3 March 1896. They are buried in Glennville Cemetery. Issue:

1. Rebecca P. Griggs m. ---- Harrison.

2. James O. Griggs.

3. Ann E. Griggs m. ---- West.

4. Ella A. Griggs m. ---- Brown.

5. George R. Griggs m. Mollie A. Foley 9 April 1868.

6. Mary F. Griggs m. Hiram A. Davis 16 Nov. 1865.

7. John C. Griggs m. Miss N. R. Kendrick 11 Dec. 1866.

8. Lizzie M. L. Griggs.

The following is the line of descent of Miss Ethel Blackmon, DAR #501089.

1. William Griggs (Revolutionary Soldier), b. 24 Jan. 1740 in Hancock Co., Va., d. ca 1779 Va., m. ---- Gardner.

2. John Gardner Griggs, b. 12 Jan. 1765 Va., d. 19 May 1839 in Harris Co., Ga., m. Rebecca Pritchett 14 March 1787. She

was born 8 Aug. 1762 Beaufort, N. C., died 17 Jan. 1827 Putnam Co., Ga..

3. James S. Griggs, b. 12 Feb. 1795 Ga., d. 8 Aug. 1866 Glenn-ville, Ala., m. (2) Martha Matilda Cox ca 1833. She was born 12 Feb. 1812 Ga., died 3 March 1869 at Midway (Bullock Co.), Ala..

4. Mary Frances Griggs, b. 17 July 1846 Putnam Co., Ga., d. 8 Sept. 1905 Midway, Ala., m. Hiram Alonzo Davis 16 Nov. 1865. He was born 7 Oct. 1835 Talbotton, Ga., died 28 Dec. 1910 Midway, Ala..

5. Mary Anna Davis, b. 6 Oct. 1869 Eufaula, Ala., d. 5 July 1921 at Eufaula, Ala., m. James Monroe Blackmon 9 Jan. 1887. He was born 7 Jan. 1866 Barbour Co., Ala., died 17 Jan. 1923 Eufaula, Ala..

Sources of information:

Barbour Co., Ala. Probate Records
Barbour Co., Ala. Census Records
Barbour Co., Ala. Cemetery Records
DAR National No. 501089

GRUBBS

In 1830, William Grubbs patented land West of Clio near the
Pike Co. line - between 1836 and 1848, Adam, Enoch, Mary and
Wineford Grubbs entered land nearby. Later Grubbs patents were
a few miles West of Eufaula.

William Grubbs, Sr. was the son of Enoch Grubbs, Sr. (a Revolutionary Soldier) who died in Fairfield Co., S. C. by Sept.
1832. The heirs of Enoch Grubbs, Sr. were his widow, Mary (Henson) Grubbs (probably his second wife) and the following children:

1. William Grubbs, Sr. - see later.
2. Mary Jennings (deceased by 1832) - her children Elizabeth,
    William, Enoch, John, James and Thomas Jennings.
3. Rhoda Hedgepath.
4. Sarah Lott (deceased by 1832) - her children Moses, George
    and Enoch Lott.
5. Enoch Grubbs - he may have died in Chester Co., S. C. in
    1844.
6. John Grubbs
7. Ashford Grubbs
8. Thomas Grubbs, b. ca 1818
9. Minerva Grubbs
10. Sirena Grubbs
11. Mithena (Martha Jane?) Grubbs
12. Lucinda Grubbs

The last six children were minors in 1831, and children by his
wife, Mary Henson. His first wife may have been Floried K.
Burton.

William Grubbs, Sr. was born 6 Oct. 1776 Chesterfield Dist.,
S. C., died 26 Feb. 1849 Barbour Co., Ala.. His wife, Elizabeth
was born ca 1778/90 S. C. - there is some confusion as to her

death date. They are buried in the Bennett-Lee Cem. near the Pike Co. line. Issue:

1. Rhoda Ann Grubbs, b. 18 March 1797 S. C., m. (1) Robert Thompson, who died by 1840 (2) Hardy Graves 7 Dec. 1847. He was born ca 1805 S. C., died by 1860. Issue (all by first husband):

   a. Elizabeth Thompson m. John Haralson - living Covington Co., Ala. in 1856.

   b. William Thompson may have married Lucinda Graves, daughter of Hardy Graves. They were living in La. in 1851.

   c. Alladin Thompson, b. ca 1818 S. C., d. 24 Jan. 1874, m. Susan N. Sutton ca 1840 (see SUTTON, page 282).

   d. Mary Thompson m. John Evans by 1840.

   e. Jane Thompson m. James Graves - they were living in Pike Co., Ala. in 1851 and in La. by 1856.

   f. Thomas Thompson - living in La. in 1851.

   g. Enoch Thompson m. Julia A. ____.

   h. John Thompson may have married Martha Thorn 16 May 1850.

   i. Sarah Thompson never married - living in La. in 1856.

   j. Rhoda Thompson m. George W. Carroll 15 Aug. 1852. In 1860, they were living in Ark..

   k. Robert Thompson m. Mrs. Lucretia Jane (Faulk) Miles 7 Feb. 1867. Her first husband was Francis Andrew Miles (see FAULK, page 84).

   l. Adam C. Thompson, b. ca 1837 Ala..

2. Hannah Grubbs, b. 24 Aug. 1798 - no further record.

3. Thomas Grubbs, b. 17 Aug. 1800 - see later.**

4. Adam Grubbs, b. 26 April 1802 S. C., d. 4 April 1888, m. Demaris ----. She was born ca 1798 S. C., died by 1860. He m. (2) Nancy J. Moats 1 Feb. 1860. She was born ca 1818 Ga., died 1897 and is buried in Louisville Cem.. Issue (all

111

by 1st wife):

a. Samuel Grubbs, b. ca 1835 Ala., not mentioned in the es-
    tate of Adam Grubbs, so may have died by 1891 and left
    children living in Leon Co., Texas.

b. Amanda Grubbs, b. 30 Sept. 1836 Ala., d. 10 Jan. 1893,
    m. (1) James W. Huey 25 April 1850. He was born 7 March
    1825 Ga., died 20 Aug. 1855. She m. (2) Benjamin C.
    Bennett 28 Dec. 1858. He was born 25 Dec. 1836 N. C.,
    died 13 Dec. 1887. They are buried in the Bennett-Lee
    Cem.. He was a son of James Bennett - no known relation-
    ship to the Luke Bennett family.

c. Green Grubbs, b. ca 1838 Ala., probably lived in Texas -
    not in estate of Adam Grubbs.

d. Alice Ann Grubbs married a Nesbitt, was living in Leon
    Co., Texas in 1888.

5. William Grubbs, Jr., b. 7 July 1804 S. C., d. 10 Nov. 1882,
    m. Nancy Parmer. She was born ca 1812 Ga., died by July
    1879 (see PARMER). Issue:

a. Mary Ann Grubbs, b. ca 1830 Ala., d. 18 July 1892, m.
    George W. Richards 11 Nov. 1847 (see RICHARDS).

b. Elizabeth Jane Grubbs, b. 20 Aug. 1831 Ala., d. 28 Feb.
    1905, m. Moses E. Bush 15 Aug. 1849. He was born 23
    Nov. 1833, died 26 Feb. 1905. They are buried in New
    Hope Cem.. (see BUSH)

c. Nancy Emeline Grubbs, b. ca 1834 Ala., d. by 1883, m.
    Abner Belcher 3 July 1851. He was born ca 1830 Ga.,
    died by Oct. 1868.

d. Sarah Amanda Grubbs, b. 18 March 1836 Ala., d. 21 July
    1908, m. John J. Price 20 Jan. 1853. He was born 29
    March 1831, died 6 May 1889. They are buried in Mt.
    Aerial Cem..

112

e. Green Grubbs, b. ca 1838 Ala., died by 1883, at which
    time his children were living in Texas.

f. Hetty Grubbs, b. ca 1840 Ala., d. by 1883, m. John D.
    Belcher 8 Jan. 1857.

g. Martha (?) Savannah Grubbs, b. ca 1842 Ala., d. after
    1883, m. James R. J. Floyd 17 Jan. 1856. He was born ca
    1835 Ala., died by 1864. She m. (2) John Vinson 18 Oct.
    1865. He died by 1866 and she married (3) Olin M. Sear-
    cy 20 March 1868. He was born ca 1832 N. C., died March
    1897.

h. Lydia Grubbs, b. ca 1845 Ala., died by 1883.

i. John W. M. Grubbs, b. ca 1849 Ala., living in 1883.

j. Worthy G. Grubbs, b. ca 1837 Ala., d. by Aug. 1862, m.
    Sarah Jane Loveless 27 April 1854. She m. (2) William
    L. Ethridge 28 Jan. 1864. In 1868, her children were
    living in Bullock Co., Ala..

6. Enoch Grubbs, b. 26 July 1806, died by 1842, m. Mary (Sas-
    ser?), born ca 1810 Ga.. Issue:

    a. Winney B. Grubbs, b. ca 1834 Ala., m. Elijah Dillard by
        1870.

    b. Elizabeth Grubbs, b. ca 1835 Ala.

    c. James Monroe Grubbs - possibly married Martha Minshew 7
        Jan. 1858 (see MINSHEW).

    d. Jefferson Worthy Grubbs, probably died by 1842.

7. Jincy Grubbs, b. 26 Aug. 1808 S. C., m. David Watson. Issue:

    a. Sarah Jane Watson, b. ca 1830 Ala., m. William J. Rollin
        11 Oct. 1846.

    b. Elizabeth Jane Watson - may have married W. E. Harper
        24 Sept. 1848.

8. Elizabeth Grubbs, b. 14 March 1810 S. C., d. by 1867, m.
    Bricey Holley - probably his second wife. He was born ca

1787 Ga., died June 1884. He m. (3) Nancy Parmer 7 Nov. 1867 (see PARMER). She died by Nov. 1868. Known issue (of Bricey Holley):

a. Mary Ann Elizabeth Holley, b. 10 Aug. 1825 Ga., d. 18 March 1900 (buried Rocky Mount Church), m. B. E. G. Parmer 23 Jan. 1851 (see PARMER).

b. Martha J. Holley, b. ca 1828 Ga., m. Cornelius Williams 3 Nov. 1853.

c. William B. Holley, b. ca 1829 Ga..

d. Thomas L. Holley, b. 22 Feb. 1834 Ga., d. 12 Feb. 1865 (buried New Hope Cem.), m. Mary E. Zorn 24 Dec. 1857.

e. Penny (Winny?) Holley, b. ca 1838 Ga., not married in 1860.

f. Luiza Jane Holley - may be the Jane Holley b. 5 Feb. 1844, d. 3 Dec. 1912, buried Rocky Mount Cem..

g. John Presley Holley, b. ca 1842 Ala..

h. (possibly) Laura Holley, b. ca 1846 Ala..*

Note: one daughter, name unknown, married a Searcy and had a son, Thomas R. Searcy.

9. Sarah Grubbs, b. 25 Jan. 1812.

10. Parthena Grubbs, b. 30 May 1814.

11. Wineford Grubbs, b. 22 Aug. 1815, died by Aug. 1846, m. Mary Ann Cadenhead 14 July 1835. She was born 10 Sept. 1816 Ga.. She m. (2) John McNair 23 July 1847. Issue (by Wineford Grubbs):

a. James Jefferson Grubbs, b. 22 May 1836 Ala., d. by 1854.

b. John Tillman Grubbs, b. 23 Oct. 1838 Jefferson (or Jackson) Co., Texas, d. 14 March 1914, m. (1) Ellen C. Lowe 4 Feb. 1866. She was born 1836, died by 1885 (buried Pea Creek Cem.). He married (2) Emma C. Smart 3 June 1885. She was born 3 March 1861 and died 17 Feb. 1924.

They are buried in Louisville Cem..

c. William Worthy Friendly Harrison Grubbs, b. 28 Aug. 1840.

d. Francis Marion Grubbs, b. 21 May 1842 Ala., d. 22 Nov. 1920, m. Martha A. Singleton 18 Aug. 1869. She was born 15 Jan. 1849 Ala., died after 1880.

e. Green Jasper Grubbs, b. 17 July 1844 Ala., d. 23 Jan. 1922, m. Mrs. Susan Sims Saunders 11 June 1865. She was born ca 1839 Fla., died Nov. 1894. He m. (2) Mrs. Mary Eliza Dillard Bundy (3) Annie Adkinson.

f. Morgan Milton Grubbs, b. 22 March 1846, probably died by Feb. 1856.

(by John McNair):

g. Phoebe Ann Elizabeth McNair, b. 16 Oct. 1848 Ala., d. 24 Feb. 1920 (buried Pea Creek Cem.), m. C. J. Lampley 1 Nov. 1874.

h. Mary Amanda McNair, b. 12 Dec. 1851 Ala., d. July 1944 Williamson Co., Texas, m. (1) William B. Moseley ca 1892 in Texas (his first wife was Susannah A. M. Grubbs). She m. (2) Paul J. Foster. She and Wm. B. Moseley are buried in Gotebo, Kiowa Co., Okla..

i. Malinda Adaline McNair, b. 7 April 1854 Ala., d. after 1931, m. J. L. Glover 1 Sept. 1878. He was born 20 June 1856 Ga., died 11 Aug. 1895 and is buried in Grubbs Church Cem..

12. Friendly Grubbs, b. 16 Oct. 1817 S. C., d. 24 Nov. 1878, m. Elizabeth J. Caroline Mabry ca 1847. She was born 16 Oct. 1817 Ga., died 15 Feb. 1888. They are buried in Clayton Cem.. They had no children but raised several nieces and nephews. Friendly Grubbs fought in the Creek Indian War in Barbour Co. in 1836, went to Texas in 1841 and returned to Barbour Co. in 1846.

13. Worthy Jordan Grubbs, b. 1 Jan. 1819 or 1820, d. 2 Aug. 1890, m. Mary A. S. ----. She was born 22 June 1822 Ga., died 26 May 1900. They are buried in Louisville Cem.. Issue:

a. Hepsey Ann Grubbs, b. 8 Nov. 1841 Ala., d. 30 Sept. 1922, m. Francis D. Veal 11 Sept. 1856. He was born 30 Sept. 1836, died 2 Nov. 1899. They are buried in Louisville Cem..

b. Mary Jane Grubbs, b. ca 1843 Ala., m. Augustus W. Cain 26 Sept. 1858.

c. William J. Grubbs, b. ca 1845 Ala., may have married Fanny C. Cox 8 Feb. 1866.

d. James F. Grubbs, b. ca 1846 Ala..

e. Winford Seth Grubbs, b. 28 March 1848 Ala., d. 23 Aug. 1878, buried Louisville Cem..

f. Samuel J. Grubbs, b. ca 1852 Ala..

g. Susannah A. M. Grubbs, b. 25 Dec. 1854 Ala., d. 5 Feb. 1890, buried Locklin Cem., Milam Co., Texas. She m. William B. Moseley 5 April 1870, who died 30 Dec. 1899. His second wife was Mary Amanda McNair.

h. Worthy J. Grubbs, Jr., b. ca 1856 Ala.

i. Laura Grubbs, b. 19 March 1857, died 25 March 1857 and is buried in Louisville Cem..

j. Ella Grubbs, born and died 20 Oct. 1858, buried Louisville Cem..

k. Emma Grubbs, born and died 20 Oct. 1858, buried Louisville Cem..

l. Adam D. Grubbs, b. 30 Jan. 1860, died 11 June 1865, buried Louisville Cem..

m. Louisa Grubbs, b. 10 Jan. 1863, died 30 Jan. 1863, buried Louisville Cem..

14. John Tillman Grubbs, b. 27 July 1824, married Lucitta Martin

116

23 April 1844. He died 20 Oct. 1895 and she filed for a CSA pension in Pike Co., Ala.. Issue (if any) not known.

15. Minerva Grubbs, b. 18 Feb. 1827.

16. ---- Grubbs (a daughter) who married James F. Watson and had issue:

    a. Madison Watson

    b. Caroline Watson

William Grubbs, Sr. also had a daughter, Mary Grubbs, who is not listed in the family Bible but is included in his estate. She was born ca 1803, m. (1) ---- McDowell and had a daughter, Elisa Jane McDowell, b. ca 1827. She m. (2) John Sloan, Sr. 22 July 1849 - his second wife. She m. (3) Benjamin Parmer 1 Oct. 1856 and (4) Mathew Laseter 24 Wept. 1857.

*In 1843, William Grubbs, Sr. gave slaves to his daughter, Elizabeth Holley and her children, viz: Winney, John Presley, Maryann Elizabeth, Seleann C., James Calvin and Luiza Jane Holley.

**The following were grandchildren of Wm. Grubbs, Sr., but there is nothing in the Barbour Co. records which gives the names of their parents - possibly they were children of the Thomas Grubbs who was born 17 Aug. 1800:

    a. Josiah Grubbs, b. ca 1826 Ala., living with Friendly Grubbs in 1850. His CSA record says he died 2 May 1894 in Russell Co., Ala., age 73.

    b. Nancy Grubbs, b. ca 1821 Ala., m. William Andrews 11 Jan. 1849.

    c. Marthena Grubbs, b. ca 1830 Al., living with Nancy Andrews in 1850.

    d. Enoch Grubbs, b. ca 1832 Ala., living with Mary (the widow of Enoch) in 1850.

Other sources:

DAR Patriot Index
Will of Enoch Grubbs, Sr., Fairfield Co., S. C.
Grubbs Bible
Cadenhead Bible
C. W. Ethridge, Columbus, Ga..

HARROD

William Harrod patented 40 acres of land Northwest of Louisville in 1829, and sold it to Thomas Warren on 16 Dec. 1833. He probably never lived in Barbour Co..

Sources of information:
Barbour Co., Ala. Probate Records

It is widely believed that the Hartzog family of Barbour Co. is descended from Daniel Hartzog (b. 1774) and his wife, Susannah Zorn, of South Carolina.

One George Hartzog died by Feb. 1838 in Barbour Co., Ala.. His wife, Sela (Celia) ----, b. ca 1811 S. C., married (2) John Mitchell 13 Aug. 1843 - she must have been his second wife. The children of this couple are not given in the Barbour Co. records, but the probable issue of George and Sela is:

1. James Washington Hartzog, b. ca 1833 S. C., d. after 1880, m. Martha A. J. Warr 2 July 1849. Known issue:

    a. William S. Hartzog, b. 1850 Ala., m. Amanda Dominey 14 Oct. 1869.

    b. George W. Hartzog, b. ca 1858 Ala., not married 1880.

    c. John A. Hartzog, b. ca 1860 Ala....did he marry S. A. Lee 23 Dec. 1884?

    d. Sarah J. Hartzog, b. ca 1866 Ala.

    e. James T. Hartzog, b. ca 1872 Ala.

    f. Timothy Hartzog, b. ca 1875 Ala.

2. Isaac Hartzog, b. ca 1835 Ala., probably died by 1860, m. Margaret A. M. Warr 6 Sept. 1856. She was born ca 1837 Ga. and was a widow in 1860.

3. Eliza A. R. Hartzog, b. ca 1836 (Ga.?), m. Zachariah Bene-field 1 Oct. 1851. Issue (from 1880 Census):

    a. William W. Benefield, b. ca 1852 Ala.

    b. John Benefield, b. ca 1853 Ala.

    c. Isaac Benefield, b. 23 Aug. 1854 Ala., d. 12 Oct. 1923 m. Malissa ----, b. 14 Feb. 1862, d. 4 Aug. 1930. Both are buried in Antioch Baptist Church Cem..

    d. James Benefield, b. ca 1857 Ala.

    e. Eliza A. R. Benefield, b. ca 1860 Ala.

f. Martha Benefield, b. ca 1864 Ala.

g. Zachariah Benefield, b. ca 1866 Ala.

h. Ansel Benefield, b. ca 1869 Ala.

4. William Henry Hartzog, b. 27 April 1837 Ala., d. 11 June 1921 Ariton, Ala., m. Mary Jane Horn 8 Sept. 1859. She was born 1 Sept. 1839 and died 8 Dec. 1918. Issue (from descendant):

a. Lydia Mae Hartzog, b. 15 June 1860 Ala., d. 25 Aug. 1932, m. Elish J. Tyler.

b. William Nathan Hartzog, b. 2 Feb. 1862 Ala., d. 19 Sept. 1919, m. Narcis Malinda Thomas 26 April 1885.

c. James Isaac Hartzog, b. 20 Feb. 1864 Ala., d. 13 April 1887, probably never married.

d. John Hartzog, b. ca 1865 Ala.

e. Alexander Hartzog, b. 12 Jan. 1868 Ala., d. 24 May 1930, m. (1) Dijah Sutton 3 Jan. 1895 (2) Missouri Briley.

f. David Wilson Hartzog, b. 20 Nov. 1869 Ala., d. 10 April 1935, probably never married.

g. Sopha Hartzog, b. 23 Sept. 1871 Ala., d. 14 April 1911, m. John Benjamin Paramore.

h. Leona Hartzog, b. 3 March 1873 Ala., d. 22 April 1900, never married.

i. Noah Hartzog, b. 29 Aug. 1878 Ala., d. 26 April 1905, never married.

j. Magnolia Hartzog, b. 1880, d. 1927, m. A. A. Sutton.

k. Thomas Albert Hartzog, b. 7 Oct. 1882, d. 10 Sept. 1963, m. Maggie Garner 8 Jan. 1911.

l. Mamie Hartzog, b. 21 Jan. 1887, m. James A. Slawson.

m. Ambrose Hartzog.

5. Martha Ann Hartzog, b. ca 1842 Ala. (living with mother, Celia Mitchell in 1870), m. William Blakey, Jr. 26 May 1859. Issue:

a. Mary A. Blakey, b. ca 1860 Ala.

b. Laura Blakey, b. ca 1861 Ala.

Also in Celia (Hartzog) Mitchell household were:

a. Mary Mitchell, b. ca 1844 Ala.

b. Hiram Mitchell, b. ca 1845 Ala., in Wm. Blakey household in 1870.

c. Julia A. Mitchell, b. ca 1850 Ala.

d. Joseph Mitchell, b. ca 1854 Ala.

Some descendants believe that this George Hartzog (who died by 1838 Barbour Co.) married (1) Sarah ---- and had:

1. Daniel Barney Hartzog, b. 15 Jan. 1815 S. C., d. 28 June 1894, m. Elizabeth (Lee?), b. 7 June 1812 S. C., d. 10 Feb. 1892. Both are buried in Pond Bethel Cem.. Known issue:

   a. Sarah E. Hartzog, b. ca 1847 Ala...may have married John W. Bedsole 10 Dec. 1869.

   b. George Wiley Hartzog, b. 16 Aug. 1848 Ala., d. 31 Oct. 1893, m. Catherine Bedsole 3 Dec. 1868. She was born 28 Nov. 1849 Ala., died 20 April 1918. They are buried in Creel Cem..

   c. Mary A. Hartzog, b. ca 1849 Ala., not married in 1880.

   d. Hepsey A. Hartzog, b. ca 1851 Ala.

   e. Daniel J. Hartzog, b. ca 1854 Ala. m. Harriett Shirah 2 Jan. 1871. (see ZORN).

2. George Wiley Hartzog, b. 1817 S. C., d. 22 April 1901, m. Epsey Lee 2 Sept. 1841 (see LEE). She was born ca 1817 S.C., died 23 May 1889. Both are buried in Pond Bethel Cem.. Known issue:

   a. Daniel Hartzog, b. ca 1841 Ala., no record after 1860.

   b. Timothy Hartzog, b. ca 1843 Ala., no record after 1860.

   c. John Hartzog, b. ca 1845/7 Ala., may have married Louisa S. ---- ca 1870.

d. James F. Hartzog, b. ca 1850 Ala., no record after 1860.

e. William Henry Hartzog, b. ca 1850 Ala., m. Anna Eudora McNair 13 Jan. 1874.

f. Nicholas Hartzog, b. 17 Aug. 1852 Ala., d. 18 Sept. 1925, m. Mary Isabella McEachern 9 Oct. 1873. She was born 14 Aug. 1855 Ala., died 7 May 1897. Both are buried in Upper Prospect Baptist Ch. Cem. (see McEACHERN).

g. Mary A. Hartzog, b. ca 1855 Ala., not married in 1880.

h. Robert Hartzog, b. ca 1859 Ala., living with brother, Henry Hartzog, in 1880.

3. Francis Hartzog, b. ca 1824 S. C., m. (1) Rebecca Zorn by 1844 (2) Betha Ann Hartzog 29 Jan. 1865, b. ca 1848 Ala.. Issue (all by 1st wife):

a. Sarah Hartzog, b. ca 1845 Ala., may have married Lewis Graves 24 July 1864.

b. George Hartzog, b. ca 1846 Ala., possibly died by 1860.

c. Jane Hartzog, b. ca 1850 Ala., not married in 1870.

d. Daniel Hartzog, b. ca 1851 Ala.

e. Henry Hartzog, b. ca 1855 Ala.

f. Molsey Hartzog, b. ca 1857 Ala.

g. James Hartzog, b. ca 1860 Ala.

Daniel Barney Hartzog and George Wiley Hartzog were living in Henry Co., Ala. in 1850. Francis Hartzog also owned land there at one time.

David Hartzog, b. ca 1796 S. C., d. ca 15 Jan. 1879 Henry Co., Ala., was in Barbour Co. from 1832 through 1850, but sold land in Henry Co. in 1860 and 1876. He probably married twice - the second time to Rebecca Henley about 1842. Issue (but 1st wife, maybe Catherine ----):

1. Rebecca Hartzog, b. ca 1825 S. C., d. after 1880, m. James Baxley 17 Sept. 1848. He was born ca 1796 S. C., died by

1880 - had probably been married before and had William (b. ca 1821 S. C.), Barnabas (b. ca 1824 S. C.), Redden (b. ca 1829 S. C.), Sarah (b. ca 1828 S. C.) and Rhoda and Riley (twins, b. ca 1833 S. C..) Issue (by Rebecca Hartzog):

a. Joseph Baxley, b. ca 1850 Ala., probably died by 1860.

b. Catherine Baxley, b. ca 1851 Ala.

c. James Baxley, b. ca 1853 Ala., may have married Martha DuBose 8 June 1873.

d. Benjamin Baxley, b. ca 1855 Ala.

(also possibly)

e. Nancy Baxley

f. Ephriam J. Baxley, m. Anna Hartzog 13 Jan. 1881.

2. Mary A. E. Hartzog, b. 25 June 1831 S. C., d. 27 Oct. 1919, m. Randall Fuqua 8 March 1849. He was born 2 March 1814 Ga., died 3 June 1896. Both are buried in the Fuqua Cem. near Louisville. Known issue:

a. Randall Fuqua, Jr., b. ca 1851 Ala., no record after 1880. He may have married Martha A. Bridges 1 Jan. 1871.

b. Margaret E. Fuqua, b. 25 July 1855 Ala., d. 22 Jan. 1942, m. R. Cain Baxley 21 Dec. 1876. He was born 29 April 1855, died 17 Feb. 1946. They are buried in Antioch Bapt. Church Cem..

c. George W. Fuqua, b. 2 Nov. 1857 Ala., d. 25 Nov. 1929, m. (1) Dicy Malissa Calsina Warr 16 Nov. 1882. She was born 23 July 1857, died 7 April 1899, buried in the Fuqua Cem.. He m. (2) Elizabeth Helms 10 Nov. 1907. She was born 12 March 1875, died after 1965. She and George W. Fuqua are buried in Upper Prospect Baptist Church Cem..

d. William Fuqua, b. ca 1860 Ala., may have married Lidia A. Benefield 27 June 1881.

e. David Fuqua, b. ca 1866 Ala., may have married Zellie Warr 31 Aug. 1884.

f. John Fuqua, b. ca 1867 Ala.. He may be the John Daniel
    Fuqua, b. 2 May 1866, d. 29 Jan. 1939, buried Texasville
    Methodist Church Cem..

g. Hepsy Fuqua, born ca 1868 Ala.

h. Mary V. Fuqua, b. 9 April 1872 Ala., d. 11 Feb. 1902,
    m. ---- Hix. She is buried in Corinth Baptist Church
    Cem..

i. Adeline Fuqua, b. ca 1873 Ala.. There was an Adeline
    Fuqua, b. 24 Feb. 1874, d. 6 Feb. 1959, m. Archie Hay-
    wood Bryan, b. 17 Oct. 1872, d. 8 Jan. 1934, maybe his
    second wife. They are buried in Corinth Baptist Church
    Cem..

j. Richmond Fuqua, b. ca 1877 Ala., may have married Zola
    Dominy 27 Oct. 1907.

k. General W. Fuqua, b. ca 1879 Ala., may have married Emma
    Floyd 1 April 1900.

3. Catharine Hartzog, b. ca 1836 Ala., probably never married.
    She may be the Catharine Hartzog, b. 8 Nov. 1837, d. 4 Sept.
    1905, buried Prospect Cem. near Edwin in Henry Co., Ala..

Issue (by 2nd wife - probably more):

4. William Hartzog, b. ca 1844 Ala.

5. Rachel M. Hartzog, b. ca 1847 Ala., m. Jacob T. Brown 29
    Oct. 1872 Henry Co., Ala.

6. Tabitha Hartzog, b. ca 1848 Ala.

7. John L. Hartzog, b. ca 1850 Ala.

8. Elizabeth Hartzog, m. L. Stephens.

Other sources:

Henry Co., Ala. Census Records
Henry Co., Ala. Cemetery Records
Information from descendants.

HARWELL

Robert Harwell entered land near Louisville in 1829. In 1834, when he sold this land, he was called "of Montgomery Co., Ala." His wife, Polly, signed this deed. In 1836, he bought some lots in Irwinton (now Eufaula), which he sold in 1837 and 1839. In the deed in 1839, he was called "of Mobile, Ala.", and the grantee was Moses Harwell of Montgomery, Ala.. Robert Harwell was not enumerated in any Barbour Co. census, so it is impossible to determine his age. However, since he patented land in 1829, he had to be born before 1808.

There was a Samuel Harwell, b. ca 1778 Va., died by Nov. 1855, who was in Barbour Co. by 1850. His wife, Burchett ----, was born ca 1788 Va., died by May 1862. This may have been a second marriage for both of them. Known issue:

1. Henry J. Harwell, died by 1857.

2. Eliza Ann Harwell m. ---- Gardner. She died by 1855, and her heirs, Frances A. and Samuel H. Gardner, were living in Pike Co., Ala.

3. Elizabeth L. (or T.) Harwell, died by 1855, m. ---- Birdsong. Issue:

    a. Frances A. Birdsong, b. ca 1829 Ga., m. William McLeod 17 June 1849.

    b. Samantha Birdsong, b. 12 April 1831, d. 6 May 1896, m. Eli C. Holleman ca 1852. He was born 28 Dec. 1800, died 28 Aug. 1874.

    c. Martha Ann Birdsong, b. ca 1836 Ga., m. John A. Jones 11 May 1856.

    d. William H. Birdsong

    e. Josephine C. Birdsong, b. ca 1846 Ala.

4. James H. Harwell, b. ca 1818 Ga., m. Caroline ---- ca 1845. Known issue:

a. Martha Harwell, b. ca 1846 Ala.

b. Mary H. Harwell, b. ca 1847 Ala., m. O. S. Wells 14 Jan. 1866.

c. Henry Harwell, b. ca 1849 Ala..

5. Samuel Warren Harwell, b. ca 1828 Ga., m. Martha C. ----.
Known issue:

a. Samuel Harwell, b. ca 1851 Ala.

b. Elizabeth Harwell, b. ca 1853 Ala.

c. John Harwell, b. ca 1854 Ala.

d. Henry Harwell, b. ca 1856 Ala.

e. Frances Harwell, b. ca 1858 Ala.

Note: James H. Harwell m. Sarah J. Martin 5 Jan. 1868.

Sources of information:

Barbour Co., Ala. Probate Records
Barbour Co., Ala. Census Records

HEAD

Richard Head, Sr. was born between 1750 and 1760, and died by September 1846. His wife, whose name is not known, was also born between 1750 and 1760, and died between 1840 and 1846.

In 1829, William Head patented land South of Clayton. In 1835 and 1836, he patented more land Northeast of Comer. In 1836, James A. Head and Joshua T. Head patented land near the present Bullock Co. line in Western Barbour Co., and in 1837, Richard Head patented land near them.

In 1848, the heirs of Richard Head, Sr. were:

1. William Head, b. ca 1783 N. C., d. 3 Feb. 1857, m. Epsey
----. She was born ca 1791 Ga., died after 1850. Issue:

   a. James M. Head, living in Apalachacola, Fla. in 1858.

   b. Elizabeth Head, died after 1858, m. (Zachariah?) Williamson.

   c. William Head, died by 1858 - left two children living in Texas.

   d. John M. Head, died by 1858, m. Lurinda (Holly) Cain 17 Nov. 1844. She was the widow of Thomas Cain.

   e. Epsey Head, b. ca 1824 Ga., m. William M. Bryant 30 Nov. 1841.

   f. Mary M. Head, b. ca 1826 Ga., m. George Bryant 28 Oct. 1841.

   g. Eliza J. Head, b. ca 1826 Ga., m. Malcom Gilchrist 31 Dec. 1846.

   h. Richard Head, living in Mississippi in 1858.

   i. Edward P. Head, b. ca 1828 Ga.

   j. Robert M. Head, b. ca 1830 Ala.

   k. Ucal Head, b. ca 1834 Ala.

   1. Eliza Head, b. ca 1843 Ala., probably died young, as she is not named in the estate settlement.

m. Neill Head.

2. Edmund Head. There was an Edmund Head in Pike Co., Ala. in 1850, but there is no proof that he was the son of Richard Head, Sr.. He was born ca 1787 Ga., m. Sarah ----. Their daughter, Nancy, probably married Jesse Faulk. (See Faulk family).

3. Temperance Head m. ---- Knight.

4. Elizabeth Head m. Joel Willis (see later).

5. Mary A. Head m. John Bullard. Known issue:

   a. William Bullard

   b. Burrella Bullard m. ---- Knight.

   c. Catherine Bullard m. ---- Kenington.

   d. James Bullard

6. Richard Head, Jr., born between 1790 and 1800. He was enumerated in Barbour Co. in 1840 with 1 male 5/10, 2 males 10/15, 2 males 15/20, 1 male 40/50, 2 females under 5, 1 female 5/10, 1 female 10/15 and 1 female 15/20. He was not in the 1850 Census of Barbour Co., but there was a Richard Head in the 1850 Census of Pike Co., Ala. as follows:

Head, Richard	age 51	born Ga.	
" , Ellender	52	born Ga.	
" , William	26	born Ala.	deaf and dumb
" , Edmund	22	born Ala.	
" , Temperance	19	born Ala.	
" , Richard	18	born Ala.	
" , Elizabeth	15	born Ala.	
" , Nancy	13	born Ala.	
" , James	8	born Ala.	

The names of the children strongly suggest a close relationship to the Head family of Barbour Co..

There were other Head families in Barbour Co., and all were probably related, but it does not show in the records.

Sources of information:

Barbour Co., Ala. Probate Records
Barbour Co., Ala. Census Records
Barbour Co., Ala. Cemetery Records
Pike Co., Ala. Census Records
"Two Centuries With a Willis Family" by D. M. Willis

Joseph Henderson patented land West of Louisville in 1828
and 1833. The date and place of his birth are not found in the
Barbour Co. records, but he migrated to Alabama from Georgia ca
1825, and died in Barbour Co. by Dec. 1833. He married Cassey
(Kissa) ----, b. ca 1798 in Ga., d. by March 1874. She m. (2)
William Edge by Feb. 1834.

1. Penelope Henderson m. Gibson J. Williams, who died in Edgefield Dist., S. C. by Nov. 1845. Issue:

   a. John Williams, living in Coffee Co., Ala. in 1874.

   b. Delaney C. Williams, living in Jackson Co., Ala. in 1874.

   c. W. H. Williams, living in Butler Co., Ala. in 1874.

   d. J. L. Williams, living in Butler Co., Ala. in 1874.

   e. Joseph Williams, living in Jackson Co., Ala. in 1874.

2. William Henderson, b. ca 1816 Ga., m. Jane ----; living in
   Pike Co., Ala. in 1850. Known issue:

   a. Kissey, b. ca 1834 Ala..

   b. James, b. ca 1835 Ala..

   c. Matthew Henderson, b. ca 1837 Ala..

   d. Joseph Henderson, b. ca 1839 Ala..

   e. Martha Henderson, b. ca 1841 Ala..

   f. Amelia Henderson, b. ca 1843 Ala..

   g. George Henderson, b. ca 1844 Ala..

   h. Zilly Ann Henderson, b. ca 1846 Ala..

   i. Penelope Henderson, b. ca 1849 Ala..

      (possibly more)

3. James Henderson, b. ca 1820 Ga., d. March 1897, age 84, at
   Mt. Andrew (Barbour Co., Ala.), m. Sarah m. ----. Issue:

   a. Henry E. Henderson, b. ca 1840 Ala..

   b. Joseph J. Henderson, b. ca 1846 Ala..

   c. Jimpsey Henderson, b. ca 1848 Ala..

d. William Henderson, b. ca 1850 Ala..

e. Daniel Henderson, b. ca 1851 Ala..

f. Harmon Henderson, b. ca 1855 Ala..

g. Thomas B. Henderson, b. ca 1859 Ala..

(possibly more).

By his second wife, a widow named Casey, he had one son, James Henderson, b. ca 1873 Ala..

4. John Henderson, living in Coffee Co., Ala. in 1874.

5. LeRoy Henderson, b. ca 1824 Ga..

6. Joseph Henderson, b. 10 Nov. 1825 Ala., d. 13 May 1880, m. Margaret McDonald 27 Oct. 1846. She was born 16 Sept. 1821 in N. C., d. 4 Jan. 1881. Both are buried in Pea River Cemetery. Known issue:

a. William, b. ca 1850 Ala., m. Margaret ----.

7. David Henderson, b. ca 1830 Ala., d. by 1874, m. Lucinda ----. Issue:

a. Joseph Henderson, b. ca 1854 Ala..

b. Daniel Henderson, b. ca 1857 Ala..

c. Isaac Henderson, b. ca 1859 Ala..

d. Mahaly Henderson.

In 1874, these children were residents of Bibb Co., Ala..

By her marriage to William Edge, Cassey Henderson Edge had:

1. Lewis Edge.

2. Eli Edge.

3. Jane Edge.

Sources of information:

Barbour Co., Ala. Probate Records
Barbour Co., Ala. Census Records
Barbour Co., Ala. Cemetery Records
Pike Co., Ala. Census Records

HILL

Abner Hill patented land just West of the Indian boundary line near Gaino in 1829, but he probably never lived in Barbour Co.. In 1834, he sold this land to Ezekiel Wise, and at that time Abner Hill was a resident of Henry Co., Ala..

He was a J. P. in Henry Co. in 1826, and on 30 May 1892, he married Mary Jones there. He died in Henry Co. by 18 Jan. 1837, on which date his will was probated. His executors were Frederick Porter, James Bennett, John Jones and Polly Hill. Issue:

1. George James Hill, a minor in 1838, died by Dec. 1847.
2. Eliza V. Hill, a minor in 1838, m. Dempsey Cawthon in Henry Co., Ala. on 30 Nov. 1847.
3. Abner Hill, Jr., a minor in 1838, died by Dec. 1847.

Mary, widow of Abner Hill, m. (2) ---- Kirven, by whom she had one son, Alford Kirven. She m. (3) Stephen Cawthon, by whom she had a daughter, Georgianna Cawthon. Mary (Jones) Hill Kirven Cawthon died in Henry Co., Ala. on 30 Nov. 1847.

Sources of information:

Henry Co., Ala. Probate Records
Barbour Co., Ala. Probate Records

HIX
(Hicks)

In 1828 and 1836, Newsom Hix patented land South of Mount A
Andrew. In 1836 Elizabeth Hix also patented land in that vicinity. There is a grave in Corinth Baptist Cemetery of Elizabeth
Allen Hicks, wife of R. J. Hicks, daughter of Bazel and Elizabeth Graves. The only date given is 13 April 1829, and there is
no indication whether it is a birth or death date. If it is a
death date, the marker must have been placed many years later.

Newsom Hix was born ca 1803 in Ga., died by Feb. 1857 in
Pike Co., Ala.. His wife, Nancy, was born ca 1810 in Ga., died
after Feb. 1857. In the 1850 Census, the following children
were living in the Newsom Hix household:

1. Morgan Hix, born ca 1832 Ala.

2. Jefferson Hix, born ca 1834 Ala.

3. Elizabeth Hix, born ca 1840 Ala.

4. Sarah Hix, born ca 1842 Ala.

5. William Hix, born ca 1845 Ala.

6. Nancy Hix, born ca 1847 Ala.

The estate settlement of Newsom Hix in 1857 names the following minor children:

1. Morgan Hix

2. Andrew Jackson Hix

3. William Jefferson Hix

4. Judy Ann Hix

5. Rhoda Ann Hix

6. Jesse Hix

7. Anon Hix (he may have been Adam Hix, born ca 1831)

8. Madison Hix

9. Newsom Hix

10. Savannah Hix

Sources of information:

Barbour Co., Ala. Probate Records
Barbour Co., Ala. Cemetery Records
Barbour Co., Ala. Census Records

HOBDY

Harrell Hobdy patented land west of Louisville, Barbour Co.,
Ala. in 1828, 1829, 1832, 1833 and 1834. Thomas Hobdy patented
land near him in 1836, as did Robert Hobdy in 1835, 1836 and
1839.

They were sons of Edmund Hobdy, b. 28 -- 1776 N. C., died
after 1850 in Pike Co., Ala.. He married Nancy (probably Harrell) who died before 1850. Their children were:

1. Joses Hobdy, b. 10 Nov. 1797, m. Lizetta Cartwright, living
    in Texas in 1850. He was born in N. C.

2. Harrell Hobdy, b. 23 Sept. 1799 N. C., d. by 21 Feb. 1865,
    when his estate was administered in Pike Co., Ala. He m.
    Jennie McNeill, b. ca 1798 Richmond Co., N. C., d. 17 Oct.
    1863 in Pike Co., Ala.. She was the daughter of John
    McNeill. Issue:

    a. Martha, b. ca 1826 Ala. (1850 Census of Pike Co., Ala.)
    b. John, b. ca 1828 Ala. (1850 Census of Pike Co., Ala.)
    c. Sarah Emeline, probably born ca 1830 Ala., m. N. Mon-
        tross Hyatt in Pike Co., Ala. on 23 Nov. 1848. He m.
        (2) Elizabeth Belcher White 12 Oct. 1859. Sarah Emeline
        (Hobdy) Hyatt had died on 10 Sept. 1855.
    d. Adeliza, b. 1834 Ala., d. 1932, m. Dr. Philip P. McRae.
        She is buried in Clayton Cemetery, Clayton, Ala..
    e. Elizabeth, b. ca 1836 Ala. (1850 Census of Pike Co.,
        Ala.)
    f. James M., b. ca 1838 Ala. (1850 Census of Pike Co., Ala.)
        There is a J. M. Hobdy, b. 15 July 1839, d. 13 May 1900,
        who is buried in Bethlehem Cemetery in Barbour Co., Ala.
    g. Robert Long, b. 22 Oct. 1840, d. 31 Dec. 1927, m. Mary
        Buford, b. 5 July 1845, d. 30 April 1903. She was the
        daughter of Jefferson and Mary Ann Rebecca (White)

Buford. Both are buried in Fairview Cemetery, Eufaula, Ala..

    h.   Edward, b. ca 1843 Ala. (1850 Census of Pike Co., Ala.) d. in Ocala, Fla. in March 1897, age 52, buried Louisville, Ala.. He was a brother of R. L. Hobdy.

    i.   Mary, b. ca 1845 Ala. (1850 Census of Pike Co., Ala.)

3. Robert Hobdy, b. 24 Aug. 1801 N. C., d. before 1847, m. Caroline ---- (she m. second ---- Dick, was living in Natchitoches Parish, La. by 1850). Issue (all minors in 1850):

    a.   John R.

    b.   Ann C.

    c.   Caroline A.

    d.   Mary Jane

    e.   Amanda

    f.   Sarah Emeline

4. William Hobdy, b. 18 Sept. 1803, living Pass Christian, Miss. in 1850.

5. Edmund Hobdy, b. 28 Nov. 1796, lived Wilcox Co., Ala., m. Martha Williams Purifoy 5 Jan. 1829 (see PURIFOY).

6. Margaret Hobdy, b. 27 April 1807 N. C., d. 24 Nov. 1834, m. Samuel G. Adams (see Adams family).

7. Eliza Hobdy, b. 19 May 1811 N. C., m. C. S. Johnson, living in Pike Co., Ala. in 1850.

8. Thomas Hobdy, b. 29 April 1812 N. C., d. by 1850/2. Issue (all minors, living in La. in 1850):

    a.   John Edward

    b.   William Lawrence

    c.   Mary Jane

9. Ivey Hobdy, b. 21 Aug. 1818, d. by 21 Sept. 1854 Pike Co., Ala., m. Eliza Reynolds. She m. (2) ---- Pickett.

10. Ira B. Hobdy, b. 21 Aug. 1818, N. C., d. 22 May 1881, buried

Oakwood Cem., Troy (Pike Co., Ala.), m. (1) Sarah Love in
Pike Co., Ala. on 29 July 1841 (2) Jane A. Nall in Pike Co.,
Ala. on 4 Nov. 1869. She was born 15 Sept. 1823, d. 10
June 1889, also buried Oakwood Cem., Troy. Issue (from 1850
Census of Pike Co., Ala.):

a. Harriet, b. ca 1844 Ala.

b. John, b. ca 1847 Ala.

c. Mary, b. ca 1850 Ala.

    (probably more)

Miscellaneous:

1850 Census of Pike Co., Ala., household #1122-1122
Hobdy, Edmund, age 73, born N. C.
Harrell, Margaret, age 68, born N. C.
Harrell, Sydney, age 45, born Ga.
Adams, John, age 20, born Ala.

Sources of information:

Dept. of Archives & History, Montgomery, Ala. - Hobdy family
    file
1850 Census of Pike Co., Ala.
Probate records of Pike & Barbour Cos., Ala.
Cemetery records of Barbour Co., Ala.

HOOD

James Hood entered land Southwest of Mount Andrew from 1828 through 1836. Daniel S. Hood entered land West of Louisville in 1835 and 1836, and Bold Robin Hood entered land adjoining him in 1837. They were all probably related, as they were still living near each other in 1838. There are not any census records on these men in Barbour Co. after 1838, but there is on record the will of Bold Robin Hood. It was written 20 Sept. 1838 and was probated 17 Oct. 1854. His heirs were:

1. Joshua T. Hood (a son), b. ca 1800 N. C., m. Elizabeth ----, b. ca 1819 N. C.. Known issue:

    a. Bold Robin Hood, b. ca 1831 N. C., m. Sarah L. Johnston 12 Sept. 1850.

    b. Sarah Hood, b. ca 1841 Ala.

    c. Elizabeth Hood, b. ca 1845 Ala.

    d. John T. Hood, b. ca 1848 Ala.

2. Daniel S. Hood m. Eliza J. ----. Known issue:

    a. Mary Jane Hood

    b. Daniel S. Hood

In 1840, the only Hood in the Census is E. Hood - 1 male 20/30, 1 female 15/20 and 1 female 50/60.

Sources of information:

Barbour Co., Ala. Probate Records
Barbour Co., Ala. Census Records

In 1829, Jacinth, Warren and William R. Jackson entered land between Clayton and Louisville, and Hiram Jackson entered land a little Southeast of them. In 1835 and 1836, Jacinth Jackson entered more land, this time close to Hiram Jackson. However, the records do not show any relationship between these men.

In 1837, Jacinth Jackson sold his lot in Clayton to John Jackson; his wife, Prudence, relinquished her dower rights. In 1839, he sold most of his farm land to John H. Miller, but no wife signed. As late as 1840, Jacinth Jackson was a County Commissioner, but he is not listed as head of a household in the 1840 Census. In 1838, his household consisted of 5 males under 21, 1 male over 21, 2 females under 21, 1 female over 21 and 27 slaves. He may have died while on a trip to the West, but there is no estate settlement for him in Barbour Co.

In 1814, Jacinth Jackson and Samuel Swilley served in the Baldwin Co., Ga. Militia. It is possible that they were the same men who later came to Barbour Co., Ala..

Jordan A. and Jasper N. Jackson, enumerated consecutively in the 1850 Census of Barbour Co. as follows, could have been sons of Jacinth Jackson:

```
Jackson, Jordan A.        age 30, born Ga.
       , Elizabeth L.         23, born Ga.
       , Jacinth O.            4, born Ala.
       , Mary J.               3, born Ala.
       , Jasper N.             2, born Ala.
       , John H.            1/12, born Ala.
Jackson, Jasper N.        age 26, born Ala.
       , Mary A.              21, born Ga.
       , James T.              2, born Ala.
       , Moses T.              1, born Ala.
```

In 1834, the land which Hiram Jackson entered (in 1829) was sold to settle a debt. At that time, he and Cary Curry were business partners, and a sawmill, gristmill and cotton gin were on the land. There is no further record of Hiram Jackson.

William R. Jackson died by 1833; his administrator was Jacinth Jackson. His wife was Lucy ----, and he had one son, John R. Jackson, a minor.

Sources of information:

Barbour Co., Ala. Probate Records
Barbour Co., Ala. Census Records

*ADDITIONS & CORRECTIONS AS OF JUNE 1, 1979:

Jacinth Jackson, b. 16 Oct. 1796, d. 5 Sept. 1869, m. Prudence Allums, b. 1797, d. 1857. He was a son of Randall Jackson, b. 1763 Brunswick Co., Va., d. 1838, m. Elizabeth Kendall, b. 1776, d. 1854.

Baldwin Co., Ga. Marriage records:

Jason (Jacinth?) Jackson m. Prudence Allums 26 May 1814

William Jackson m. Nancy Springer 29 July 1807

James Allums m. Sarah Jackson 25 April 1811

John Beasley m. Martha Allums 9 March 1820

William Beasley m. Temperance Jackson 3 Dec. 1814

JERNIGAN

Blake Jernigan patented land West of Louisville in 1827. On
17 Dec. 1827, Jos. Henderson sold land to Blake Jernigan - at
the time, the land was in Pike Co., but was later cut in Barbour
Co.. On 29 Nov. 1836, Blake Jernigan sold his land to the heirs
of Joseph Henderson, deceased. His wife, Winney Jernigan, signed
her dower relinquishment in Escambia Co., Fla.. Blake Jernigan
later went to Santa Rosa Co., Fla..

The following is the probable ancestry of Blake Jernigan:

I.   Lame David Jernigan, died ca 1793 Wayne Co., N. C., his
      son

II.   Josiah Jernigan married Mary Jernigan. They had sons
      Blake and David.

III. David Jernigan m. Milly, daughter of Thomas Toler (who died
      ca 1812 in Wayne Co., N. C.)

IV.   Blake Jernigan married Winney, also a daughter of Thomas
      Toler.

Blake Jernigan was listed in the 1820 Census of Wayne Co.,
N. C., age 26/44, with a wife and one son. Blake and Winnie
Jernigan had a son, Silas, b. 1812 N. C., who married Anna Cole-
man in 1837 in Conecuh Co., Ala.. They later moved to Escambia
Co., then to Santa Rosa Co., Fla.

There was a Milly (Emily) Jernigan, b. ca 1792 N. C., d.
Feb. 1867, who is buried in Mount Aerial Church Cemetery. She
was listed as head of a household in the 1840 Census of Barbour
Co., age 50/60, with 1 male 15/20. In 1850 and 1860, she was
enumerated in the household of William Jernigan. It is very
likely that she was the wife of David Jernigan, brother of Blake.
In the 1838 Census, David Jernigan was head of a household, with
a wife and two males under 21.

There is little doubt that Milly Jernigan was the mother of
142

Wm. M. Jernigan. He was born 12 Sept. 1823 Ala., d. 1 July 1902, m. Martha Deshazo 12 March 1845 (see Deshazo family). She was born 30 Nov. 1826 Ga., died 25 July 1896. Both are buried in Mount Aerial Church Cemetery. Probable issue:

1. Jason J. Jernigan, b. 1843 Ala., d. 1911, m. Martha E. Craddock 22 Sept. 1867. She was born 1846, died 1920. Both are buried in Mount Aerial Church Cemetery. They moved to Texas about 1871, but returned to Alabama about 1878.

2. Stephen Decatur Jernigan, b. ca 1847 Ala., m. Mary Jane Skipper 19 Dec. 1869.

3. Mary Jane Jernigan, b. ca 1849 Ala.

4. Lucinda C. Jernigan, b. ca 1851 Ala., m. John P. Duncan Wilkerson 20 Nov. 1872.

5. Savannah Jernigan, b. ca 1853 Ala., m. Tom J. Coats 28 Jan. 1872.

6. Lela Emaline Jernigan, b. 23 July 1855 Ala., d. 7 March 1925, m. Dave A. Walden 21 Dec. 1876. He was born 11 Sept. 1847, died 16 Feb. 1926. Both are buried in East Side Cemetery, Headland, Ala..

7. Malinda M. Jernigan, b. ca 1857 Ala., m. A. Reed Adams 29 Sept. 1886.

8. William Clahorn Jernigan, b. ca 1859 Ala., m. Henriette Bush 28 Dec. 1881. She was born 1 Dec. 1848, died 10 Nov. 1937, and is buried in Mount Aerial Church Cemetery.

9. Emily Jernigan, b. ca 1860 Ala.

10. Fern B. Jernigan, b. ca 1862 Ala., m. G. Anna Pittman 24 Dec. 1882.

11. Alpheus Baker Jernigan, b. ca 1866 Ala., m. Leola Cora Eulala Texas Lee 25 Dec. 1887.

Other Jernigan families in Barbour Co. at this time were:
James Jernigan - in 1840, he was head of a household which

included himself (age 40/50), 1 male under 5, 2 females under 5, 2 females 5/10, 3 females 10/15 and 1 female 20/30. In 1846, James W. Jernigan patented land West of Mount Andrew.

S. L. Jernigan - in 1840, he was head of a household (age 20/30), with 1 female age 20/30.

On 23 Oct. 1840, George W. Trainham gave livestock to his grandson, William H. Jernigan.

Sources of information:

Barbour Co., Ala. Probate Records
Barbour Co., Ala. Census Records
Barbour Co., Ala. Cemetery Records
Henry Co., Ala. Cemetery Records
Information from descendants.

JOHNSON
(Johnston)

Nicholas Johnson patented land North of Gaino in 1828. He was enumerated in the 1838 Census as 1 male under 21, 1 male over 21 and 1 female over 21. In the 1840 Census, his household consisted of 2 males under 5, 1 male 40/50 and 1 female 30/40. There are no further records of him in Barbour Co..

In "Georgia Landmarks" by Knight, it is stated that one Nicholas Johnson was an early settler of Troup Co., Ga.. In the 1805 Georgia Land Lottery, a Nicholas Johnson of Oglethorpe Co., had 2 draws. And in Camden Co., Ga., a Nicholas Johnson married Mrs. Elizabeth Norton on 23 Feb. 1824. However, there is nothing to prove that any of these men were related to Nicholas Johnson of Barbour Co., Ala..

Another Johnson family in Barbour Co. was that of Stephen Johnson.* He entered land South of Clayton in 1836. In 1808, he was living in Lexington Co., S. C., where he made deed-of-gift to his children, viz: Sarah, Mary, Elizabeth, Jesse and Nancy Johnson. He married (1) Mary (Lindsay?) (2) Rosanna Williams, born 17 Jan. 1785, died 18 Jan. 1837. She was the daughter of Capt. Jeremiah Williams, Jr. (1755-1830), a Revolutionary Soldier, and Nancy Jane Graham, born 30 Jan. 1756, died 11 April 1829. Stephen Johnson was born 11 Nov. 1776 Newberry Dist., S. C., died 20 Aug. 1836. He may have been the son of William Johnson, Jr. and Winefred ----. Issue of Stephen Johnson (by 1st wife):

1. Sarah Johnson, b. 14 June 1793, m. Benjamin Sawyers.
2. Mary Johnson, b. 7 March 1795, m. Daniel Creel.
3. Alexander Johnson, b. 13 May 1797 - not named in deed-of-gift, so may have died young.
4. Elizabeth Johnson, b. 7 March 1799 S. C., m. Timothy Johnson,

son of Phillip Johnson who migrated to Ala. from S. C.
Known issue:

a. William Johnson, b. ca 1830 Ala.

b. Phillip R. Johnson, b. ca 1833 Ala.

c. Jacob E. Johnson, b. ca 1835 Ala.

d. Timothy Johnson, b. ca 1838 Ala., m. Elizabeth ----.

e. Mary M. Johnson, b. ca 1843 Ala.

5. Thomas Johnson, b. 21 Jan. 1801. He was not named in the
   deed-of-gift, so may have died young.

6. Jesse Johnson, b. 11 June 1806 S. C., died 1854, m. Sarah
   ----. Issue:

   a. William W. Johnson, b. 20 Oct. 1828 Ala., may have mar-
      ried Sarah J. Brown 20 Sept. 1866.

   b. Rachel A. Johnson, b. ca 1830 Ala., d. ca 16 Oct. 1914,
      m. Jacob Utsey. He died 13 Nov. 1913; both are buried
      in Clayton Cemetery (see Utsey).

   c. Emanual Johnson, b. ca 1832 Ala., d. 1856, m. Ann Eliza-
      beth Hightower 5 Sept. 1854.

   d. *Louisa A. Johnson, b. ca 1834 Ala., m. (1) Archibald P.
      McLeod 30 Dec. 1857 (2) ---- Reid.

   e. Mary Elizabeth Johnson, b. ca 1836 Ala., m. William E.
      Ventress 18 Aug. 1859.

   f. Julia A. Johnson, b. ca 1838 Ala., m. (1) Spence L.
      McCracken 29 Nov. 1860 (2) G. D. Helms 15 Nov. 1880.

   g. James H. Johnson, b. ca 1840 Ala.

   h. Lidia Eudora Johnson, b. 25 Nov. 1842 Ala., d. 18 July
      1939, m. William E. Cox 20 Sept. 1862 (see Cox family).

   i. Frances H. Johnson, b. ca 1844 Ala., m. Louis B. Bush
      16 Nov. 1869 (see Bush family).

   j. Sarah (or Laura) Johnson, b. ca 1846 Ala.*

   k. Jesse Robert Johnson, b. ca 1850 Ala.

1. Virginia J. Johnson, b. ca 1852, not married in 1914.

By 2nd wife:

7. Nancy Johnson, b. 25 Feb. 1808, m. Eli Harrod 23 Aug. (or Oct.) 1829.

8. Rachel Johnson, b. 24 Oct. 1809 S. C., d. 20 Feb. 1886, m. Jimpsey Cox. He was born ca 1808 Ga.. Known issue:

    a. Rose Ann Cox, b. 6 Oct. 1834 Ala., d. 20 Feb. 1886, m. Lewis V. Norton 23 Dec. 1852. He was born ca 1832, died 27 Nov. 1867. Both are buried in Bethlehem Cemetery.

    b. Nancy Cox, b. 16 Oct. 1836 Ala., d. 30 June 1920, m. R. J. Richards 6 Jan. 1861. He was born Feb. 1827, died 17 March 1895. Both are buried in Bethlehem Cemetery.

    c. Mary A. M. Cox, b. 16 March 1839 Ala., d. 31 Oct. 1903, m. I. B. Braxton. She is buried in Bethlehem Cemetery.

    d. Sarah A. Cox, b. ca 1841 Ala.

    e. Rachel A. Cox, b. ca 1844 Ala.

    f. Julia A. Cox, b. ca 1848 Ala., m. J. J. Floyd 14 Oct. 1869. He was born 1 Nov. 1843, died 26 July 1881, is buried in Bethlehem Cemetery.

9. Lucinda Johnson, b. 30 April 1811 S. C., d. by 1892, m. Daniel A. Norton, b. ca 1813 S. C., d. 1897. Known issue:

    a. William Asbury Norton, b. 8 March 1836 Ala., d. 10 July 1865.

    b. James Norton, b. 11 May 1837 Ala., d. 2 April 1864 in Civil War.

    c. Mary Eliza Norton, b. 16 May 1839 Ala., d. 6 Nov. 1851.

    d. Julia Ann Norton, b. 22 May 1840 Ala., d. 26 Jan. 1908.

    e. Lewis Fletcher Norton, b. 26 Oct. 1843 Ala., d. Nov. 1862 (CSA).

    f. Ann Elizabeth Norton, b. 28 May 1846 Ala., d. Arcadia, La..

g. Josephine Palestine Norton, b. 4 Aug. 1848 Ala., d. 17 Oct. 1908, m. John Burt.

h. Frances C. Norton, b. 16 Dec. 1850, d. 15 Jan. 1915, m. Langdon Perrett.

10. Barsheba Johnson, b. 9 Feb. 1813, d. y.

11. Alexander Johnson, b. 24 Oct. 1814, d. 15 Oct. 1891, m. Elizabeth Collins 19 Dec. 1838. Known issue:

a. Alexander T. Johnson, b. ca 1838 Ala..

b. Amanda Johnson, b. 1 June 1841 Ala..

c. Wilson Johnson, b. 1 Sept. 1842 Ala.

d. Martha C. Johnson, b. 15 Feb. 1846 Ala..

12. Lewis A. T. Johnson, b. 23 March 1817 S. C., d. 7 Aug. 1891 La., m. (1) Patience Elizabeth Norton 3 Dec. 1837, daughter of William Norton, Jr. and Lucretia ---. She was born ca 1822 S. C., died 10 May 1863 (2) Eliza Jane Burleson 8 Oct. 1865. Known issue:

By 1st wife:

a. Nancy Ann Johnson, b. 28 July 1838 Ala., d. 29 July 1892, buried in Fairview Cemetery, Eufaula, Ala.. She married Wm. McLeod 30 Sept. 1856. He married (2) Julia Cade.

b. Felder Johnson, b. ca 1842 Ala., died in Civil War.

c. Elizabeth Johnson, b. 10 May 1845 Ala., d. 11 Sept. 1913, m. John W. Blair 31 Aug. 1865. He was born 25 Oct. 1836, died 19 June 1900. She is buried in Fairview Cemetery, Eufaula, Alabama, and he is buried in Bishop-Blair Cemetery.

d. Rosanna Johnson, b. ca 1847 Ala., died in La..

e. Thomas Johnson, b. 15 June Ala., d. 10 April 1909 La., m. Julia A. Perrett in La..

f. William Ardis Johnson, b. 21 Dec. 1853 Ala., d. 28 July 1925 in La..

g. Mary Johnson, b. ca 1856 Ala.

h. Emma Leola Johnson, b. 5 Nov. 1858 Ala., m. William
    Berry Madden.

By 2nd wife:

i. Louis Nathaniel Daniel Johnson

j. Lily Johnson

k. Stephen Richard Johnson

l. Ella Elizabeth Johnson

m. Lucinda S. Johnson

n. Joseph Francis Johnson

o. Rastus Fouts Johnson

13. Barshaba Johnson, b. 27 Dec. 1818. She is not named in the
    estates of Stephen or Rosanna Johnson, so she must have died
    before 1836.

14. Marina Johnson, b. 22 Oct. 1820 S. C., d. 22 May 1883, m.
    Samuel Benton 18 July 1845. He was born 30 Jan. 1826, died
    14 Oct. 1866. Both are buried in Bethlehem Cemetery. Known
    issue:*

a. Sarah Benton, b. ca 1846 Ala.

b. Mary Benton, b. ca 1848 Ala.

c. Lucinda Benton, b. ca 1850 Ala., m. John Elbert Warr.

15. Felder Benejah Johnson, b. 13 Sept. 1823, d. ca 16 May 1916
    in Pike Co., Ala., m. Julia A. Ellis 29 Jan. 1843. She was
    born 6 Dec. 1823, died 3 Jan. 1902. Issue:

a. Martha Ann Johnson, b. 16 Nov. 1845, d. 5 Nov. 1871, may
    have married ---- Moore.

b. William Henry Johnson m. Martha M. ----.

c. Mary Elizabeth Johnson, m. Judge Donald Gillis 14 April
    1867, lived in Pike Co., Ala.

d. Margaret Rosanna Johnson, b. 15 Sept. 1847, d. 15 Feb.
    1931, m. T. J. Daniel. They lived in Pike Co., Ala..

e. Nancy Lucinda Johnson, b. 28 March 1849, died 1 June 1941, lived in Pike Co., Ala..

f. Julia Frances Johnson, b. 19 Oct. 1850, m. ---- McLane.

g. Rachel Ann Mirandy Johnson, b. 5 April 1852.

h. Lewis Alexander Johnson, b. 11 Jan. 1854, d. 9 June 1855.

i. Annie Johnson, m. ---- Bryant, lived in Pike Co., Ala.

j. Susan Rebecca Johnson, b. 24 Dec. 1855, m. ---- Blackmon.

k. Felder Bena T. Johnson, b. 22 Nov. 1857

l. Elijah L. Johnson, b. 25 June 1859, d. 15 July 1878.

m. Thadeus A. Johnson, b. 30 Nov. 1860, lived in Pike Co., Ala.

n. James Fletcher Johnson, b. 31 July 1867, d. 26 Sept. 1869.

There were also three brothers, Isham, Miles M. and Andrew N. Johnson. Andrew N. Johnson died in Leon Co., Fla. between Dec. 1840 and Dec. 1846. His wife was Mary ---, b. ca 1798 Ga., d. 1856. Probable issue:

1. John Washington Johnson, b. ca 1822 Ga., m. Louisa Ball 18 Aug. 1844.

2. Andrew Jackson Johnson

3. Isham Lafayette Johnson, b. ca 1827 Fla.

4. William Lauren Johnson, b. ca 1830 Fla.

5. David White Johnson, b. ca 1833 Fla.

6. Caroline Johnson, b. 10 Oct. 1819, d. 24 May 1845, buried in Tennell Chapel Cemetery. She married Hugh A. Blount 5 Nov. 1835.

7. Joseph Marcain Johnson, b. ca 1836 Fla.

8. Mary Johnson, b. ca 1840 Fla.

Isham Johnson died between May and Nov. 1846. His wife, Elizabeth, was born ca 1800 in Ga.. Issue:

1. Catherine Johnson (called Purnetty Jane in will), b. ca 1823

Fla., m. Cornelius J. M. Andrews, b. ca 1821 Ga.

2. Allen R. Johnson

3. Richard M. Johnson, b. 24 May 1831 Fla., d. 26 May 1855,
    buried in Tennell Chapel Cemetery.*

There is no record of Miles M. Johnson in Barbour Co., so he
evidently never lived here.

Isaiah Johnson, b. Aug. 1790, d. 2 July 1879 Leon Co., Fla.
He had been living there since 1828. There is nothing to show
that he was related to the other Johnson families of Leon Co.,
Fla., but his obituary was run in a Barbour Co. newspaper, so
there must have been some kinship.

Sources of information:

Barbour Co., Ala. Probate Records
Barbour Co., Ala. Census Records
Barbour Co., Ala. Cemetery Records
"Georgia Landmarks" by Knight
Camden Co., Ga. Records
Stephen Johnson family Bible
"Alabama Series", Vol. II, by Helen S. Foley.

*ADDITIONS & CORRECTIONS AS OF JUNE 1, 1979:

Louisa A. Johnson m. Archibald P. McLeod 30 Dec. 1857. She was
born 28 Nov. 1836 and died 28 July 1893. He was born 22 March
1834 and died 5 March 1907. Both are buried in Cunningham Cem.
In all available records, she is called "Louisa", but her tomb-
stone inscription says "Sarah". Archibald P. McLeod m. (2)Alice
V. Howell. She was born 1875, died 1913 and is buried in Rocky
Mount Cem.

In addition to the children listed (a, b & c), Marina and Samuel
Benton had twins, Rosa and Alex.

Laura Johnson m. Jim Reid and moved to Texas. He died there and
she and her two sons returned to Barbour Co.. She died 9 April
1919 and is buried in Clayton Cem..

In 1874, the heirs of Richard Madison Johnson were: M. A.,
J. P. and R. M. Johnson. His widow, Amanda J., had married
_____ Gaston.

Johnson family cemetery, Barbour Co., Ala.
   Stephen Johnson, b. 11 Dec. 1766, d. 20 Aug. 1836
   Rosanna Johnson, b. 17 June 1787, d. 18 Jan. 1837
   Alexander Johnson, b. 1814, d. 1891. His obit says he came
      to Barbour Co. ca 1820 (then Pike Co.).

JOHNSTON

Although John Johnston was not one of the earliest settlers of this area, he is included because of the many marriages between his family and the families of the earliest settlers. He was born ca 1785 Horry Co., S. C. and died 3 Sept. 1853 Barbour Co., Ala. (his estate was not settled until 1879). He married Mary (Molsie) Hodges of S. C.. She was born ca 1792 Horry Co., S. C. and died 1879 Barbour Co., Ala.. Issue:

1. Margaret C. Johnston, b. 4 Oct. 1808 Horry Co., S. C., d. 30 July 1864, m. James Russell Norton (see NORTON).

2. Molsie Johnston, b. 1813 S. C., d. 10 May 1840, m. Edward Grantham in S. C.. He married (2) Prudence Johnston, her sister. He was born ca 1820 in N. C. and was living in Simpson Co., Miss. in 1860. He died near D'Lo, Miss. Issue (by first wife):

   a. John Grantham, b. 22 Oct. 1838 S. C., d. 28 March 1907, m. --- Floyd. He was living in Miss. in 1879.

   b. Edward Grantham, b. 10 May 1840 S. C., m. Caroline DuBose, lived Eureka, Texas.

3. Celia Johnston, b. 1 Aug. 1815 S. C., d. 22 Jan. 1872, m. Robert E. Price in 1831. He was born 1811 S. C., d. 27 April 1899. Both are buried in Mt. Aerial Cem.. Known issue:

   a. John J. Price, b. 29 March 1831 S. C., d. 6 May 1889, m. Sarah Amanda Grubbs 20 Jan. 1852. She was born 18 March 1836 and died 21 July 1908 (see GRUBBS). They are buried in Mt. Aerial Cem..

   b. William Price, b. ca 1834 S. C., not married in 1860, living in Pike Co., Ala. in 1879.

   c. Mary A. Price, b. ca 1836 S. C., not married in 1879.

   d. Martha Johnston Price, b. ca 1838 S. C., not married

153

in 1860.

e. Patience Price, b. ca 1841 S. C., not married in 1860, may have died by 1879.

f. Margaret Price, b. ca 1843 S. C.

g. James (Jimpsey?) Price, b. ca 1845 S. C., may have m. Penny J. Loveless 19 Feb. 1867.

h. Caroline Price, b. ca 1847 Ala.

i. Celia A. Price, b. ca 1850 Ala.

j. Robert J. Price, b. ca 1851 Ala., d. after 1891, m. Amanda A. Belcher 30 Aug. 1877. He was born ca 1857, died 30 Jan. 1891, buried Mt. Aerial Cem..

4. Elizabeth Johnston m. William Williams. In 1853, they were living in Horry Co., S. C. - he died by 1854.

5. Jane Johnston m. Joseph Griffin. In 1853, they were in Horry Co., S. C.

6. Prudence Johnston, b. ca 1821 S. C., d. 10 Nov. 1843, m. Edward Grantham (whose first wife was her sister, Mary Johnston). Issue:

a. Johnston Grantham, b. 3 Aug. 1841 S. C., living in Simpson Co., Miss. in 1860, m. Eliza Floyd.

b. Daniel Grantham (twin to Johnston Grantham), b. 3 Aug. 1841 S. C., living in Simpson Co., Miss. in 1860. He married (1) S. Margaret Williams 4 March 1869 in Barbour Co., Ala. (2) Lula Williams 29 Feb. 1884, both daughters of George Walker Williams (see WILLIAMS).

c. Mary Jane Grantham, b. 10 Nov. 1843 S. C., d. 6 Oct. 1918, m. Lemuel L. Wise 29 Nov. 1860 (see WISE).

7. Mary Ann Johnston, died by 1853, married D. R. Anderson. Known issue (living in Horry Co., S. C. in 1854):

a. John J. Anderson.

b. Margaret K. Anderson, m. Arch'd Hammond.

     c. Morgan A. Anderson.

     d. David Russell Anderson.

     e. Samuel P. Anderson.

     f. G. W. Anderson. (George W.)

     g. G. J. Anderson. (Gilbert J.)

     h. J. T. Anderson. (James T.)

     i. Mary Anderson

8. --- Johnston (female), b. ca 1825.

9. --- Johnston (female), b. ca 1827.

10. James "Jimpsey" Johnston, b. 1828 S. C., d. 16 Aug. 1864 in
the Civil War, m. Harriet A. Crews 17 Dec. 1846, daughter
of Arthur Anderson Crews (see CREWS). In 1850, they were
living in Cato Springs, Miss. and in 1860 they were in Simpson Co., Miss.. Known issue:

     a. Mary C. Johnston, b. ca 1848 Ala., possibly died young.

     b. John Arthur Johnston, b. 27 Aug. 1849 Ala., d. 5 Apr.
        1924, m. Josephine Watson. She was born 2 Jan. 1854,
        died 5 Feb. 1928. Both are buried in Rocky Mount Cem..

     c. Cinthia Johnston, b. ca 1852 Ala., m. John Wilson 8 Jan.
        1868.

     d. James W. Johnston, b. 22 Nov. 1853 Miss., d. 5 June 1912,
        m. Sarah C. Watson 13 Jan. 1880. She was born 21 April
        1852, died 21 June 1925. They are buried in Rocky Mount
        Cem..

     e. Margaret Johnston, b. ca 1856 Miss., m. W. F. Rollins
        5 Dec. 1872.

     f. George A. Johnston, b. 1858 Miss., d. 1929, m. Clifford
        Bishop 15 Jan. 1891. She was born 1867, died 1933.
        They are buried in Clayton Cem..

     g. William Yancy Johnston, b. ca 1861 Miss., living in 1903.
After the Civil War, the family of James Johnston returned

to Barbour Co., Ala..

11. Patience Johnston, b. 18 Aug. 1825 (?) S. C., d. 12 Jan. 1894, m. Marion Mullion Watson 12 Sept. 1850. He was born 22 April 1829 Ga., died 13 Feb. 1907. They are buried in Rocky Mount Cem.. Known issue:

   a. Frances Victoria Watson, b. 1854 Ala., d. 1920, m. J. Edward Wise 26 Oct. 1870. He was born 1846 Ala., d. 1913 (see WISE).

   b. John W. Watson, b. 1856 Ala., d. 1928, may have married Mrs. Mary E. Thomas 8 May 1886. She was born 1856, died 1929. They are buried in Rocky Mt. Cem..

   c. Margaret Leonora Watson, b. 27 Nov. 1857, d. 4 Sept. 1913, never married, buried in Rocky Mt. Cem..

   d. Mary Ella Watson, b. ca 1860 Ala., not married 1913.

12. John W. Johnston, b. ca 1832 S. C., d. 1 June 1862, m. Georgia Ann Williams 9 Nov. 1859, daughter of George Walker Williams (see WILLIAMS). She was born ca 1842 Ala., died 9 July 1900. Issue:

   a. Sarah V. Johnston, b. ca 1861 Ala., m. James W. Floyd 12 Oct. 1879.

   b. John W. Johnston, Jr., b. ca 1864 Ala.. This date is from the census records and may not be accurate.

13. George W. Johnston, b. 25 Feb. 1835 S. C., d. 26 July 1905, m. Margaret Leonora Kennedy 6 May 1856. She was born ca 1834 S. C.. In 1860, they were living in Simpson Co., Miss. and died near D'Lo, Miss. Issue:

   a. Mary Frances Johnston, b. ca 1857.

   b. James Rhea Johnston, b. ca 1859.

   c. Nancy Johnston.

   d. Patience Johnston.

   e. Georgia Ann Johnston.

f. Margaret Johnston.

g. Leonora Johnston.

Other sources:

Price Family History by Pauline Price Cliats
CSA records

JONES

Arial Jones entered land near Rocky Mount Church from 1829 through 1835. In the 1840 Census, his household consisted of 2 males under 5, 2 males 5/10, 1 male 15/20, 1 male 50/60, 1 female under 5, 1 female 5/10 and 2 females 20/30. He is not in the 1850 Census, so he must have died by that time. There is no estate settlement for him in the Barbour Co. records.

In 1838, James W. Jones and William K. Jones entered land North of Rocky Mount Church. William K. Jones was enumerated next to Arial Jones in the 1830 Census of Pike Co., Ala., but is not in any Barbour Co. census.

James W. Jones, Jr., b. 17 April 1810 N. C., d. 28 July 1862, m. Susannah S. ---. She was born 19 Oct. 1817 N. C., died 31 Oct. 1895. They are buried in Rocky Mount Cemetery. She may have been his second wife. Known issue of James W. Jones, Jr.:

1. Leroy Jones, b. ca 1836 Ala..
2. Thomas Jones, b. ca 1837 Ala..
3. James Jones, b. ca 1839 Ala..
4. William Jones, b. ca 1841 Ala..
5. Wiley Jones, b. ca 1843 Ala..
6. John Jones, b. ca 1845 Ala., may have died young.
7. Martha Jones, b. ca 1846 Ala..
8. Nancy Jones, b. ca 1848 Ala..
9. Susan Jones, b. ca 1849 Ala..
10. John C. Jones, b. ca 1853 Ala..
11. Frances C. Jones, b. ca 1855 Ala..
12. Emma L. Jones, b. ca 1861 Ala..

Aerial Jones was enumerated next to James W. Jones in 1850. He was born ca 1820 N. C., died after 1880, married Matilda Baker 17 Jan. 1841. She was born ca 1824 N. C. or S. C., died 1880. He could have been a son of the Arial Jones who entered land in 1829. Known issue:

1. Retus Jones, b. ca 1841 Ala.

2. Josephus Jones, b. ca 1843 Ala.

3. Mary Jones, b. ca 1845 Ala.

4. Americus Jones, b. ca 1847 Ala.

5. Sarah Jones, b. ca 1849 Fla.

6. Frances Jones, b. ca 1852 Ala.

7. Gatsey E. Jones, b. ca 1854 Ala.

8. Missouri Jones, b. ca 1856 Ala.

9. Dixon A. Jones, b. ca 1858 Ala.

10. Hilliard E. Jones, b. ca 1859 Ala.

11. Margaret Jones, b. ca 1864 Ala.

12. Barney Jones, b. ca 1870 Ala.

   In 1827, John B. Jones entered much land in Barbour Co.. He does not appear in any of the Census records, so he may have been a land speculator. By 1832, he and his wife, Elizabeth, were living in Lowndes Co., Miss..

Sources of information:

Barbour Co., Ala. Probate Records
Barbour Co., Ala. Census Records
Barbour Co., Ala. Cemetery Records
Pike Co., Ala. Census Records

LEE

There were two Lee families in Barbour Co. at a very early date that were probably distantly related, as there were Needham Lee's in both.

Thomas Lee, b. 3 Dec. 1729 Northumberland Co., Va., d. Hawkins Co., Tenn. by June 1816, m. Mary Bryan 15 Mar. 1761. She was born 4 Nov. 1745 N. C. and died 3 March 1821 Hawkins Co., Tenn. Issue:

1. Thomas Lee, b. 9 Dec. 1761

2. John Lee, b. 10 May 1763 Hawkins Co., Tenn., d. ca 1820 Wilkinson Co., Ga. (see later).

3. William Lee, b. 15 Nov. 1764

4. Richard Lee, b. 3 April 1766

5. James Lee, b. 20 Oct. 1768

6. Needham H. Lee, b. 4 Nov. 1770 Johnston Co., N. C., m. Susan Bailey. They lived in Shelby Co., Ala..

7. Lewis Lee, b. 1772

8. Zilpha Lee, b. 3 Jan. 1773

9. Willis Lee, b. 13 Feb. 1775

10. Winifred Lee, b. 1 Jan. 1778

11. Mary Lee, b. 20 July 1779

12. Luanna Lee, b. 2 Aug. 1781, d. 2 Sept. 1782

13. Edward Lee, b. 3 Jan. 1788.

John Lee, b. 10 May 1763 Hawkins Co., Tenn., d. ca 1820 Wilkinson Co., Ga., m. Elizabeth Farrar (?). She was born 14 Aug. 1769, m. (2) John Fairchild. Issue:

1. Lewis Lee, b. 1782, m. Jane Triplett 22 Feb. 1802 - lived in Wilkinson and Quitman Cos., Ga..

2. Needham Lee (Sr.), b. 6 Aug. 1786, d. 28 Nov. 1852 (see later)

3. Lovard Lee, b. 25 Sept. 1791, m. Elizabeth McNair (see

160

later).

4. Greenberry Lee

5. John Lee, Jr.

6. Godfrey Lee

7. Winefred Lee, b. ca 1798 S. C., m. Jesse Pierce, lived Wilkinson Co., Ga. and Barbour Co., Ala.

8. Sarah Lee, b. 1805 S. C., m. A. M. McNair. She also was in Barbour Co., Ala. by 1850.

9. Mary Lee, never married.

Lovard Lee (son of John Lee and Elizabeth Farrar) was born 25 Sept. 1791 S. C., died 1 Nov. 1870, m. (1) Elizabeth McNair (daughter of Gilbert McNair of Cochran, Ga.?). She was born 22 March 1795 Ga., died 7 March 1855. They are buried in a field near Prospect Cem.. In their household in 1850 was Lewis J. Lee, an infant. Lovard Lee m. (2) Sarah J. Polk 26 June 1859. She m. (2) J. M. Danford. In their household in 1860 was Lovard W. Lee, b. ca 1846 Ala., who later married Martha Bounds. Probable issue (by 1st wife):

1. Elizabeth Lee, b. 18 Aug. 1814 Ga., d. Pike Co., Ala., probably married James Galloway. He married (2) Rebecca Black. Issue (all by 1st wife):

   a. Mary Galloway, b. ca 1833 Ga.

   b. George G. Galloway, b. ca 1835 Ga., m. Salany E. Cooper 4 Jan. 1855.

   c. James Galloway, b. ca 1837 Ga.

   d. Lovard Galloway, b. ca 1839 Ga.

   e. Elizabeth Galloway, b. ca 1841 Ala.

   f. Benjamin Galloway, b. ca 1843 Ala.

   g. Leroy Galloway, b. ca 1845 Ala.

   h. Wellborn Galloway, b. ca 1847 Ala.

   i. Thomas J. Galloway, b. ca 1849 Ala.

j. Susan Frances Galloway, b. 27 Aug. 1853 Duval Co., Fla.

2. Susannah Lee, b. 10 March 1816 Ga., d. 17 April 1885 Leesburg, Fla., m. Evander McIver Lee (son of Arthur Lee) of
Leesburg, Fla. on 18 Oct. 1838. Arthur was probably a brother of Timothy Lee (see later). Issue:

a. George Marion Lee, b. 18 Aug. 1839, d. 1 Aug. 1905, m.
    Margaret Jane Gamble 5 Jan. 1860. She was born 14 Sept.
    1837, died 27 May 1873.

b. Jason J. Lee, b. 8 Dec. 1840, killed in Civil War.

c. Louisa Lee, b. 24 Sept. 1842 Barbour Co., Ala., d. 3
    Jan. 1899, m. Obed Fussell 6 Jan. 1862 Leesburg, Fla.
    He was born 20 March 1844, died 1 March 1916.

d. Lovard Bryant Lee, b. 29 Oct. 1844, d. 28 Oct. 1907, m.
    Sarah Catherine Clark 5 Nov. 1867. She was born 2 Dec.
    1848, died 23 April 1889.

e. Molcey Lee, b. 28 Oct. 1844, m. John Love.

f. Pleasant Arthur Lee, b. 13 Sept. 1847, d. 1930, never
    married.

g. Elizabeth Lee, b. 24 Oct. 1849, d. 1 June 1924, m.
    Mathew W. Dozier, b. 3 Jan. 1847, d. 5 May 1882.

h. Needham C. Lee, b. 2 Feb. 1853, m. (1) Commens Fontaine
    Bouknight 14 Nov. 1872 (2) Mary Galloway (3) Frances
    Isabella James.

3. Godfrey Lee, b. 10 July 1819 Ga., m. (1) unknown (2) Sarah
A. A. McNair 1 Aug. 1850. Known issue (by 1st wife):

a. William B. W. Lee, b. ca 1839 Ala., d. May 1903, m.
    Louisa Jane Pierce 10 Dec. 1857. She was his cousin,
    a daughter of Jesse and Winefred (Lee) Pierce.

b. John P. Lee, b. ca 1840 Ala., probably died by 1870,
    may have married Margaret McLeod 27 Sept. 1860.

c. Mary Lee, b. ca 1842 Ala.

162

d. Molsey Jane Lee, b. ca 1843 Ala., d. 18 Nov. 1907, m. W. Taylor Lott by 1876. He was born 8 July 1851, died 18 Oct. 1904. They are buried in Antioch Baptist Church Cem..

e. Lovard Lee, b. ca 1845 Ala.. He could be the same as the one in Lovard Lee's household in 1860, m. Martha Bounds 9 May 1861.

f. Lewis Lee, b. ca 1850 Ala. - could be the Lewis J. Lee in the household of Lovard Lee in 1850, in which case he was enumerated twice.

4. Mary S. Lee, b. 29 Oct. 1821.

5. Needham G. Lee, b. ca 1825 Ga., no record after 1857, m. Alice Boylston 17 Sept. 1844. Known issue:

a. Anara L. Lee, b. ca 1845 Ala.

b. General Taylor Lee, b. ca 1846 Ala.

c. Margaret Elizabeth Lee, b. ca 1849 Ala.

d. Ellen Caroline Lee

e. Joseph Lovard Lee

f. Susan Eugenia Lee

g. Alice Virginia Lee

6. Winefred Lee, b. 4 July 1827.

7. Sarah Lee, b. 8 March 1830, probably married Daniel Cameron McEachern (see McEACHERN).

Issue (by 2nd wife):

8. Emily Lee, b. ca 1862 Ala.

9. Susanah Lee, b. ca 1866 Ala.

10. Columbus C. Lee, b. 1 Nov. 1869, d. 20 March 1939, buried in Upper Prospect Baptist Cem., possibly m. (1) Camilla Stevens 20 Dec. 1885 (2) Emma Wright 20 Jan. 1892.

Needham Lee, Sr. (son of John Lee and Elizabeth Farrar) was born 6 Sept. 1786 Tenn., died 28 Nov. 1852. He is buried in a family cemetery near Louisville, Ala.. He m. (1) Lydia Pryor ca 1806, who probably died between 1817 and 1834 and he married a second wife (name unknown) who died ca 1846/50. He then married (3) Sarah Ann Sloan 16 Oct. 1850. She was born 9 Aug. 1811 Ga., died 30 Aug. 1881 Lake City, Fla.. Issue (by 1st wife):

1. John B. Lee, b. 18 Feb. 1807, possibly died by 1856, may have married Amy Allen 12 March 1829 Jefferson Co., Ga..

2. Robert S. Lee, b. 30 Sept. 1808, probably died young as he is not mentioned in the will of Needham Lee, Sr.

3. Elizabeth Lee, b. 1 Oct. 1810, d. after 1852, m. John W. W. Jackson. Possible issue:

   a. Margaret Jackson, b. ca 1833 Ga.

   b. William Walker Jackson, b. 13 April 1831 (?) Ala., d. 28 Sept. 1859, buried Louisville Cem..

   c. Needham Wellborn Jackson, b. 15 April 1837 Ala., d. 25 Sept. 1860, buried Louisville Cem..

   d. George Jackson, b. ca 1839 Ala.

   e. Louisianna Jackson, b. ca 1845 Ala., d. 24 Sept. 1853, buried Louisville Cem..

4. Needham Lee, Jr., b. 28 Aug. 1813 Ga., d. 24 Feb. 1887, m. Emeline Lewis 19 Nov. 1835. She was born 8 Oct. 1816 N. C., died 4 May 1871. Both are buried in Louisville Cem.. Issue:

   a. Mary A. Lee, b. 8 Sept. 1836 Ala., d. 20 March 1892, m. B. F. Petty, Sr. 27 June 1854 (his second wife). He was born 2 Sept. 1806 N. Y., died 3 Sept. 1876. They are buried in Clayton Cem..

   b. Jefferson L. Lee, b. 15 May 1838 Ala., m. Mary Lurena Faulk 27 Sept. 1860 (see FAULK). In 1909, they were living in Thorndale, Texas.

   c. Nancy Lee, b. 28 July 1840 Ala., d. 4 April 1907, never married, buried in Louisville Cem..

d. Lycurgus L. Lee, b. 13 July 1842, d. 15 Jan. 1915 Milam Co., Texas (living in Texas by 1872). He married Mary Susan (Gunter) Grubbs, b. 27 May 1847, d. 18 Sept. 1901 Milam Co., Texas, widow of Samuel Jackson Grubbs (see GRUBBS).

e. Sarah Lee, b. 29 Feb. 1844 Ala., d. 10 Feb. 1888, buried Clayton Cem.. She m. (1) C. Lilly 14 Jan. 1869 (2) --- Ham. In 1908, her children were in Grants, New Mexico.

f. Robert Monroe Lee, b. 19 Aug. 1846 Ala., d. 3 Sept. 1929, m. Annie T. Reynolds 19 Jan. 1881. She was born 9 July 1857, died 10 June 1948, daughter of Dr. John A. Reynolds and Elizabeth Huey. Both are buried in Pea River Cem..

g. George Washington Lee, b. 2 Dec. 1848 Ala., d. 4 March 1907, m. Ann Eliza Ventress 13 May 1875. She was born 26 March 1855, died 20 Nov. 1908, daughter of Thomas Ventress and Mary Ann Norton (see VENTRESS). They are buried in Clayton Cem..

h. Virginia Lee, b. 19 Jan. 1851 Ala., d. 24 July 1914, m. William Owen Drury 19 Nov. 1878. He was born 20 Aug. 1853, died 26 June 1904. They are buried in Louisville Cem..

i. Needham Lee, b. 31 July 1853 Ala., d. 8 Feb. 1939, m. (1) Etta Cora Lampley 3 April 1892 (b. 28 May 1870, d. 2 Aug. 1893). He m. (2) Irene T. ----, b. 24 June 1863, d. 27 Feb. 1946. They are buried in Louisville Cem..

j. Luthur Lee, b. 19 April 1856, d. 30 Sept. 1857.

k. Joseph G. Lee, b. 8 March 1859 Ala., d. 1 June 1878, buried in Louisville Cem..

l. Benjamin F. Lee, b. 16 Aug. 1860 Ala., d. 1945, m. Avonia B. ----. She was born 1859, died 1943. Although they were living in Temple, Texas in 1909, they are buried

165

in Pea River Cem. in Barbour Co..

    m. Alpheus Jackson Lee, b. 24 Feb. 1863, d. 19 Feb. 1928, m. Janie Miles. She was born 2 Nov. 1865, died 13 April 1948. Both buried in Louisville Cem..

5. Louisianna Lee, b. 17 June 1815 Ga., d. by Oct. 1857, m. Grandberry H. Hudson 5 May 1830 Jefferson Co., Ga.. Issue:

    a. Needham A. Hudson, b. ca 1832 Ga., probably married Nancy A. Harris 3 April 1853.

    b. Elizabeth Hudson, b. ca 1834 Ga., m. William Smith 31 July 1856.

    c. Jonathan Hudson, b. ca 1836 Ga.

    d. Abigail Hudson, b. 1840 Ala., m. John Bass 25 Oct. 1859.

    e. Amazon Hudson, b. ca 1842 Ala., probably died by 1857.

    f. Irwin Hudson, b. ca 1846 Ala.

    g. Missouri Hudson, b. ca 1849 Ala.

    h. Robert Hudson

    i. Louisianna Hudson, b. ca 1856 Ala., living with Lovard and Susan E. Lee in 1860 and 1870.

6. Lovard L. Lee (known as Lovard Lee, Jr.), b. 10 Nov. 1817 Augusta, Ga., d. 6 June 1896, m. Susan Emeline Lovelace 24 Oct. 1842. She was born 25 Oct. 1823 Ga., died 6 Jan. 1877. They are buried in Clayton Cem.. Issue:

    a. Alto Vela Lee, b. 28 Dec. 1843 Ala., d. 27 Oct. 1911, m. Lillie Ildegert Lawrence 19 Dec. 1865, possibly in Tuscaloosa, Ala.. She was born 2 March 1845 Ala., died 13 Dec. 1909, daughter of Judge W. H. Lawrence of Tuscaloosa, Ala.. They are buried in Clayton Cem..

    b. Julia A. Lee, b. ca 1848 Ala., d. Sept. 1881, m. A. T. Williams 20 Oct. 1870.

Issue (by 2nd wife):

7. Martha Ann Lee, b. 7 Dec. 1834 Ala., m. James W. Stokes 20

Dec. 1854. In 1856, they were living in Henry Co., Ala..

8. John Godfrey Boswell Lee, b. 7 June 1837, d. May 1840, buried in the Lee family cemetery.

9. Joseph Peeples Lee, b. 11 Dec. 1838, d. May 1840, buried in the Lee family cemetery.

10. Mary Jane Lee, b. 24 Nov. 1840 Ala., d. 26 Sept. 1859, m. J. F. Harrison 10 Nov. 1858. She is buried in the Lee family cemetery. No known issue.

11. Sarah Ann Lee, b. 21 June 1842 Ala., d. 30 July 1921, m. George Newman 19 Nov. 1857. He was born 26 April 1826, died 23 March 1869. They are buried in Abbeville Cem., Henry Co., Ala.. Issue:

    a. Leonora Evelin Newman, b. 4 Sept. 1858 Ala., d. 12 Nov. 1932, m. John Bird Ward. He was born 31 Aug. 1853, died 13 June 1941. They are buried in Abbeville Cem., Henry Co., Ala..

    b. Mollie Newman, b. ca 1863 Ala., m. ---- Martin.

    c. Robert Newman, b. ca 1865 Ala.

    d. Laura Newman, b. ca 1867 Ala., m. ---- Dowling.

    e. Winefred Newman, m. ---- Robson.

12. Christopher Columbus Lee (Rev.), b. 24 Jan. 1844 Ala., d. after 1880, m. Leona Williams 9 July 1871. Known issue:

    a. Anna Lee, b. ca 1872 Ala.

    b. Paul W. Lee, b. ca 1875 Ala.

    c. Samuel P. Lee, b. ca 1877 Ala.

    d. Omand (?) K. Lee, b. Sept. 1879 Ala.

13. Winefred Lee, b. 6 Feb. 1846 Ala., d. 17 Dec. 1931, buried in Clayton Cem., m. Adelbert Pope Robson 21 Dec. 1869. He was born 5 Feb. 1847 Shellman, Ga., died 23 July 1899, buried Louisville Cem.. In 1881, they were living in Lake City, Fla., but evidently returned to Barbour Co.. Issue:

a. Lee Robson, b. 20 Aug. 1876, d. 22 Nov. 1900, buried in
    Louisville Cem..

14. William Lee, b. 12 Feb. 1853, d. 13 July 1854 or 1859, bur-
    ied in the Lee family cemetery.

Also buried in this cemetery is W. T. Hurcey (1881-1885),
son of L. C. Hurcey.

Another Lee family, probably distantly related to Lovard and
Needham Lee, was that of Timothy Lee, b. 2 July 1773, d. 22 May
1845. His wife, Elizabeth Muldrough of Darlington, S. C., was
born 23 Dec. 1781, died 31 Jan. 1848. These dates are from the
Lee family Bible - dates from the Lee cemetery are: Timothy
Lee, b. 3 July 1772, d. 22 May 1845; wife Elizabeth Lee born 23
Oct. 1781, died 20 Jan. 1848.

It is thought that Timothy Lee had brothers Redding Lee who
married Patsy Hicks and Arthur Lee, b. 16 Aug. 1785, d. Nov.
1856 (wife Mary[1], daughter of Simon Lee) who came to Barbour Co.
with Timothy Lee but moved to Florida about 1849 and is buried
in Sumter Co., Fla.. Issue (of Arthur and Mary Lee):

1. Evander McIver Lee, b. 7 Dec. 1813 Sumter Co., S. C., d. 12
    Jan. 1881 Leesburg, Fla., m. Susannah Lee 18 Oct. 1838 in
    Barbour Co., Ala., daughter of Lovard Lee and Elizabeth
    McNair. She was born 10 March 1816 Ga., died 17 April 1885
    Leesburg, Fla..

2. Joseph (or Josiah) Aiken Lee, b. 4 Sept. 1824, d. 2 Sept.
    1885 Gainesville, Fla., m. Mary Ann Cassidy 25 Sept. 1847.

3. Eliza Lee, b. 24 April 1810, d. before Nov. 1866 in Sumter
    Co., Fla., m. Robert William Hays, b. 1809, d. 1868 Sumter
    Co., Fla..

4. Rebecca Lee, b. 20 July 1814, never married, buried in
    Sumter Co., Fla.

5. Molcie Lee, b. 24 July 1811, d. 10 Sept. 1889 Sumter Co.,

Fla., m. George M. Condrey 24 April 1834.

6. Elizabeth Lee, b. 17 Feb. 1816, d. 12 July 1882, m. Hansford Dyches in 1837.

7. Margaret Gilly Ann Lee, b. 22 Feb. 1818, d. 10 Jan. 1889, m. Duncan Stivender. He died in Barbour Co. and she moved to Florida.

8. Julaney Lee, b. 1 March 1826, d. 22 Oct. 1878, m. James M. Condrey.

9. John Calvin Lee, b. 31 March 1831 Abbeville S. C., d. 22 Oct. 1878 Leesburg, Fla., m. Eliza Caruthers ca 1856.

10. Arthur Lee, b. 21 June 1822, never married.

(Information on Arthur Lee family of Florida from "Three Lee Lines" by Margie L. Holbrook, a descendant of Arthur Lee).

Probable issue of Timothy Lee and Elizabeth Muldrough:

1. James Lee (see later)

2. David Lee

3. Andrew V. Lee (see later)

4. Epsey Lee m. George Wiley Hartzog 2 Sept. 1841 (see HARTZOG).

5. Robert (E.?) Lee (see later)

6. Timothy Lee, Jr. (see later)

7. Mary Ann (Molcie) Lee m. ---- DuBose

8. Elizabeth Lee m. Daniel Barney Hartzog (see HARTZOG).

9. Agnes Lee may have married ---- Coler

10. Nancy Lee may have married ---- Aires

James Lee (son of Timothy Lee and Elizabeth Muldrough) was born ca 1807 S. C., m. Sarah ----. Issue (from 1850 Census):

1. Harvey Lee, b. ca 1832 S. C., probably married Nancy Wise 1 Aug. 1853 (see WISE).

2. Irving Lee, b. ca 1838 Ala.

3. Thomas Lee, b. ca 1846 Ala.

Andrew V. Lee (son of Timothy Lee and Elizabeth Muldrough)

was born ca 1810 S. C., m. Nancy McLeod. Known issue:

1. Martha J. Lee, b. ca 1837 Ala.

2. Mary A. Lee, b. ca 1842 Ala.

3. Lucinda E. Lee, b. ca 1844 Ala.

4. Nancy Arincey Lee, b. ca 1846 Ala.

5. William A. S. Lee, b. ca 1851 Ala.

6. Thomas M. Lee, b. ca 1857 Ala.

Robert (E.?) Lee (son of Timothy Lee and Elizabeth Muldrough)
b. 11 Dec. 1822 S. C., d. 7 June 1903, m. (1) Mary Pary Parmer
15 Dec. 1842 (see PARMER). She was born ca 1820 Ga., died 24
Oct. 1884. He m. (2) Ida Griffin 27 Sept. 1887, who m. (2) John
Foy Adams. She was born 30 Oct. 1869, died 25 Nov. 1957. They
are all buried in Pond Bethel Cem.. Issue (by 1st wife):

1. Needham T. Lee, b. 22 Sept. 1843 Ala., d. 7 Jan. 1906, buried
    Pond Bethel Cem.. He married Ann E. Bryan 11 July 1872.
    Issue (from 1880 Census):

    a. William D. Lee, b. 24 May 1874 Ala., d. 5 March 1961, m.
        Leonora Wood. She was born 5 May 1887, died 31 May
        1946. They are buried in Pond Bethel Cem..

    b. Mary Lee, b. ca 1876 Ala.

    c. James F. Lee, b. 2 Nov. 1878 Ala., d. 18 Feb. 1940,
        buried Pond Bethel Cem..

    d. Margaret Lee, b. ca 1880 Ala., d. 1957, m. Barlow D.
        Wood. He died 1926 - both buried Pond Bethel Cem..

    e. John D. Lee (probably), died 24 April 1955, buried
        Pond Bethel Cem..

2. Almira P. Lee, b. ca 1846 Ala., m. James F. Creel 28 Aug.
    1867. In 1903, they were living in Bluffton, Ga..

3. Matilda A. Lee, b. 24 Nov. 1847, d. 18 Dec. 1925, m. Joseph
    B. C. Searcy. He was born 8 Feb. 1846, died 11 Aug. 1925.
    Both buried Pond Bethel Cem..

4. Mary A. E. Lee, b. 10 July 1850 Ala., d. 10 Sept. 1917, m. George W. Zorn 11 Feb. 1869. He was born 9 April 1846, died 25 Dec. 1922. They are buried in Pond Bethel Cem..

5. Martha J. Lee, b. 24 Oct. 1853, d. 9 Nov. 1857, buried in the family cemetery with Timothy Lee.

Issue (by 2nd wife):

6. Jeffie E. Lee (female), b. ca 1889.

7. Edna I. Lee, b. ca 1894.

8. Robert E. Lee, b. ca 1897, m. Mayme Delle Bruner 24 Dec. 1919.

Timothy Lee, Jr. (son of Timothy Lee and Elizabeth Muldrough) b. ca 1826 S. C., m. Nancy B. Parmer 14 Nov. 1845 (see PARMER). Issue:

1. Narcissa Victoria Lee, b. 25 Oct. 1847 Ala., d. 26 March 1899, m. Malcolm Gillis 29 Jan. 1868. He was born 27 Jan. 1839, d. 2 Feb. 1917. Both are buried in Louisville Cem. (see GILLIS). Issue:

   a. John Thomas Gillis

   b. Robert Timothy Gillis

   c. Henry Gillis

   d. Christian Gillis

   e. Ida Gillis

   f. Cora Gillis

   g. Fannie Gillis, b. 30 Sept. 1875, d. 29 May 1953, m. Clifford Anderson Glover 6 Jan. 1895. He was born 20 Aug. 1873, d. 13 Jan. 1942.

   h. Nannie Gillis

   i. Margaret Gillis, b. 1874, never married, buried in Louisville Cem..

   j. Mary Gillis

   k. Carrie Gillis

1. Lawrence Gillis, b. 27 July 1890, d. 9 Jan. 1891, buried in Louisville Cem..

2. Lehman David Lee, b. 7 June 1849 Ala., d. 7 Jan. 1936, m. Margie Antnett Jimmerson 22 Dec. 1870. She was born 7 March 1851 Ga., died 28 Nov. 1917. Both are buried in Belcher Bethel Cem.. Issue:

   a. James Edward Lee, b. ca 1873 Ala.

   b. Charles Anderson Lee, b. 19 March 1874 Ala., d. 7 March 1958, buried in Belcher Bethel Cem.. He married Ada D. Ray 31 Oct. 1897.

   c. John Maxie Lee, b. ca 1875 Ala.

   d. Lehman Augustus Lee, b. ca 1877 Ala.

   e. Nancy Margaret Lee, b. 9 March 1879 Ala., d. 8 Sept. 1950, m. James Anderson Smith 6 Oct. 1894. He was born 16 May 1872, died 17 Jan. 1957. They are buried in Rocky Mount Cem..

   f. Marion Leander Lee, b. 14 Feb. 1881, d. 13 July 1882, buried Belcher Bethel Cem..

   g. Rosanna Lee, b. 29 April 1884, d. 18 Oct. 1884, buried Belcher Bethel Cem..

   h. Ludie Lee

   i. Birdie Lee

   j. Lucy Evelyn Lee

3. Martha Ann Margaret Lee, b. 24 March 1851 Ala., m. Jesse Daniel Walker.

4. Epsey Ann Rebecca Lee, b. 19 May 1853 Ala., m. John Shirley 6 Dec. 1868. He was born 10 Oct. 1845, died 3 Oct. 1893 and is buried in Pond Bethel Cem..

5. William Anderson Lee, b. 7 March 1854 Ala., m. Margie A. Wise 21 Jan. 1877 (see WISE). Probable issue:

   a. A. Casper Lee, b. ca 1877 Ala.

b. William E. Lee, b. ca 1879 Ala.

c. Marvin Lee

d. Risdon Lee

e. Nettie Lee

f. Jim Lee

6. John Andrews Lee, b. 6 Aug. 1856.

7. Jacob Timothy Lee, b. 3 March 1859 Ala., may have married Martha Caroline White. Probable issue:

a. Minta Lee m. W. P. Deshazo 23 Dec. 1900.

b. Ola Lee m. Charles Lucas 9 Dec. 1900.

c. Tempie Lee m. Jim Harrison.

d. Rosa Lee m. Oscar Carter.

e. Albert Lee m. Ouida Byrd.

f. Everett Lee

8. Robert David Beauregard Lee, b. 6 Sept. 1861, may have married Liddie White. Probable issue:

a. Alto Lee

b. Cora Lee

c. Mattie Lee

d. Mamie Lee

e. Jesse Lee

f. Lilla Mae Lee

g. Addie Lee

h. Bessie Lee

9. William Barney Lee, b. 3 July 1867 Ala.

10. Leola Cora Eulala Texas Lee, b. 17 Aug. 18-- Ala., m. Alpheus Baker Jernigan 25 Dec. 1887 (see page 143).

Another Lee family, unrelated to the foregoing, was Durham Lee, b. ca 1795/8, d. Dec. 1842, m. Mary Williams 14 June 1813 Jones Co., Ga.. She was born ca 1797 N. C., died 12 July 1861 Hinds Co., Miss. They came to Barbour Co. (then Indian

173

Territory) ca 1823 with Mark Williams and his son, Floyd, Henry
Ledbetter, Floyd Lee and John DeLochiou Thomas. Some of the
above stayed in Eufaula but Durham Lee evidently continued on to
Marianna, Fla.. In the 1830's, he returned to Eufaula where he
established a mercantile business. He died in Dec. 1842 and his
wife and some of their children moved to Hinds Co., Miss. ca
1853. In 1858, John C. and Alexander D. Williams were there
also - they may have been brothers of Mary (Williams) Lee.
Issue:

1. John Floyd Lee, b. 14 March 1814 Ga., d. ca 1886/7, m. Mar-
    tha Ann Tate ca 1834. She was born 14 April 1814, died 18
    Sept. 1875 Hinds Co., Miss. Known issue:
    a. W. D. Lee, b. 7 Oct. 1837, m. Amanda Williams 19 April
        1866, possibly in Miss..
    b. Mary A. Lee, b. 9 April 1845.

2. Mary Ann Lee, b. 29 May 1816 Ga., d. after 1870, m. Lauchlin
    McLean 22 Dec. 1835. He was born 24 Sept. 1808 N. C., died
    25 Nov. 1874. They lived in Eufaula Ala.. Issue:
    a. Margaret E. McLean, b. 20 Feb. 1850 Ala., may have mar-
        ried John N. Kelly 23 Feb. 1866.
    b. Mary Lee Ellen McLean, b. 1 Nov. 1856 Ala.

    Also in this household in 1850 and 1860 was Eugenia McLean,
b. ca 1842 Ala.. She was enumerated last both times, so may not
have been a daughter of Lauchlin and Mary Ann (Lee) McLean.

3. Andrew Jackson Lee, b. ca 1818 Ga., d. 7 March 1856 Hinds
    Co., Miss. m. Harriet West of Texas 10 April 1853.

4. William Butler Lee, b. ca 1820, went to California in 1849.

5. a son, died in Florida by 1827.

6. Bessie Lee, died in Florida by 1827.

7. Bryant Q. Lee, b. ca 1828/30, d. 1910 Hinds Co., Miss.

8. Lucinda Jane Lee, b. ca 1831 Fla., to Miss. 1853, d. ca

174

1900, m. ---- Owens 21 Dec. 1869.

9. Rufus Sewell Lee, b. ca 1834, d. ca 1885 (Hinds Co., Miss.?),
   m. Rebecca Jones 8 Dec. 1869 (Hinds Co., Miss.?)

Most of the above information taken from the McLean-Lee Bible.

Other sources:

Mr. Oates Caraway
Dictionary of Ala. Biography, page 1031
Henry Co., Ala. Cemetery Records by Scott
Story of Ala., Vol. IV, page 12
Lee family Bibles
DAR Nos. 131747 and 218683
Wilkinson Co., Ga. Historical Collections by Mattox

1. Mary, wife of Arthur Lee, was born 16 Nov. 1786 died 27 Nov.
   1852. She and Arthur Lee are buried in Adamsville Cem.,
   Sumter Co., Fla..

ADDITION AS OF JUNE 1, 1979:

It has long been assumed that Needham, Lovard, Sarah and Winefred Lee of Barbour Co. were children of John Lee who died in
Wilkinson Co., Ga. and grandchildren of Thomas Lee who died in
Hawkins Co., Tenn.. It has now been established that John Lee
(son of Thomas) died in Maury Co., Tenn. in 1843. Although it
has not been conclusively proven, it appears that the father of
the above named children was Godfrey Lee who died in Jefferson
Co., Ga. by March 1806. He was a son of Robert Lee of Johnston
Co., N. C., who was probably a brother of Thomas Lee who died in
Hawkins Co., Tenn.

LEWIS

In 1829, Daniel B. Lewis patented land where Clayton is now located. When the town of Clayton was formed, he gave the land. He wrote his will 9 June 1830, and it was probated 27 July 1833. His wife was Sarah ----, b. ca 1775 S. C., d. after 1850. His heirs were:

1. Kendall Lewis, who married the daughter of a Creek Indian Chief, Big Warrior, and lived at Fort Bainbridge (near the present Russell-Macon Co. line) from about 1814 until 1826, where he ran a tavern. He is probably buried there.

2. Catharine (Kitty) Lewis

3. Mary (Polly) Lewis

4. John E. Lewis, who also had an Indian wife.

5. Harrison W. Lewis, b. ca 1805 Ga., m. Mahala ----. In 1840, his household contained 1 male under 5, 1 male 5/10, 2 males 15/20, 1 male 40/50, 1 female under 5, 1 female 10/15, 1 female 15/20 and 1 female 30/40. In 1850, there was only one child in his household - Francis M. Lewis, b. ca 1833 Ala..

6. Seaborn L. Lewis, b. between 1800 and 1810. In a deed dated 19 Aug. 1833, his wife was Delilah. In 1840, his household was as follows: 1 male under 5, 1 male 30/40, 1 female 5/10, 1 female 10/15 and 1 female 20/30. On 2 Nov. 1841, Seaborn Lewis married Susan Wheeler. However, there is nothing to show whether this was a second marriage for Seaborn Lewis (above) or another man of the same name. There is no Seaborn or Delilah Lewis in the 1850 Census of Barbour Co., nor is there an estate settlement for either of them.

7. Harriet Lewis.

Sources of information:

Barbour Co., Ala. Probate Records
Barbour Co., Ala. Census Records
"Alabama Historical Quarterly", Vol. 21

McEACHERN

The McEachern family came to Barbour Co. from Richmond Co.,
N. C. in the 1820's and settled in the Pea River section called
"Little Scotland". Gilbert McEachern, born ca 1792 Scotland,
died 1 Feb. 1864, married Catharine Cameron 8 Oct. 1818 in Richmond Co., N. C.. She was born ca 1795 Scotland and died 12
April 1872. In 1860, Mary Judie (b. ca 1790 in N. C.) was living with Gilbert and Catharine McEachern. According to the
McEachern Bible, she died 14 Feb. 1875, but there is no indication of her relationship to them. Issue:

1. Mary Catharine McEachern, b. 25 Aug. 1819 Richmond Co., N.C.,
   d. 4 Nov. 1857, m. Allen Byrd 25 Aug. 1839. He was born ca
   1820 N. C.. After the death of Mary Catharine McEachern,
   he married Sarah Butts 20 May 1858. Possible issue of Allen
   Byrd and Mary McEachern:

   a. William Jackson Byrd, b. ca 1840 Ala.

   b. Alexander Byrd, b. ca 1842 Ala.

   c. Margaret Byrd, b. ca 1843 Ala.

   d. Gilbert L. Byrd, b. ca 1845 Ala.

   e. Richard D. Byrd, b. ca 1846 Ala.

   f. Mary Byrd, b. ca 1847 Ala.

   g. Gracie E. Byrd, b. ca 1848 Ala.

   h. Thomas Byrd, b. ca 1849 Ala.

   i. James B. Byrd, b. ca 1856 Ala.

2. Daniel Cameron McEachern, b. 7 March 1821 Richmond Co., N.C.,
   d. 17 March 1894, m. Sarah Lee 18 July 1850 (see LEE). She
   was born 8 March 1830, died Aug. 1884 Leesburg, Fla.. Known
   issue:

   a. Lovard Lee McEachern, b. ca 1854 Ala.

   b. Gilbert L. McEachern, b. ca 1856 Ala., d. 2 Aug. 1884
      Leesburg, Fla..

c. Isabella McEachern, b. ca 1857 Ala.

d. John D. (C.?) McEachern, b. ca 1863 Ala.

3. Isabel C. McEachern, b. 28 April 1823 Richmond Co., N. C.,
d. 3 Oct. 1854 Palestine, Texas, m. George Keahey 1 Jan.
1852. The Keahey's lived in Dale Co., Ala..

4. Margaret Cameron McEachern, b. 19 June 1825 Richmond Co.,
N. C. - no further record.

5. Anna C. McEachern, b. 29 April 1827 Ala., d. 14 May 1910,
buried Louisville Cem., m. Henry Smith 21 Sept. 1854. He
was born ca 1830 Ga., killed 25 March 1865 Petersburg, Va.
in the Civil War. Issue:

a. Sarah J. Smith, b. 28 Oct. 1855 Ala., d. 29 April 1927,
never married. She is buried in Louisville Cem..

b. Mary Smith, b. ca 1858 Ala.

c. Catherine Cornelia Smith, b. 17 June 1860 Ala., d. 3
Dec. 1909.

d. Henry G. Smith, b. 4 Oct. 1862, d. 25 Dec. 1929, never
married. He is buried in Louisville Cem..

6. Catharine C. McEachern, b. 4 Oct. 1829 Ala., d. 17 March
1907, buried in Louisville Cem.. She never married.

7. Malcolm McNair McEachern, b. 27 June 1831 Ala., d. 5 Aug.
1863 Chattanooga, Tenn. in the Civil War, m. Nancy Green 4
Aug. 1853. She was born 18 May 1839 Ala., died 26 Jan. 1922,
buried Upper Prospect Cem.. Issue:

a. Mary J. McEachern, b. ca 1856 Ala. *

b. Thomas Archibald McEachern, b. ca 1857 Ala., m. (1) Mary
J. Price 24 Oct. 1878 (granddaughter of Burrel Price).
She was born 26 Jan. 1859, died 25 Feb. 1885. He m.
(2) Rosanna A. Benton 22 Dec. 1885. She was born ca
1860, died 15 Dec. 1888, buried in Upper Prospect Cem..

c. Margaret Ann McEachern, b. 16 June 1858, d. 29 March

179

1943, m. Adam Sylvester Warr 12 Jan. 1876. He was born
1 Nov. 1853 and died 21 Aug. 1897. They are buried in
Upper Prospect Cem..

d. Amanda E. McEachern, b. 4 March 1860 Ala., d. 15 Sept.
1948, m. Wm. W. Andrews. He was born 22 April 1859 and
died 29 Aug. 1930. They are buried Louisville Cem..

e. William Henry McEachern, b. 1861 Ala., d. 1936, m. (1)
Anna Andrews 29 Nov. 1883. She was born 16 Feb. 1862
and died 14 Sept. 1888, buried in Upper Prospect Cem..
He m. (2) Nancy Jane Walker 30 April 1893. He is buried
in Louisville Cem..

f. Malcolm M. McEachern, b. 15 Sept. 1863, d. 19 Sept. 1944,
m. Sarah Elizabeth Blakey 27 Feb. 1889. She was born
1871 and died 1952 - both buried Louisville Cem..

8. Sarah Jane McEachern, b. 10 Jan. 1835 Dale Co., Ala., - no
further record.

9. John Cameron McEachern, b. 1 Jan. 1837 Dale Co., Ala., d. 8
May 1903, m. Victoria Williams 11 Jan. 1868 (see WILLIAMS).
She was born 25 April 1842 Ala. and died after 1880. Issue:

a. Judge Norman McEachern, b. 19 March 1869, died 18 June
1870, buried Clayton Cem..

b. Maxey Cameron McEachern, b. 25 July 1870, d. 2 Jan. 1872,
buried Clayton Cem..

c. Richard Malcolm McEachern, b. 7 Feb. 1872 Ala., d. 20
Sept. 1957, m. Ruby Dunbar 4 Sept. 1907. They are
buried in Fairview Cem., Eufaula, Ala..

d. Victoria Williams McEachern, b. 6 Jan. 1874, m. Dr. Mercer Davie, Jr. 27 June 1901.

10. Gilbert Columbus McEachern, b. 5 Aug. 1839 Dale Co., Ala.,
d. 13 Nov. 1862 Red Clay, Ga. on his way home from the
Civil War.

The following McEachern family is included because they
lived so near the Barbour Co. line and are connected by marriage
to the Barbour Co. family.

I.   Daniel McEachern, b. Scotland, d. Cumberland Co., N. C.

II. John McEachern, moved to Sumter Co., Ga. ca 1837, then to
     Pike Co., Ala. near Hobdy's Bridge in 1840. He m. Eliza-
     beth Conaly (who d. 1879). They had eight children but
     three sons and one daughter stayed in N. C..

III. James D. McEachern, b. 25 Sept. 1825 Robinson Co., N. C.,
     m. (1) Hasseltine J. Anderson 1861. She was born 9 Feb.
     1835 Troup Co., Ga., died 5 July 1866. He m. (2) Mrs.
     Mildred Corley Anderson, daughter of M. C. and Mahala Cor-
     ley of Edgefield Dist., S. C. and Chambers Co., Ala..
     Issue (by 1st wife):

     a.   John A. McEachern, b. 1 Oct. 1862, d. 5 Jan. 1915.

     b.   Hasseltine J. McEachern, m. Wm. C. VanHoose.

     c.   William C. McEachern, b. 24 Aug. 1854, d. 26 Oct. 1931.
     Issue (by 2nd wife):

     d.   Hodley A. McEachern, b. 1869, d. 1945.

     e.   Conaley P. McEachern.

     f.   Mary L. McEachern, b. 9 Aug. 1874, d. 17 Dec. 1915, m.
          Dr. George Oscar Wallace, b. 28 Feb. 1868, d. 7 Sept.
          1948, buried Pea River Presbyterian Church Cem.. They
          were the parents of George Corley Wallace and grand-
          parents of Gov. George Corley Wallace.

Other sources:

McEachern Bible
Dictionary of Ala. Biography, Vol. 4, page 111
Memorial Record of Ala., page 847
Pike Co., Ala. Cemetery Records (Ala. Hist. Quarterly,
   Vol. XXXV)

*Mary J. McEachern m. Nicholas Hartzog 9 Oct. 1873.

McGILVRAY

James McGilvray patented land North of Oateston from 1829 through 1836. From 1835 through 1848, John McGilvray entered land in the same neighborhood. There were two men by the name of John McGilvray in the 1840 Census. In 1836, Duncan McGilvray entered land near County Line Church on the Henry-Barbour Co. line.

John McGilvray, b. 1798 Scotland, d. 27 Oct. 1857, m. Margaret Gillis, daughter of Hugh and Mary Gillis. Margaret Gillis was born in 1813 in Scotland, died 20 Jan. 1885. They are buried in Old Scotch Cemetery. Issue:

1. Hugh H. McGilvray, b. ca 1833 Ala., m. Effie McLeod 10 Sept. 1854. She was born 1834 S. C., died 1895. Both are buried in Old Scotch Cemetery. Known issue:

   a. Daniel McGilvray, b. ca 1855 Ala.

   b. John D. McGilvray, b. ca 1858 Ala.

   c. Norman Whitfield McGilvray, b. ca 1860 Ala.

   d. Malcom J. McGilvray, b. ca 1866 Ala.

   e. Catherine A. McGilvray, b. ca 1875 Ala.

2. Norman McGilvray, b. 19 Jan. 1835 Ala., d. 4 Oct. 1857, buried in Old Scotch Cemetery.

3. Malcom McGilvray, b. ca 1836 Ala., m. Cybtha Reeves 30 Sept. 1858. Known issue:

   a. Mary McGilvray, b. ca 1859 Ala.

4. Mary McGilvray, b. 16 Jan. 1837 Ala., d. 15 Oct. 1857.

5. Margaret McGilvray, b. ca 1844 Ala., m. William Alexander Woods 12 Nov. 1868.

James McGilvray, b. 1789 Scotland, d. 27 Aug. 1863, m. Anna McNeill 4 July 1846, daughter of Daniel and Abigail McNeill. She was born 1817 S. C., died 6 April 1881. Both are buried in Old Scotch Cemetery. Issue:

1. Mary Jane McGilvray, b. ca 1850 Ala., m. Benjamin Dickens 29
    Oct. 1867.

2. Daniel McGilvray, b. 22 Aug. 1852 Ala., d. 22 Jan. 1925, m.
    Ella Harrison 12 Feb. 1880. She was born 22 Oct. 1861, died
    8 March 1942. They are buried in Bethlehem Cemetery.

Also buried in Old Scotch Cemetery are David McGilvray, b. 1792,
d. 9 April 1837 and Mary McGilvray, b. 1781, died 1831.

In 1850, James McGilvray, b. ca 1820 N. C., was living with
James and Anna (McNeill) McGilvray. He could have been a son of
James McGilvray by an earlier marriage. James McGilvray, b. ca
1820 N. C., m. Sarah J. Walker 27 Nov. 1867. She was born 1838,
died 1935 and is buried in Creel Cemetery.*

Martin McGilvray, b. ca 1802 Scotland, d. between 1850 and
1860, m. Sarah Gillis, b. ca 1820 N. C., d. after 1880. She was
probably his second wife. Known issue:

1. Daniel McGilvray, b. ca 1829 N. C.

2. Elizabeth McGilvray, b. ca 1831 N. C.

3. Catherine McGilvray, b. ca 1832 N. C.

4. Angus McGilvray, b. ca 1838 N. C.

5. Flora A. McGilvray, b. ca 1840 Ala.

6. William Alexander McGilvray, b. ca 1841 Ala.

7. John W. McGilvray, b. 13 Dec. 1845, d. 5 Nov. 1921, m. Mary
    Ann Norton 6 Jan. 1867, b. 26 April 1846, d. 4 Sept. 1911.

8. Neill McGilvray, b. 19 Jan. 1847 Ala., d. 30 Dec. 1898, m.
    Addie Beasley 19 Jan. 1873.

9. Martin Luther McGilvray, b. 1850 Ala., m. Margaret Ann Box-
    tic 31 Dec. 1872.

10. James F. McGilvray, b. ca 1855 Ala.

In March 1848, Martin McGilvray deeded his share of the
estate of John McGilvray to Mrs. Janet McGilvray. The land de-
scribed in this deed was patented to John McGilvray in 1835. In

the deed, he mentioned a brother, Alexander McGilvray. Mrs. Janet McGilvray was born ca 1786 in Scotland and died by March 1856. She deeded her entire estate to Roderick C. Chisholm and his sister, Janet.

Duncan McGilvray was born ca 1814 N. C., died after 1880. In 1836, he entered land near the Henry-Barbour Co. line. He was administrator of the estate of John McGilvray in 1857 and James McGilvray, Sr. in 1863.

In 1850, he was head of the household which consisted of his mother, Mary McGilvray (b. ca 1785 Scotland, d. between 1860 and 1870) and the following brothers:

John McGilvray, b. ca 1816 N. C., died after 1880.

Daniel McGilvray, b. ca 1818 N. C., died between 1860 and 1870.

Malcolm McGilvray, b. ca 1820 N. C., died between 1860 and 1870.

There is no record to show that any of these brothers married.

Another James McGilvray married Sarah Jane Thomas 8 April 1841. She died in March or April 1859 in Dale Co., Ala. and he died by 1860. On 27 Feb. 1861, Jonathan Thomas was appointed guardian of their minor children, who were living with him in 1860. These children were:

1. Zilpha Ann McGilvray, b. ca 1850 Ala. or Ga., m. John W. T. Gibbons 12 Oct. 1869.

2. Mary Mozelle McGilvray, b. ca 1852 Ala., m. George Hubbard 12 June 1881 and moved to Fla., then to Cullman Co., Ala.

3. Charity McGilvray, b. ca 1856 Ala., d. ca 1870.

4. Joseph Eldredge McGilvray, b. ca 1854 Ala., m. Mary T. Holly 7 Aug. 1887, lived near Hartford, Ala.

5. Thomas Jefferson McGilvray, b. 14 Feb. 1859 Dale Co., Ala., d. 24 Nov. 1945 Barbour Co., m. (2) Jennie Lee Smith 8 March

1891. She was born 6 May 1871, died 17 Aug. 1941, buried
Pond Bethel Cemetery.

Sources of information:

Barbour Co., Ala. Probate Records
Barbour Co., Ala. Census Records
Barbour Co., Ala. Cemetery Records
Henry Co., Ala. Cemetery Records
"History of Barbour Co., Ala." by Thompson

*ADDITIONS & CORRECTIONS AS OF JUNE 1, 1979:

Sarah J. Walker, wife of James McGilvray, may have been the
Sarah Jane Carroll who married Daniel S. Walker 24 Nov. 1858
at Jno. Carroll's.

McINNIS

Miles McInnis patented land North of Clio in 1827, 1835 and 1836. John McInnis patented land next to him from 1832 through 1849, and William and Hector McInnis patented land in the same area in 1835 and 1836.

Miles McInnis was born 1796 in Richmond Co., N. C., died 15 July 1876. His first wife was Sarah (McInnis?), born 5 June 1790 Richmond Co., N. C., died 11 April 1861. He married (2) Sarah A. McDonald on 8 April 1862. She was born 5 June 1826 N. C., died 20 Feb. 1895. They are all buried in Pea River Cemetery. By his second marriage, Miles McInnis had one daughter, Janett McInnis, b. ca 1871. In his will, Miles McInnis named a nephew, Miles McInnis of S. C., son of his brother, Angus McInnis. He also named a niece, Susannah Jones. She was born ca 1860 in Ala..

John McInnis was born 1794 Richmond Co., N. C., died 9 March 1870, married Christian ----. She was born 1806 Richmond Co., N. C., died 29 May 1887. Both are buried in Pea River Cemetery. Issue:

1. Jackson McInnis, b. 7 Aug. 1834, d. 1846, buried in Pea River Cem..

2. Daniel C. McInnis, b. 29 July 1836 Ala., d. 22 Sept. 1908, m. Margaret McRae 28 Feb. 1867. She was born Feb. 1845 N.C., died 11 Jan. 1900. They are buried in Pea River Cemetery. Known issue:

    a. Annabella (?) McInnis, b. ca 1868 Ala.

    b. Christian McInnis, b. ca 1870 Ala.

    c. Flora McInnis, b. ca 1871 Ala.

    d. John D. McInnis, b. 20 Sept. 1872 Ala., d. 10 Sept. 1901, buried Pea River Cemetery.

    e. Mary Lucy McInnis, b. ca 1874 Ala.

186

f. Alex McInnis, b. ca 1877 Ala.

g. Murdock McInnis, b. Sept. 1879 Ala.

3. John Martin McInnis, b. 28 July 1839 Ala., d. 9 Oct. 1899,
    m. Margaret (Jane?) ----. She was born ca 1845 N. C.. They
    are buried in Pea River Cemetery. Known issue:

    a. Christian McInnis, b. ca 1864 Ala.

    b. Anna McInnis, b. ca 1867 Ala.

4. Catherine McInnis, b. 30 May 1840 Ala., d. 25 May 1919, m.
    John Shaw 23 Dec. 1866. He was born 18 Nov. 1840, died 17
    June 1910. Both are buried in Pea River Cemetery. Known
    issue:

    a. Mary F. Shaw, b. ca 1867 Ala.

    b. Marcella Shaw, b. 14 Sept. 1869 Ala., d. 28 Oct. 1954,
        m. Robert T. Johnston 2 Nov. 1916.

    c. John W. Shaw, b. 15 Nov. 1871 Ala., d. 24 Aug. 1940.

    d. Arch Shaw, b. 23 Aug. 1874 Ala., d. 7 Sept. 1890.

    e. Robert C. Shaw, b. 1 May 1877 Ala., d. 19 June 1959, m.
        Annie E. Helms 9 Nov. 1913.

    f. James Martin Shaw (possibly), b. 19 Aug. 1880, d. 21
        Feb. 1947.

5. Jane McInnis, b. ca 1842 Ala., not married in 1880.

6. Elizabeth McInnis, b. 9 April 1847 Ala., d. 11 Oct. 1874.
    She never married and is buried in Pea River Cemetery.

    Hector McInnis, b. 10 Feb. 1801 N. C., d. 14 Feb. 1850, was
a brother of John B. McInnis who died in 1865. He married
Janett McInnis, sister of Duncan McInnis who died 27 March 1857.
She was born 4 March 1805 N. C., died 4 Feb. 1870. Both are
buried in Pea River Cemetery, as are most of their children.
Issue:

1. Peter McInnis, b. 24 Aug. 1824 N. C., d. 25 Nov. 1911, n.m.

2. Malcom McInnis, b. 4 March 1828 Ala., d. 24 Aug. 1917, m.

Marian Shaw 23 Dec. 1858. She was born 3 Dec. 1838 Ala.,
died 7 April 1938. Known issue:

a. John Lang McInnis, b. 27 Sept. 1859 Ala., d. 4 Sept.
1953.

b. Martha Jane McInnis, b. ca 1862 Ala.

c. William R. McInnis (M. D.), b. 13 Feb. 1866 Ala., d. 18
April 1950, m. (1) Eliza Elizabeth Stephens 23 Dec. 1903
(2) Lillie Baxter 26 Jan. 1921.

d. Flora Ann McInnis, b. 5 Dec. 1868 Ala., d. 27 Feb. 1959.

e. Mary Emma McInnis, b. 8 July 1871, d. 25 Aug. 1949.

f. Jane McInnis, b. ca 1877 Ala.

3. Catherine A. McInnis, b. 18 March 1832, d. 15 March 1895,
n.m.

4. Jane McInnis, b. 25 Sept. 1834, d. 28 Aug. 1918, n.m.

5. Margaret McInnis, b. 27 July 1839, d. 4 Feb. 1920, n.m.

Duncan McInnis, b. ca 1810-1813 N. C., d. 27 March 1857. He
is buried in Pea River Cemetery. His heirs were Miles McInnis,
John McInnis, Sarah McInnis, Mary (wife of John B. McInnis) and
Janet (widow of Hector McInnis), all of Barbour Co., Ala., also
Neal McInnis, Angus McInnis, Margaret McInnis, Elizabeth McInnis,
Flora (wife of Daniel Stewart) and Alexander McInnis, all of
North Carolina - probably his brothers and sisters. Miles, John,
Mary and Janett are included in this chapter.

John B. McInnis, b. ca 1790 Richmond Co., N. C., d. 5 June
1865, m. Mary McInnis, sister of Miles, John and Duncan McInnis.
She died 27 Sept. 1858. Both are buried in Pea River Cemetery.
All of their children died in infancy. The heirs of John B.
McInnis were:

1. Children of his deceased brother, Hector McInnis.

2. Sister Effie Dawkins.

3. Sister Nancy McLean of Richmond Co., N. C.

4. Sister Sarah McNall (or McKeller) of Barbour Co., Ala..

5. Niece Matilda Curry.

6. Niece Jane Danford.

Samuel N. McInnis, b. ca 1830 N. C., came to Barbour Co. between 1850 and 1860 from Richmond Co., N. C.. His wife, Catherine Stokes, was born ca 1840 N. C.. Their known children were Hugh, Margaret, Mary Jane, Isabella, Elizabeth, M. Daniel and Philip. In 1880, Isabella Currie, aunt of Samuel N. McInnis, was living with them.

Angus McInnis, b. Scotland, m. Catherine McInnis, also born in Scotland. They migrated to N. C., then to the Scotch Presbyterian settlement near Pea River Church in what is now Barbour Co. about 1825. Known issue:

1. Nancy McInnis, b. 10 March 1810 N. C., d. 29 March 1893, m. Lewis Walker, son of Solomon Walker. Lewis Walker was born 6 Jan. 1791 N. C., died 23 Nov. 1877. They are buried in the Walker family cemetery, as are most of their children. Issue:

   a. Maisy Catherine Walker, b. 21 Dec. 1832 Barbour Co., Ala. d. 17 Jan. 1889, m. Arthur Crews 12 May 1863.

   b. Nancy Jane Walker, b. 16 March 1835 Barbour Co., Ala., d. 23 Aug. 1929, n.m.

   c. Solomon Miles Walker, b. 14 Aug. 1837 Barbour Co., Ala., d. 10 Nov. 1837.

   d. Mary Walker, b. 6 Oct. 1838 Barbour Co., Ala., d. 18 March 1925, m. George H. Thomas 7 Feb. 1866.

   e. John Alexander Walker, b. 14 March 1841 Barbour Co., Ala., d. 9 Nov. 1862.

   f. Amanda Walker, b. 1 Jan. 1844 Barbour Co., Ala., d. 13 Oct. 1931, m. J. M. Keahey 3 July 1884.

   g. David Lewis Walker, b. 1 Sept. 1846 Barbour Co., Ala.,

d. 20 March 1935. He was not married in 1880.

    h. James Franklin Walker, b. 30 March 1849 Barbour Co., Ala. d. 29 Jan. 1945, m. David A. Wilson 25 Jan. 1870. He was born 12 April 1846, died 28 June 1909.

2. Mary McInnis, b. ca 1815 N. C., m. William Keahey, a Presbyterian elder. Known issue:

    a. George W. Keahey, b. ca 1830 Ala., m. Sallie Wiggins.

    b. Margaret Keahey, b. ca 1831 Ala.

    c. Nancy Emeline Keahey, b. ca 1833 Ala., d. 1916.

    d. Miles L. Keahey, b. ca 1836 Ala., moved to Texas ca 1870.

    e. James D. Keahey, b. ca 1838 Ala., killed in Civil War.

    f. Martha Keahey, b. ca 1840 Ala., m. Levi Foxworth.

    g. William Greene Keahey, b. ca 1842 Ala., killed in Civil War.

    h. John Keahey, b. ca 1844 Ala., killed in Civil War.

    i. Sarah Keahey, b. ca 1846 Ala.

3. Catherine McInnis m. William Berry Thomas (see Thomas family).

4. *Christian McInnis m. William French. Known issue:

    a. James Edward French m. Mrs. Nancy Stimson Goff of Dale Co., Ala.

    b. Jefferson French.

    c. Nancy Jane French m. ---- Jones.

    d. Angus French m. ---- Vickers of Elba, Ala.

    e. Frances French m. ---- Clowers of Pike Co., Ala.

5. Miles McInnis, d. y.

6. Margaret McInnis, d. y.

There was also an Angus McInnis, b. ca 1808 N. C., m. Unity Ellis 20 May 1851. There is nothing to show his connection, if any, to the others of this name in Barbour Co.. In the 1850 Census of Henry Co., Ala., Angus McInnis, age 40, born N. C.,

had in his household Unity McInnis, age 21, born Tenn. and Elizabeth McInnis, age 3, born Ala..

Sources of information:

Barbour Co., Ala. Probate Records
Barbour Co., Ala. Cemetery Records
Barbour Co., Ala. Census Records
Henry Co., Ala. Census Records
History of Barbour Co., Ala. by Thompson
Dale Co., Ala. Census Records
Walker Bible Records
Pea River Presbyterian Church Records

*ADDITIONS & CORRECTIONS AS OF JUNE 1, 1979:

Mrs. Christian French died at Tarenton (Pike Co., Ala.?), daughter of Angus McInnis. She was born in Barbour Co. about 78
years ago, the youngest of four sisters, and married William
French in Dale Co. (Ala.). They moved to Florida and later to
Miss. where he died in 1857 and she returned to Ala.. She
leaves a son, James E. French, once Mayor of Brundidge. She is
buried in St. John's Cem.. From "Brundidge News", 1 June 1895.

McKENZIE

Daniel McKenzie was born 25 Nov. 1805 N. C., died 19 Jan. 1886, married Amanda Burch ca 1834 (see BURCH). She was born ca 1821 Ga., died 1869. They are buried in Bethlehem Cemetery. He was a son of Kenneth McKenzie, who was born in Scotland and came to America with his parents in 1784, settling in Richmond Co., N. C.. Kenneth McKenzie had three sons: James, Daniel and Bethune Bostick McKenzie (who married Abagail, daughter of Angus and Catharine Currie). Bethune B. McKenzie stayed in North Carolina, but Daniel McKenzie migrated to Barbour Co., Ala. about 1828 with Angus and Catharine Currie. Issue:

1. James McKenzie, died 1836, buried Louisville Cem..

2. Bethune Bostick McKenzie, b. 11 Oct. 1837 Ala., d. 1915, m. Caroline Elizabeth Flournoy 14 Oct. 1858. She was born 1840 Ala., died 1928. They are buried in Fairview Cem., Eufaula, Ala.. In 1885, they may have been living in Butler Co., Ala.. She was a daughter of Gen. Thomas Flournoy and Caroline Elizabeth Rogers of Eufaula; granddaughter of Josiah Flournoy and Martha Manley of Edenton, Ga.; great-granddaughter of John Manley, a Rev. Soldier. Known issue:

    a. Edgar Flournoy McKenzie, b. 1860 Ala., m. Lena A. Lampley 11 March 1884 in Barbour Co., Ala., at which time he was living in Baton Rouge, La..

    b. Caroline F. McKenzie, b. ca 1862 Ala., m. Uriah C. Vinson in Oct. 1883 at Georgiana, Ala..

    c. Amanda McKenzie, b. 29 June 1861, d. Oct. 1861, buried in Bethlehem Cem..

    d. Anna Josephine McKenzie, b. ca 1865 Ala., m. Samuel T. Suratt and lived in Montgomery, Ala..

    e. Amanda M. McKenzie, b. 1866 Ala., d. Aug. 1904, buried in Fairview Cem., Eufaula, Ala., m. Dr. W. W. Mangum.

192

f. Daniel Burch McKenzie, b. 7 Jan. 1870 Ala., m. Esther Downing of Brewton, Ala. in June 1905.

g. Fannie Flournoy McKenzie, b. ca 1872 Ala., m. E. M. Loveless and lived Brewton, Ala..

h. Mary Lou McKenzie, b. 1874 Ala., d. 1951, m. (1) Edgar Hugh Roberts 28 Feb. 1901. He died Dec. 1903 - they are buried in Fairview Cem., Eufaula, Ala.. She m. (2) J. E. Methvin 12 Nov. 1907.

i. Jennie Mae McKenzie, b. 30 May 1876, d. 8 July 1877, buried in Bethlehem Cem..

j. Kenneth B. McKenzie, b. 1875 or 1877, d. 1952, m. Annie Clyde Methvin 21 April 1908. She was born 1881, died 1955 - both buried Fairview Cem., Eufaula, Ala..

k. Susan Dean McKenzie m. John Alexander Copeland 19 April 1913. They lived in Atlanta, Ga..

3. Susan B. McKenzie, b. 21 April 1838 Ala., d. 6 Nov. 1889 (buried Bethlehem Cem..), m. Robert Flournoy 30 Sept. 1856. He was born ca 1835 Ga., died by 1868. Known issue:

a. Walter D. Flournoy, b. ca 1859 Ala., m. Susan B. ----. She was born 21 April 1868, died 6 Nov. 1889 and is buried in Bethlehem Cem..

b. Charles M. Flournoy, b. April 1860, d. Nov. 1864, buried in Bethlehem Cem..

c. Ava Flournoy, b. ca 1864 Ala.

d. Robert Flournoy, b. ca 1867 Texas.

4. Anna McKenzie, b. 4 March 1841 Ala., d. 20 Oct. 1874, m. Dr. Wm. U. Morton 13 Jan. 1867. He married (2) Wealtha M. Feagin 26 June 1878. Known issue:

a. Thomas J. Morton, b. ca 1867 Ala..

5. Louisianna McKenzie, b. ca 1843 Ala., d. after 1890, m. James M. Hobdy 28 Nov. 1863 (see HOBDY). He was born 15

July 1839, died 13 May 1900, buried in Bethlehem Cem..
Known issue:

    a. Clifton Hobdy, b. 15 March 1865, d. 3 Nov. 1865, buried in Bethlehem Cem..

    b. Janet Hobdy, b. ca 1872 Ala.

    c. Harold Hobdy, b. ca 1877 Ala.

    d. a son, born ca 1879 Ala...name unknown.

6. William McKenzie, died 1846, buried Bethlehem Cem..

7. Elizabeth McKenzie, b. ca 1849 Ala., d. 1885, m. Edward O. Petty 18 Nov. 1868. He was born ca 1845 Ala.. They moved to Arkansas in Nov. 1883. Known issue:

    a. Zula Petty, minor in 1890.

    b. Cora Petty, minor in 1890.

    c. Charles Petty, minor in 1890.

    d. Edna Petty, minor in 1890.

8. Emma McKenzie, b. ca 1855 Ala., d. after 1890, m. Wm. H. Norton 20 Nov. 1877. In 1886, they were living in Warrenton, Ga.. Issue unknown.

9. John McKenzie, who lived in Meridian Miss., may have married Nancy McLeod 16 Nov. 1848. Issue:

    a. William C. McKenzie, b. ca 1849 Ala.

    b. John A. McKenzie, b. ca 1855 Ala.

    c. Andrew G. McKenzie, b. ca 1857 Ala.

    d. Daniel McKenzie, b. ca 1859 Ala.

Other sources:

DOWNING Bible
Dict. of Ala. Biography, Vol. 4, page 1123
Memorial Record of Ala., Vol. I, page 567
"My Folk" by Elanor McSwain

McLEAN
(McLain, McClain)

There were several families of this name in Barbour Co. before 1850, but there is nothing to show that they were all related.

Daniel C. McLean, b. ca 1797 Scotland, died by 1854, leaving
his estate to his brothers and sisters, viz: John McLean, Hugh
McLean, Sibly (Cebie) McLean and Christian, wife of John Cameron.
In 1855, John and Christian (McLean) Cameron were living in
Alexandria, Canada.

In the 1840 Census of Barbour Co., there was a Hector McLean,
born between 1770 and 1780. He could have been the father or
the brother of the above family group.

*Hugh McLean, b. 1782 Scotland, d. 1 Aug. 1880, m. Margaret
----, b. 1805 Scotland, d. 15 Sept. 1870. They are buried in
Pond Bethel Cemetery. Known issue:

1. *Hugh McLean, Jr., b. 1820 Scotland, d. 1903, m. Amanda
   Stricklin 3 July 1870. She was born 1846, died 1928. Both
   are buried in Pond Bethel Cemetery.
2. Catharine (Christian?) McLean, b. ca 1832 Scotland, m. John
   Gillis, Jr. 28 Jan. 1857.
3. Sarah McLean, b. ca 1836 Scotland, was not married in 1880.
4. Nancy McLean, b. ca 1840 Scotland, was not married in 1870.
5. Mary A. McLean, b. ca 1842 New York.
   Sibly (Cebie) McLean was born ca 1780/90 Scotland, died
   after 1870. She never married.

In 1827, John McLean entered land in the Southeastern section of Barbour Co., near the Henry Co. line. He was born ca
1795 in Scotland and died between 1860 and 1870. His wife,
Catharine, was born ca 1805 Scotland, died between 1870 and
1880. Probable issue:

1. *Daniel McLean, b. ca 1841 Ala., m. Matilda ---- ca 1865.

2. *Hector McLean, b. ca 1843 Ala., m. Mary ---- ca 1868.

3. Nancy McLean, b. ca 1846.

Another Daniel McLean died by June 1843, leaving wife Mary (b. ca 1807 N. C.) and daughter, Elizabeth (b. ca 1840 Ala.). By 1845, Mary McLean married Micah Mixon (or Nixon). On 24 May 1852, Elizabeth McLean married John S. Hamilton. Lachlin McLean was the administrator of the estate of this Daniel McLean.

*Lachlin McLean, b. ca 1810 N. C., d. after 1870, m. Mary W. (Lee?), b. ca 1813 Ga., d. after 1870. Known issue:

1. Eugenia McLean, b. ca 1842 Ala.

2. Margaret E. McLean, b. ca 1850 Ala.

3. Mary L. McLean, b. ca 1857 Ala.

In the 1870 Census, Lachlin McLean stated that his father was of foreign birth. An entry in the Eufaula newspaper states that Lachlin McLean died there on 25 Nov. 1874, over 70 years of age. He was born in Scotland, and came to Eufaula in 1836, where he was the bridgekeeper. Perhaps he was the father of Lachlin McLean who was born in 1810.

Another McLean family was John W. McLean, b. 1795 N. C., died 5 May 1870. He married Margaret, daughter of Angus and Catharine Curry. She was born 1 Nov. 1798 N. C., died 5 Feb. 1870. They are buried in Pea River Cemetery, as are most of their children. Probable issue:

1. Daniel W. McLean, b. 13 April 1826 N. C., d. 7 May 1898, m. Sidney D. ----, b. 14 July 1840 Ala., d. 7 May 1898.

2. Mary A. McLean, b. 6 June 1828, d. 11 Feb. 1900, m. Thomas F. Baxter 6 Dec. 1846. He was born 16 June 1827, died 26 Feb. 1908. Although they died in Clio, Ala., they are buried in East Side Cem., Headland, Ala..

3. Catharine C. McLean, b. ca 1837 Ala., not married in 1880.

196

, 4. Eliza J. McLean, b. ca 1839 Ala., not married in 1880.

5. John W. McLean, Jr., b. 10 Aug. 1839 Ala., d. 15 July 1862.

6. Angus A. McLean, b. 6 Jan. 1842 Ala., d. 3 March 1905, m.
   Mary ----.

In 1829, Duncan McLean patented land North of Louisville.
In 1833, he sold this land, with his wife, Catharine, also sign-
ing. He died in Pike Co., Ala. between March and December,
1848. Issue:

1. Lauchlin Crawford McLean.

2. Duncan Washington McLean.

3. Patrick McLean

4. ---- McLean, a daughter, not married in 1848.

5. ---- McLean, a daughter

Sources of information:

Barbour Co., Ala. Probate Records
Barbour Co., Ala. Census Records
Barbour Co., Ala. Cemetery Records
Pike Co., Ala. Probate Records
Henry Co., Ala. Cemetery Records
"Alabama Series", Vol. II by Helen S. Foley

*ADDITIONS & CORRECTIONS AS OF JUNE 1, 1979:

Hugh and Margaret McLean also had a son, Alexander McLean, b.
ca 1823 Scotland. Also, Amanda (wife of Hugh McLean, Jr.) was
nee Hudley and the widow of Green Strickland.

Hugh McLean died ca Nov. 1903, age 73, and is buried in Pond
Bethel Cem.. He was born in Scotland but had lived in Barbour
Co. for 40 years. He leaves a wife and eight children.

From Lee-McLean Bible:

Lauchlin McLean, b. 24 Sept. 1808, d. 25 Nov. 1874, m. Mary Ann
Lee 22 Dec. 1835. She was born 29 May 1816, died Nov. 1901.

Her obit states that she died in Eufaula but was buried beside her mother in Crystal Springs, Miss. Possible issue:

1. Eugenia McLean, b. ca 1842 Ala.. (She is in the 1850 Census but not in the Bible record).

2. Margaret E. McLean, b. 20 Feb. 1850, d. 27 Sept. 1859.

3. Mary Lee Ellen McLean, b. 1 Nov. 1856, not married in 1901. She was living with her mother in 1901.

Other McLean's included in this Bible record were:

    Daniel C. McLean, d. 9 May 1843

    Hector McLean, d. 16 Oct. 1843

    Hugh McLean, d. 17 Oct. 1843

No birth dates are given for these three, so it is impossible to know if they were adults or children.

McLEOD

The McLeod family groups in this chapter were put together primarily from estates, census records, cemetery records, Bible records and information from descendants. In some instances, there is no documentary proof of a relationship except a combination of the above records. There were also more McLeod families here that were probably related to the ones in this chapter but they are not included because the relationship would be purely guesswork.

In 1835, Alexander, Angus, Daniel and Margaret McLeod patented land within a mile of one another. John and William McLeod patented land a few miles away, also in 1835.

Daniel McLeod, b. ca 1770/80, d. by 1843, m. Sarah ----. She was born ca 1770/80, died after Dec. 1844. The following heirs each received an equal share:

1. John McLeod, b. ca 1808 N. C., d. by Jan. 1857, m. Sarah ----. She was born ca 1815 Ga., probably died after 1870. Issue (from census):
   a. William McLeod, b. ca 1845 Ala., no record after 1850.
   b. Mary McLeod, b. ca 1846 Ala., not married in 1880.
   c. George McLeod, b. ca 1848 Ala., not married in 1880.
   d. John McLeod, b. ca 1847 Ala., no record after 1850.
   e. Martha McLeod, b. ca 1855 Ala., not married in 1880.
2. William McLeod, b. 30 Jan. 1810 Cumberland Co., N. C., d. ca July 1877. He moved with his father to Washington Co., Ga. ca 1828, to Stewart Co., Ga., then to Barbour Co., Ala. He married Frances E. Birdsong 17 June 1849 (see page 126). She was born ca 1829 Ga., died after 1891. Known issue:
   a. William F. McLeod, b. ca 1852 Ala., m. C. A. Matthews 5 Jan. 1876.
   b. Effy Elizabeth McLeod, b. 2 May 1855 Ala., d. 6 Dec.

1886, m. John T. Brown 11 April 1880 at Georgetown, Ga..
He was born 12 Aug. 1835 S. C. and came to Eufaula from
Macon, Ga.. He died here 15 April 1885. They are buried
in Fairview Cem., Eufaula, Ala.

    c. Mary McLeod, b. 5 Jan. 1858, d. 8 Aug. 1859, buried in
        Fairview Cem., Eufaula, Ala.

    d. Sarah A. McLeod, b. ca 1860 Ala.

    e. Henry John (Jack) McLeod, b. ca 1863 Ala., living in
        Columbus, Ga. in 1901.

    f. Carrie E. McLeod, b. ca 1869 Ala., d. ca Oct. 1901 in
        Columbus, Ga., m. John Brady 22 Feb. 1887. They were
        living in Columbus, Ga. by 1891.

    g. Edward S. (L.?) McLeod, b. ca 1872 Ala.

3. Daniel McLeod, b. ca 1815 Ga., m. Nancy Smith 10 April 1841.
    She was born ca 1821 in Ga.. They may have moved to Rome,
    Ga. after 1860. Issue (from 1850 & 1860 Census):

    a. Margaret E. McLeod, b. ca 1842 Ala.

    b. Sophronia C. McLeod, b. ca 1844 Ala.

    c. Martha (Laura?) McLeod, b. ca 1846 Ala.. She probably
        married Neill McLeod - they were living in Dawson, Ga.
        in 1891.

    d. John W. McLeod, b. ca 1848 Ala.

    e. Mary McLeod, b. ca 1850 Ala., probably married Jack
        Moore and lived in Rome, Ga..

    f. Daniel McLeod, b. ca 1853 Ala., living Rome, Ga. 1891.

    g. William McLeod, b. ca 1855 Ala., living Rome, Ga. 1891.

    h. James McLeod, b. ca 1859 Ala., living Rome, Ga. 1891.

Also in this household in 1850 was Sarah McLeod, b. ca 1778 N.C.,
probably the mother of Daniel McLeod.

4. Janet McLeod, b. ca 1816 Ga., m. John C. Bryant ca 1837.
    They moved to Rome, Ga. ca 1870 and he died there in 1891.

Issue:

a. William Bryant, b. ca 1839 Ala., living Rome, Ga. 1891.

b. John D. Bryant, b. ca 1840 Ala.

c. Sarah Bryant, b. ca 1841 Ala.

d. Francis M. Bryant, b. ca 1843 Ala.

e. Daniel D. Bryant, b. ca 1845 Ala., living Rome, Ga. 1891.

f. Mary J. Bryant, b. 1850 Ala., m. ---- Sharp, living Rome, Ga. 1891.

g. Tabitha A. Bryant, b. ca 1857 Ala., m. Tom Moore, living Rome, Ga. 1891.

5. Mary McLeod, b. ca 1821 Ga., d. by 1859 m. Alexander G. Smith ca 1844. He m. (3) Mary J. Turpin 19 Dec. 1866 and (2) Annie E. Johnson 10 Feb. 1859. Issue (by Mary McLeod):

a. Louisianna Smith, b. ca 1846 Ala., not married 1870.

b. Henrietta Smith, b. ca 1849 Ala., m. J. F. Fortner 29 Oct. 1874. They were living in Livingston, Texas 1891.

c. Mary J. Smith, b. ca 1851 Ala.

d. Alexander Smith, b. ca 1853 Ala.

e. Richard Smith, b. ca 1855 Ala.

f. Jesse Smith, b. ca 1855 Ala.

Issue (by Mary J. Turpin):

g. Fannie Smith, b. ca 1860 Ala.

h. Thomas Smith, b. ca 1861 Ala.

Issue (by Annie E. Johnson):

i. Georgia Smith, b. ca 1868 Ala.

6. Whitson Pugh, b. ca 1837 Ala., d. 2 July 1863 in the Civil War. He was probably a grandson.

Angus McLeod, probably a brother to the preceeding Daniel McLeod, was born ca 1781 Scotland, died by 1868 (maybe before 1860). In 1850, Margaret McLeod (b. ca 1782 Scotland) was in his household, probably his wife. They are not in any later

Barbour Co. census and his estate does not mention her. However, there was a Margaret McLeod, b. ca 1779 Scotland, in the household of Mary Winslett in the 1860 Census of Pike Co., Ala.. The estate of Angus McLeod was not settled until 1891, when heirs were:

1. Mary (Polly) McLeod, b. ca 1814, m. Joel Winslett (see WINSLETT).

2. Alexander McLeod, b. ca 1816 N. C., d. 14 July 1891 Terrell Co., Ga., m. (1) Catharine McIntosh 20 June 1841. She was born 13 June 1820 Kershaw Dist., S. C., died 9 June 1856. He m. (2) Catharine Stewart 5 Jan. 1862. She was born 22 April 1833, died 27 Aug. 1887. They are buried in Palmyra ·Cem.. Issue:

    a. Mary A. McLeod, b. 12 Sept. 1842 Ala., d. 29 Nov. 1908, m. Sam C. Woods 29 Nov. 1866. They are buried in Palmyra Cem. but there are no dates on his grave.

    b. Neill McLeod, b. ca 1844 Ala., living in Dawson (Terrell Co.), Ga. in 1891. He may have married his cousin, Laura McLeod, daughter of Daniel McLeod and Nancy Smith.

    c. William McLeod, b. ca 1847 Ala., living Terrell Co., Ga. in 1891. He probably married Laura H. Goodson 14 Oct. 1873.

    d. John McLeod, b. ca 1854 Ala., living Terrell Co., Ga. in 1891.

    e. Ida McLeod, b. ca 1867 Ala., no record after 1870.

3. John McLeod, b. 1819 S. C., d. ca Oct. 1886, m. Jane Cunningham 26 May 1842, daughter of Duncan Cunningham. She was born 8 Jan. 1825 Ala., d. 2 May 1901. They are buried in Palmyra Cem.. Issue:

    a. Catharine A. McLeod, b. 10 Oct. 1843 Ala., d. 4 Feb. 1917, m. Charles Franklin Stewart 7 July 1868. He was

born 15 March 1837 and died 1 Oct. 1908. They are buried in Mt. Serene Cem..

4. Sarah Elizabeth (Herrod?), b. ca 1844 Ala., m. Harrell Flowers by 1870. She could have been a granddaughter of Angus
McLeod. Harrell Flowers m. Elizabeth Herrod 13 Aug. 1861 -
she was a daughter of Sarah Herrod, b. ca 1810 N. C..

5. Jane (Herrod?), b. ca 1840 N. C., m. Thomas S. Moffett 15
Dec. 1858. He was killed 17 Jan. 1864 in the Civil War. In
1870, Jane Moffett was in the household of Sarah Herrod, b.
ca 1814. Also in this household was William Moffett, b. ca
1859 Ala., who married Vickie Laseter 9 July 1884 and William
McLeod, b. ca 1850 Ala..

6. Hugh Gillis, probably a grandson (son of Daniel Gillis and
Catharine McLeod - see GILLIS).

7. Neill Gillis, probably a grandson (son of Daniel Gillis and
Catharine McLeod - see GILLIS).

Daniel D. McLeod, Sr., b. 1783 Isle of Skye, Scotland, d.
1856, m. Mary Catharine Douglas in Robeson Co., N. C.. She was
born 1789 N. C., d. 14 Oct. 1853. They moved to Kershaw Dist.,
S. C., then to Barbour Co., Ala.. Both are buried in Palmyra
Cem.. Issue:

1. Nancy L. McLeod, b. 3 July 1813 S. C., d. 30 Jan. 1892 (or
1897) in Clairette, Texas. She married Andrew Lee 3 June
1836 and they moved to Hico (Early Co.), Texas by 1856 (see
LEE). Issue:

a. Martha Jane Lee, b. 8 Nov. 1836

b. Catharine Christian Lee, b. 30 March 1839

c. Mary Ann Lee, b. 24 Jan. 1841

d. Isabell Caroline Lee, b. 3 Feb. 1843

e. Lucinda Elizabeth Lee, b. 16 Jan. 1845

f. Nancy Arincy Lee, b. 8 May 1847

g. William Andrew Lee, b. 25 Jan. 1852

h. Margaret Fran Lee, b. 30 April 1854

i. Thomas McLeod Lee, b. 7 Sept. 1857

2. Christian McLeod, b. ca 1816 S. C., m. John Kennedy Norton
(see NORTON). In 1891, her heirs were:

a. John Douglas Norton, b. ca 1837

b. Jane (Nancy A.) Norton, b. ca 1840, m. James R. Eidson
20 Dec. 1860

c. Mary Elizabeth (Lizzie) Norton, b. ca 1844, m. ----
Jackson.

d. Manerva (Viney) Norton, b. ca 1847, m. Dionitius D.
Burkhalter 30 Nov. 1865.

3. Daniel McLeod, Jr., b. 2 Jan. 1824 Kershaw Dist., S. C., d.
24 Feb. 1911, m. Pamelia Retta McGill 31 Oct. 1848. She was
born 16 Oct. 1832 Abbeville Dist., S. C., died 21 Dec. 1917.
They are buried in County Line Cem.. Issue:

a. William McLeod, b. ca 1850 Ala.

b. Mary Catharine McLeod, b. 14 April 1851, d. 19 July 1852,
buried Palmyra Cem..

c. John C. McLeod, b. ca 1853 Ala., probably buried County
Line Cem. but no dates. He is believed to have married
four times - possibly to (1) Mrs. Nancy Baker 20 Feb.
1877 (2) Miss Mary J. Baker 16 Feb. 1881 (3) Sarah J. S.
Cooper 25 April 1882. The name of his fourth wife is
not known.

d. Carrie Isabella McLeod, b. 12 Sept. 1855 Ala., d. 25 May
1911, buried County Line Cem., m. George M. Howell. At
one time, they lived in Anniston, Ala..

e. Daniel D. McLeod, b. ca 1857 Ala., d. Feb. 1899 Anniston,
Ala., never married. He was a lawyer.

f. Ella V. McLeod, b. ca 1860 Ala., m. S. F. Jenkins 11

Sept. 1900.

g. Coleman Beauregard McLeod (Rev.), b. ca 1862 Ala., d. Frisco City, Ala.. He once lived at Faunsdale, Ala.

h. Archibald N. McLeod, b. ca 1869 Ala., never married.

i. Edward Thornton McLeod, b. 14 Nov. 1871 Ala., d. 10 Jan. 1900, buried County Line Cem..

j. Robert E. McLeod, b. 23 April 1877 Ala., d. 9 Aug. 1903, buried County Line Cem..

4. William E. McLeod, b. 1826 Kershaw Dist., S. C., d. 8 Sept. 1907, buried Batesville Bapt. Cem. (no dates), m. (1) Nancy Ann Johnson 30 Sept. 1856. She was born 28 July 1838, died 29 July 1892 (see page 148). She is buried in Fairview Cem., Eufaula, Ala.. He married (2) Julia Cade 22 Dec. 1895. Issue (by 1st wife):

a. Mary Lenora McLeod, b. 10 Aug. 1857, d. 8 Nov. 1937 in Birmingham, Ala., m. James Silvester Watson 27 Dec. 1877. He was born 23 Oct. 1853, died 13 Oct. 1895 and is buried in Prospect Cem. in an unmarked grave.

b. James Coleman McLeod, b. 10 Oct. 1859, d. 10 Aug. 1900 (or 1901), buried Fairview Cem., Eufaula, Ala.. He never married.

c. Alice Adella McLeod, b. 7 Feb. 1862, d. 24 April 1952, m. (1) J. E. Howell 27 Feb. 1894, He was born 5 Aug. 1857, died 21 Feb. 1902. They are buried in Fairview Cem.. She married (2) James W. Grubbs 28 Dec. 1902.

d. Sarah Elizabeth McLeod, b. 10 Feb. 1866, d. 4 July 1947, never married. She is buried in Fairview Cem..

e. Leona Christian McLeod, b. 28 Jan. 1868, d. 11 March 1951, m. John Wesley King 18 Dec. 1886. He died 6 March 1929. They are buried in Birmingham, Ala..

f. Marion (Kittie Mae) McLeod, b. 2 Oct. 1870, d. 27 Feb.

1917, buried Fairview Cem., m. Wm. F. Rose 30 May 1893.

g. Willa Ann McLeod, b. 8 Jan. 1873, d. 16 Jan. 1942 in Columbus, Ga., m. Robert E. Calhoun 29 Jan. 1900. They were living in Pittsview, Ala. in 1907.

h. Ruby Celestia McLeod, b. 14 Nov. 1875, d. 18 Nov. 1952, buried Fairview Cem., m. Robert Dunbar.

i. Elle Ree McLeod, b. 19 April 1878, d. 1 Nov. 1878.

j. Rosa Louise McLeod, b. 15 Dec. 1879, d. 25 April 1945, m. Crawford Clay Davis 3 Dec. 1902. They were living in Amory, Miss. in 1907, later moved back to Atlanta. He died 26 Oct. 1942 - both are buried in Atlanta, Ga..

k. Kathren Blanche McLeod, b. 27 March 1882, presently living in Sylacauga, Ala., m. Winfield Wesley Stanton 10 June 1903. He was born 16 Dec. 1878, died 4 Jan. 1954 and is buried in Fairview Cem., Eufaula, Ala.

Issue (by 2nd wife):

l. William Dozier McLeod, minor in 1907, never married.

m. Mary Lou McLeod m. Buford S. Warr 18 Sept. 1921.

5. Archibald P. McLeod, b. 22 March 1834 Kershaw Dist., S. C., d. 5 March 1907 Polk Co., Ga., m. (1) Sarah Louisa A. Johnson 30 Dec. 1857 (see page 146). She was born 28 Nov. 1836 and died 28 July 1893. They moved to Polk Co., Fla. ca 1884, but are buried in Palmyra Cem., Barbour Co., Ala.. He m. (2) Alice V. Howell 14 Sept. 1897. She was born 1875, died 1913 and is buried in Rocky Mount Cem. (see WISE).

Issue (by 1st wife):

a. Jesse D. McLeod, b. ca 1859 Ala., d. by 1912, m. Ida ----. He lived in Florida.

b. William E. McLeod, b. 21 July 1861 Ala., d. 20 Aug. 1900, m. Angie Sparks 15 Feb. 1888. She was born 27 Nov. 1869 and died 25 July 1895 - both buried Fairview Cem.,

Eufaula, Ala..

    c. Merritt A. McLeod, b. ca 1868 Ala., not in estate settlement in 1912.

    d. Solon McLeod, b. ca 1870 Ala., m. Bertha Cox.

Issue (by 2nd wife):

    e. Archibald Howell McLeod, a minor in 1913.

    f. Douglas Groover McLeod, b. 1906, d. 1918, buried in Rocky Mount Cem..

    g. Kate McLeod, a minor in 1913.

6. Isabel Jane McLeod, b. 11 May 1837, d. 12 Feb. 1856, buried Palmyra Cem..

Norman McLeod died by Jan. 1842 in Anson Co., N. C., leaving wife, Mary, and other heirs. His will was also recorded in Barbour Co., Ala. in 1847. Some of the heirs named in his will were enumerated here in 1850, including his wife. Issue:

1. Alexander McLeod, b. ca 1800 N. C., may have married Pamelia ----. There is no record of him after 1850.

2. Duncan McLeod

3. Daniel McLeod

4. Angus McLeod, b. ca 1823 N. C., d. Nov. 1864 (CSA), buried at Ft. Gaines, Ga.. He married Josephine Brown, who died in Durant, Okla.. Issue:

    a. Pauline McLeod

    b. Susan McLeod

    c. Almira McLeod

    d. Angus Irene McLeod

5. John McLeod

6. Catharine McLeod m. ---- Douglas.

7. Janet McLeod, b. 26 Feb. 1806 Anson Co., N. C., d. 5 June 1868, m. John C. McRae 21 Sept. 1826 Anson Co., N. C. He was born 18 Feb. 1806 Anson Co., N. C., died 11 April 1891 (see page 212).

8. Isabel McLeod, b. ca 1818 N. C., m. ---- McNabb.

9. Mary McLeod, b. ca 1828 N. C., living with Angus McLeod in
    1850.

10. Christian McLeod, b. 18 Feb. 1814 N. C., d. 3 April 1889, m.
    George Washington McRae 20 Feb. 1845. He was born 24 April
    1811 Anson Co., N. C., died 5 April 1878. They are buried
    in Pea River Presbyterian Church Cem..

11. Ann Beverly (McLeod?)

12. Margaret McLeod, died by 1841, m. ____ Fields.

13. Elizabeth McLeod. She may have married John G. McLendon.

Other sources:

McRae Bible
McLeod Bibles
Family Records

Alexander McRae patented land near Pea River Church in 1827
and 1829. Duncan (or Daniel) McRae patented land near him in
1827. William McRae patented land in 1827 and 1835, also in
this area.

It is extremely difficult to establish the exact relation-
ships of the members of this family, as they intermarried fre-
quently, and also used the same given names in all branches of
the family.

Christian McLeod McRae died by 1844 in Barbour Co.. Her husband, Phillip McRae, died in North Carolina ca 1824. Issue:*

1. Farquhar A. McRae, b. 1796 N. C., d. 11 Dec. 1858, m. Mary
   McRae, daughter of Christopher and Mary McRae. She was born
   1796 N. C., died 25 May 1854. Both are buried in Pea River
   Church Cemetery. Issue:

   a. Harvey A. McRae, b. 20 Oct. 1823 N. C., d. 10 Oct. 1890,
      m. Lucy Shipman 25 March 1849. She was born 17 July
      1828 Ala., died 1 April 1877.

   b. Phillip P. McRae, b. ca 1828 N. C., living in Texas by
      1860.

   c. John L. McRae, b. ca 1829 N. C.

   d. Lillian Ann McRae, b. 29 Aug. 1831 N. C., d. 12 June
      1910, m. William C. Bostwick 22 Oct. 1857. He was born
      22 July 1829, died 20 June 1884. They are buried in
      Pea River Church Cemetery.

   e. Christian McRae, b. 2 March 1834 N. C., d. 13 Jan. 1913,
      and is buried in Pea River Church Cemetery. She m. John
      DeBardelaben.

   f. *Charles M. McRae, b. 24 Nov. 1840 Anson Co., N. C., m.
      ---- Hobdy.

2. Isabella McRae m. Farquhar McRae.

3. *John E. McRae, b. ca 1784 N. C., m. Christian ----, b. ca
   1794 N. C.. Known issue:

   a. Elizabeth McRae, b. ca 1825 N. C.

   b. John McRae, b. ca 1827 N. C.

   c. Harriett McRae, b. ca 1833 N. C., m. Paul McCall 2 July
      1857.

   d. Isabella McRae, b. ca 1836 N. C.

   e. Christian McRae, b. ca 1840 N. C.

4. Nancy McRae m. Alexander McLendon. They were living in N.C.
   in 1844.

5. *Daniel McRae - he was dead by 1844, and the following heirs
   were living in Miss.:

   a. Farquhar McRae

   b. Colin McRae

   c. Daniel McRae

   d. Catherine McRae

   e. Alexander McRae

   f. John McRae

6. Elizabeth McRae, died by 1844, m. ---- McRae. Issue:

   a. Isabella McRae, b. ca 1800, m. William Teal.

   b. Margaret McRae, b. ca 1800, d. by 1850, m. Allen Teal.

7. Colin E. McRae, died by 1844. Known issue:

   a. Ann McRae, b. ca 1826 N. C., m. M. A. Patterson.

   b. James McRae, who was living in Early Co., Ga. in 1846,
      later moved to Randolph Co., Ga..

   c. Sarah C. McRae, b. ca 1830 Fla., m. Henry H. Field, Jr.
      3 Nov. 1853.

   d. Mary McRae, b. ca 1833 Fla.

   e. Martha McRae, b. ca 1835 Fla.

   f. Elizabeth McRae, b. ca 1838 Ga.

8. Alexander McRae died by 1850. His wife may have been

Margaret ----. Known issue:

a. John C. McRae, living in S. C. in 1850 (see later).

b. Ann McRae, b. ca 1819 N. C., not married in 1860.

c. Winney McRae, b. ca 1815 N. C., m. Donald McKay, b. ca 1812 Scotland.

d. Christian McRae m. John Hair (or Harris). They were living in N. C. in 1850.

Christopher McRae died by 1837. His will was written 26 June 1837 in Anson Co., N. C. and probated there in April 1837. It was recorded in Barbour Co., Ala. 31 March 1840. His wife was Mary ----, b. ca 1765/75 N. C., d. by Feb. 1861. Neither will was very explicit, but the heirs were:

1. Mary McRae, a daughter, who married Farquhar A. McRae, son of Christian McRae.

2. Daniel McKay, grandson of a sister of Christopher McRae.

3. John G. McLendon, a nephew, born ca 1806 S. C.. Mary McRae lived with him from 1850 until her death.

4. Daniel McRae, a grandson, and his daughter, Elizabeth.

5. Isabella, wife of William Teal (relationship not given).

6. Margaret, wife of Allen Teal (relationship not given).
   (Note: Isabella and Margaret were daughters of Elizabeth McRae, granddaughters of Christian McRae.)

7. Mary Capel, relationship not given. She was born 22 Jan. 1815 N. C., died 9 Oct. 1886, m. James Capel. He was born 25 Jan. 1800, died 9 Oct. 1886. They are buried in Pea River Church Cemetery.

8. Caty ----, relationship not given, who m. James Boyt (or Brock).

9. Gilbert McRae, relationship not given.

10. Colin McRae, who moved to Union Co., Ark. ca 1843.

John C. McRae, b. 18 Feb. 1806 Anson Co., N. C., d. 11 April

1891, m. Janet McLeod, daughter of Norman and Mary McLeod in Anson Co., N. C. 21 Sept. 1826. She was born 26 Feb. 1806 N. C.,
died 6 June 1868. They are buried in Fairview Cemetery, Eufaula,
Ala., as are most of their children. Issue:

1. Jabez A. McRae, b. 25 June 1827 Anson Co., N. C., m. Josephine McKay.

2. John McLeod McRae, b. 13 Nov. 1838 Marlboro, S. C., d. 1901,
   m. Amanda Matilda Williams 18 Dec. 1862. She was born 1841
   Ga., died 17 April 1916.

3. Mary Jane McRae, b. 16 Aug. 1833 Chesterfield Dist., S. C.,
   d. 29 Sept. 1904, m. James T. Kendall 13 Nov. 1851 Cheraw,
   S. C.

4. Mariah Marshall McRae, b. 2 Dec. 1840 Marlboro, S. C., d. 2
   May 1924, m. Henry Augustus Young 5 June 1860. He was born
   22 Oct: 1835, died 19 Feb. 1863, son of Edward B. and Ann F.
   Young.

5. Julia Hawes McRae, b. 17 Aug. 1844 Chesterfield, S. C., d.
   18 Aug. 1862 in Knoxville, Tenn..

6. Daniel McRae, b. 18 May 1829 Anson Co., N. C., d. 12 May
   1859.

Also buried with this family in Fairview Cemetery is Elizabeth
McRae, born 25 June 1837, died 5 June 1857.

William McRae, b. 8 Jan. 1798 N. C., d. 10 Dec. 1886, m.
Margie ----. She was born 10 March 1792 and died 10 July 1875.
They and most of their children are buried in Pea River Church
Cemetery. In 1840, there was a female, age 60/70, living in
this household, but she must have died by 1850, as she is not
included in that census. Probable issue:

1. Farquhard C. McRae, b. ca 1817 Ala., m. Mary Ann E. Cameron
   27 July 1854.

2. John C. McRae, b. ca 1821 Ala., m. Martha ----.

3. Daniel C. McRae, b. ca 1823 Ala., not married in 1880.

4. *Catherine McRae, b. ca 1830, m. John N. McRae 25 Jan. 1852.
   He was the son of Donald and Catharine McRae of N. C.. He
   was born 10 May 1827 N. C., died 16 June 1864 at Griffin,
   Ga. (CSA). Known issue:

   a. Jane C. McRae, b. ca 1854 Ala..

   b. Phillip McRae, b. 14 Nov. 1855 Ala..

   c. Duncan Franklin McRae, b. July 1857 Ala..

   d. Mary F. McRae, b. March 1861.

   Also in this household in 1860 was Daniel McRae, b. ca 1824
N. C..

5. Murphy McRae, b. 28 Jan. 1832 Ala., d. 4 Sept. 1900, probably never married.

6. Washington McRae, b. 5 Oct. 1836 Ala., d. 14 Nov. 1913, m.
   Katie H. ----. She was born 27 Oct. 1831, died 3 March 1911.

   John R. McRae, b. ca 1785 N. C., d. after 1860, m. Comfort
Keane. She was born ca 1795 N. C., died by 1860. Known issue:

1. *Alexander Keane McRae, b. ca 1823 Anson Co., N. C., m. Winnie Elder Jones, daughter of Henry and Nellie (Payne) Jones.
   She was born 3 Nov. 1835.

2. George McRae, b. ca 1830 N. C.

3. John P. McRae, b. ca 1833 Ga.

4. Elizabeth McRae, b. ca 1835 Ga., m. Alexander D. McRae 15
   Dec. 1853. He died by 1860.

5. Margaret McRae, b. ca 1838 Ga.

6. *Possibly Sarah McRae, b. ca 1830 N. C., m. ---- Arrington.

   George Washington McRae, b. 24 April 1811 Anson Co., N. C.,
d. 5 April 1878, m. Christian McLeod 20 Feb. 1845. She was born
18 Feb. 1814 N. C., died 3 April 1889. They are buried in Pea
River Church Cemetery. Known issue:

1. William N. McRae, b. ca 1847 Ala., m. Mary C. McCraney 13
   June 1871.
2. Mary C. McRae, b. ca 1847 Ala.
3. Duncan McRae, b. 1850 Ala.
4. Martha J. McRae, b. ca 1853 Ala.

   Christopher M. McRae, b. 27 Dec. 1819 N. C., d. 23 May 1883,
m. Abigail ----. She was born 8 Feb. 1820 Anson Co., N. C.,
died 27 Oct. 1895. They are buried in Pea River Church Cemetery.
Issue:
1. Nancy McRae, b. ca 1844 N. C.
2. Catherine McRae, b. ca 1845 Ala.
3. Christopher Columbus McRae, b. ca 1847 Ala.
4. Henrietta McRae, b. ca 1850 Ala.
5. Mary McRae, b. ca 1852 Ala.
6. Washington McRae, b. ca 1855 Ala.
7. Christian McRae, b. ca 1860 Ala.

   Christopher C. McRae, b. 18 Dec. 1823 Anson Co., N. C., d.
18 Nov. 1861, m. Nancy Ann Campbell 8 Aug. 1850. She was born
26 June 1832 Anson Co., N. C., d. 28 May 1910. They are buried
in Pea River Church Cemetery. Known issue:
1. Thomas W. McRae, b. ca 1852 Ala.
2. James McRae, b. ca 1855 Ala.
3. Mary A. McRae, b. ca 1857 Ala.
Also in this household in 1850 were John J. (or C.) McRae, b.
24 April 1826 Anson Co., N. C., d. 17 May 1904 and Catherine
(or Caroline) McRae, b. 9 June 1836 N. C., d. 3 Feb. 1905. John
J. McRae was still there in 1860. They are buried in Pea River
Church Cemetery.
   John McRae, b. ca 1816 S. C., m. (1) Virginia ----, b. ca
1825 Ga., (2) C. G. ----, b. ca 1839 Ga.. Known issue:

1. Mary C. McRae, b. ca 1847 Ga.

2. Amanda A. McRae, b. ca 1848 Ala.

3. Sarah J. McRae, b. ca 1849 Ala.

4. Malcom A. McRae, b. ca 1851 Ala.

5. Reubin S. McRae, b. ca 1852 Ala.

6. John J. McRae, b. ca 1853 Ala.

Colon W. McRae, b. ca 1810 N. C., m. Harriett ----, b. ca 1813 N. C. They came to Ala. after 1855. Known issue:

1. Martha McRae, b. ca 1839 N. C.

2. Elizabeth McRae, b. ca 1843 Ga.

3. John McRae, b. ca 1845 Ga.

4. Colon McRae, b. ca 1848 Ga., m. Drucilla Thomas 17 March 1868.*

5. Margaret McRae, b. ca 1849 Ga.

6. Sarah McRae, b. ca 1851 Ga.

7. Stephen McRae, b. ca 1853 Ga.

8. Lotty (Lena?) McRae, b. ca 1855 Ga.

Sources of information:

Barbour Co., Ala. Probate Records
Barbour Co., Ala. Census Records
Barbour Co., Ala. Cemetery Records
Pea River Presbyterian Church Records
"The Storied Kendall's" by Walker
McRae Family Bible

*ADDITIONS & CORRECTIONS AS OF JUNE 1, 1979:

According to the will of Phillip McRae, dated 6 Oct. 1825, recorded Anson Co., N. C. Will Book A, page 122, he and Christian had the following children:

1. Alexander J. McRae

2. Margaret McRae (who m. Daniel McRae)

3. Isabel McRae (who m. Farquhar McRae)

4. Betsy McRae

5. John McRae (who had a son, Phillip McRae)

6. Colin McRae

7. Farquhar McRae (who had a son, Phillip McRae)

8. Nancy McRae (who m. Alexander McLendon)

In his will, Phillip McRae also named a sister, Flora ----.

Charles M. McRae m. Addie Hobdy, sister of R. L. Hobdy and
niece of John McNeill (from "Backtracking in Barbour Co., Ala."
by Walker). They lived in Pike and Bullock Cos., Ala..

John E. McRae, b. 1785 N. C., d. 1869 Mt. Holly, Ark. m. Christian McRae, lived Anson Co., N. C., Barbour Co., Ala. and Mt.
Holly, Ark.. Issue:

a. Elizabeth McRae, buried Mt. Holly, Ark.

b. John B. McRae, b. 1827 Anson Co., N. C., d. 1901 Mt. Holly,
   Ark., m. Mary Strain.

c. Harriett McRae m. Paul McCall, moved to Mt. Holly, Ark.

d. Isabella McRae - to Mt. Holly, Ark.

e. Christian McRae m. ---- Eagleton - to Mt. Holly Ark.

Daniel McRae was not a son of Phillip and Christian (McLeod)
McRae - he was the husband of their daughter, Margaret. (Will
of Phillip McRae, Anson Co., N. C.)

Mrs. Kittie (Catherine) McRae of Clio died March 1897. She was
the mother of Frank (Duncan Franklin), Phillip, Jane (not married in 1897) and Mary McRae (not married in 1897).

A. K. McRae, an old citizen of Barbour Co., died Dec. 1893.

Sarah McRae m. James Albert Arrington at age 13. He committed
suicide before she was 20, leaving her with four children, one
of which died young:

216

a. Mary Arrington m. N. J. Evans 31 Aug. 1866 Barbour Co., Ala.

b. Sarah Arrington m. James W. Smith 16 Dec. 1867 Barbour Co., Ala.

c. James M. Arrington m. Margaret E. Smith 14 Aug. 1867 Barbour Co., Ala..

From A. D. Beasley, Rossville, Ga.

Mrs. Drucilla McRae, age 65, died at the home of her nephew, C. D. Bush, buried New Hope Cem.. She leaves one son, Colon McRae.

McSWEAN

Roderick C. McSwean, b. 1791 Isle of Skye, Scotland, sailed
to the United States on the "Duke of Kent" with his parents in
1802. He died 28 Jan. 1862. His wife was Mary (Gillis?), b.
1795 Richmond Co., N. C., d. 16 Dec. 1861. They are buried in
Louisville Cemetery. He patented land West of Bakerhill from
1829 through 1836. Issue:

1. Catharine McSwean, b. 25 Feb. 1822 N. C., d. 25 Jan. 1902,
   m. (1) William B. Crews 8 DEc. 1842. He was born 8 Dec.
   1816 Ga., died 20 July 1865. She m. (2) Rev. William H.
   Chambers 7 Jan. 1868. She and her first husband are buried
   in New Hope Church Cemetery. Issue (by 1st husband):
   a. Mary V. Crews, b. ca 1843 Ala., m. James J. Winn 9 June
      1868.
   b. Nancy J. Crews, b. ca 1849 Ala.

2. Nancy McSwean, b. ca 1823 N. C., m. (1) Dr. Thomas F. Pugh
   on 26 Feb. 1850. They were living in Jefferson, Texas in
   1852. She m. (2) Isaac F. Culver on 15 Dec. 1860. In 1862,
   they were living in Henry Co., Ala.. Known issue:
   a. James Francis Pugh, b. 26 Sept. 1851, d. 20 Oct. 1852,
      buried in Louisville Cemetery.
   b. Thomas Pugh, b. 14 March 1853, d. 1 July 1854, buried
      in Louisville Cemetery.

3. Angus McSwean, b. ca 1825 N. C., m. Christian L. Beverly 30
   Aug. 1867 at the home of Jno. G. McLendon. She was born ca
   1834 N. C..

4. John C. McSwean, b. ca 1828 N. C., m. Mary A. McLendon 11
   Dec. 1866 at the home of Jno. G. McLendon. She was born ca
   1847 Ala.. Known issue:
   a. Mary E. McSwean, b. ca 1868 Ala..

5. Christian Caroline McSwean, b. 11 March 1829 Ala., d. 2

April 1853. She is buried in Louisville Cemetery.

6. Colen McSwean, b. 26 Jan. 1832, d. 24 Aug. 1910, m. Josephine, b. 17 Sept. 1837, d. 21 July 1891.

7. Sarah J. W. McSwean, b. ca 1834 Ala., may have married Thomas W. Persons 30 Jan. 1866.

Daniel McSwean patented land near the Dale Co. line in 1848 and 1849. He was born ca 1776 Scotland, died by 1860, m. Mary ----. She was born ca 1778 N. C., died after 1860. Possible issue:

1. Roderick McSwean, b. ca 1812 N. C., m. Catherine ----, b. ca 1816 N. C.. Known issue:

    a. Finley McSwean, b. ca 1838 N. C..

    b. Mary McSwean, b. ca 1840 Ala..

    c. John McSwean, b. ca 1843 Ala..

    d. Daniel McSwean, b. ca 1846 Ala..

    e. Catherine McSwean, b. ca 1847 Ala..

    f. Archibald McSwean, b. ca 1814 N. C..

2. Daniel McSwean, Jr., b. ca 1814 N. C..

3. Angus McSwean, died ca 13 Feb. 1863, may have married Mary Lee 2 March 1843. They probably lived in Henry Co., Ala.. Known issue:

    a. Isabella McSwean

    b. Finley McSwean

    c. John Robert McSwean

    d. Christian McSwean

    e. A. McSwean

    f. Catherine McSwean

4. Nancy McSwean, b. ca 1826 N. C.

5. Malcolm McSwean, b. ca 1828 N. C., m. Sarah Elizabeth Horn 28 Dec. 1854. Known issue:

a. Eli McSwean, b. ca 1857 Ala., m. Leola (or Leonora) Johns on Oct. 1882. She died 13 March 1883.

b. Sarah J. McSwean, b. ca 1860 Ala.

c. Daniel McSwean, b. ca 1862 Ala.

d. Robert McSwean, b. ca 1864 Ala.

e. William McSwean, b. ca 1867 Ala.

f. Mary McSwean, b. Aug. 1869 Ala.

Sources of information:

Barbour Co., Ala. Probate Records
Barbour Co., Ala. Cemetery Records
Barbour Co., Ala. Census Records

Gilbert, Watts and William B. Mann entered land near Gaino from 1829 through 1836.

Gilbert Mann was born ca 1774 S. C. and died 11 July 1854. He was married, but the name of his wife is not in the records of Barbour Co.. At the time of his death, his "only kin" was a son, Robert Mann. On 26 Sept. 1840,*Robert Mann deeded his land and cattle to Ryan Bennett in trust for his wife, Harriett.

William B. Mann, b. ca 1800, m. Bethsadie (or Bathsheba) ----. They had at least five sons and three daughters, according to the 1838 and 1840 Census records. This family must have left Barbour Co. about 1845, as they sold much land about that time, and they do not appear in the 1850 Census. William B. Mann once owned land in Walker Co., Ga., which he sold to Hosea Bailey in 1841.

Watts Mann and James W. Mann were listed on the 1818 Tax List of Conecuh Co., Ala.. Watts Mann was enumerated in the 1830 Census of Pike Co., Ala., as were William B., John W., Lewis and Gilbert Mann. In 1838 and 1840, Watts Mann was enumerated in Barbour Co., Ala., with three males under 21 and two females under 21, besides himself (b. ca 1780) and his wife (b. ca 1780). He is not in the 1850 Census, nor is there an estate settlement for him in Barbour Co.

Cooly Mann entered land South of Clayton in 1833, and John Watts Mann entered land in the same vicinity in 1831.

Sources of information:

Barbour Co., Ala. Probate Records
Barbour Co., Ala. Census Records
Pike Co., Ala. Census Records
1818 Tax List of Conecuh Co., Ala.

*ADDITIONS & CORRECTIONS AS OF JUNE 1, 1979:

Robert Mann married Harriett Bennett, who had brothers Ryan,
Redmund and Orren Bennett and sisters Siney Bennett (who m.
Elisha Davis) and Elizabeth Bennett (who died by 1859). They
may have been children of Luke and Elizabeth Bennett. Data from
Winfred Horne, Clayton, Ala.

MINSHEW

The first man of this name to patent land in Barbour Co. was Philip Minshew, who entered land in the Southwest corner in 1830. Jacob, Nathan, John, Isaac and Joseph Minshew entered land in the same area over the next twenty years. It is of interest that Isaac, Jacob, John, Kiziah and Nathan Minshew were enumerated in the 1790 Census of Dobbs Co., N. C. It was discontinued in 1791 and Green Co. was formed from part of it.

Jacob Minshew, Sr. was born ca 1770/80, died by May 1842. His wife (at the time of his death) was Sarah Holmes, b. ca 1780/90, died after 1848. Issue:

1. Sarah Minshew, b. ca 1800 N. C., m. James Graves, b. ca 1785 S. C. In 1850, they were living in Pike Co., Ala..

2. John M. Minshew, b. ca 1800 N. C., m. Harriet ----, b. ca 1810 Ga.. They later lived in Rusk Co., Texas. Issue:

   a. Merrick Minshew, b. ca 1826 Ala., m. Elizabeth A. ---- ca 1854.

   b. Eliza Minshew, b. ca 1830 Ala.

   c. Nicey Minshew, b. ca 1832 Ala., m. Hezekiah Huggins 7 Sept. 1851.

   d. Lawson Minshew, b. ca 1833 Ala.

   e. Martha Minshew, b. ca 1835 Ala., m. James Grubbs 7 Jan. 1858.

   f. John Minshew, b. ca 1836 Ala.

   g. Harriet Minshew, b. ca 1840 Ala.

   h. Samantha Minshew, b. ca 1843 Ala.

   i. Mary Minshew, b. ca 1845 Ala.

   j. Sarah Minshew, b. ca 1846 Ala.

   k. Jane Minshew, b. ca 1848 Ala.

3. Feriba Minshew, m. George Nichols.

4. Jacob Minshew, b. ca 1808 N. C., m. Mary Dansby (see page

). Issue (from 1850 Census)

a. Catherine Minshew, b. ca 1837 Ala.

b. Melissa Minshew, b. ca 1838 Ala.

c. Lorenzo Minshew, b. ca 1840 Ala.

d. Julia Minshew, b. ca 1841 Ala.

e. Alonzo Minshew, b. ca 1844 Ala.

5. Wineford Minshew, b. ca 1810 Ga., m. Garie King (probably
his second wife). He was born 18 Sept. 1801 and died 28
Jan. 1844. She married (2) Elisha Rumbley by 1849. He died
by Sept. 1853 and she married (3) Isaac H. Harrell 29 July
1855. Issue (by 1st husband - some may be his by his first
wife):

a. John W. King, b. ca 1829 Ala., m. Sarah Skiner 31 March
1853.

b. Gabriel N. King, b. ca 1830 Ala., m. Mary Spurlock 21
Jan. 1855, daughter of Solomon Spurlock.

c. Winney S. A. King, b. 27 Jan. 1832, d. Oct. 1846, buried
in King Cem. near the Pike Co. line.

d. Nancy M. King, b. ca 1833 Ala.

e. Daniel J. King, b. 3 March 1837, d. 4 June 1849, buried
in the King Cem..

f. Necy S. J. (Smithey?) King, b. ca 1840 Ala.

g. Louisa L. L. King, b. 3 Jan. 1842, d. 23 Oct. 1846,
buried in the King Cem..

6. Nicey Minshew, b. ca 1811 (Ga.?), m. William Black, b. ca
1811 Ga.. In 1850, they were living in Pike Co., Ala..
Issue (from 1850 Census Pike Co., Ala.):

a. Martha Black, b. ca 1829 Ala.

b. Abraham Black, b. ca 1832 Ala.

c. Nancy Black, b. ca 1834 Ala.

d. Henry Black, b. ca 1836 Ala.

e. Rebecca Black, b. ca 1838 Ala.

f. William Black, b. ca 1840 Ala.

g. Isaac Black, b. ca 1842 Ala.

h. James Black, b. ca 1844 Ala.

i. Edmond Black, b. ca 1845 Ala.

j. Almira Black, b. ca 1847 Ala.

k. Mary Black, b. ca 1850 Ala.

Also in this household in 1850 were Jane Graves, b. ca 1847 Ala. and Stephen Graves, b. ca 1849 Ala..

7. Isaac Minshew, b. ca 1818 N. C., m. Sarah ----, b. ca 1821 Ga.. Issue (from 1850 Census):

a. Jane Minshew, b. ca 1845 Ala.

b. Isaac Minshew, b. ca 1847 Ala.

c. Jacob Minshew, b. ca 1849 Ala.

One Nathan Minshew (called Nathan Minshew, Sr. in OR 2) died by 1847. Records of this estate are fragmentary, but the following heirs are mentioned:

1. Ava Minshew, b. ca 1802 N. C., m. Ephriam Hill, b. ca 1807 Ga.. Issue (from 1850 Census):

a. Martha Hill, b. ca 1833 Ga.

b. Woodruff Hill, b. ca 1844 Ala.

Also in this household in 1850 was Margaret Minshew, b. ca 1833 Ga..

2. Children of Joseph S. Minshew (see later). In 1847, Joseph S. Minshew was appointed guardian of his children (not named), the minor heirs of Nathan Minshew, Sr.. It is possible that he married a daughter of Nathan Minshew, Sr., so he is not given here as a son.

Another Nathan Minshew was born ca 1803 N. C., died by July 1860, m. Elizabeth (Moreland?), b. ca 1816 N. C.. Issue:

1. Catherine Minshew, b. ca 1833 Ga., m. Allen Daniels 6 March 1853. In 1860, they were living in Monroe Co., Ala.

2. Bryant Minshew, b. ca 1837 Ga., probably never married.

3. Martha A. Minshew, b. ca 1838 (Ga.?), m. Dempsey G. W. Warrick 12 Aug. 1858.

4. Margaret A. S. Minshew, b. ca 1839 Ala., m. John Roundtree 26 Feb. 1857. In 1860, they were in Pike Co., Ala.

5. Mary E. Minshew, b. ca 1840 Ala., probably died by Oct. 1860 as she is not in the list of heirs on that date.

6. Ailsey Ann Rebecca Minshew, b. ca 1841 Ala., d. by 1870, m. John Pitts by Oct. 1860, at which time they were living in Dale Co., Ala.

7. Virgil Irwin Minshew, b. ca 1842 Ala., m. Jude (?) Andrews 19 June 1866.

8. Clarissa Ann Minshew, b. ca 1843 Ala., d. by 1870, m. George Dansby 30 Aug. 1860 (see page 56).

9. Charlotte Minshew, b. ca 1844 Ala., m. Elsey F. Powell 7 Jan. 1867.

10. Caroline Minshew, b. ca 1845 Ala.

11. James Andrew Minshew, b. ca 1846 Ala., may have married Julia F. Sasser 4 Dec. 1867.

12. Hulda Minshew, b. ca 1850 Ala., m. Richard W. Scroggins 5 Dec. 1867.

13. Nancy A. Minshew, b. ca 1851 Ala., m. William J. Green 8 Jan. 1868.

14. Benjamin Alfred Minshew, b. ca 1853 Ala., may have married Martha Scroggins 14 Nov. 1875.

15. Alfred Benjamin Minshew, b. ca 1853 Ala., probably twin to Benjamin Alfred Minshew.

Also in this household in 1860 was N. M. Minshew (male), b. ca 1795 N. C. and H. B. E. Minshew (female), b. ca 1858 Ala.

Joseph S. Minshew, b. ca 1809 N. C., m. Mary (Minshew?), b. ca 1810. Issue (from 1850 Census):

1. Martha Minshew, b. ca 1827 Ga.

2. Elizabeth (Lovely?) Minshew, b. ca 1829 Ga.

3. Caleb Oliver Minshew, b. ca 1830 Ga.

4. Henry Minshew, b. ca 1831 Ga.

5. Margaret (or Missouri) Minshew, b. ca 1833 Ga.

6. Daniel Minshew, b. ca 1834 Ga.

7. Mary A. Minshew, b. ca 1836 Ga.

8. Nathan Minshew, b. ca 1837 Ala.

9. Robert Minshew, b. ca 1838 Ala.

10. Clarissa Minshew, b. ca 1840 Ala.

11. Joseph Minshew, b. ca 1841 Ala.

12. Servilla (Gracy?) Minshew, b. ca 1845 Ala.

13. William Minshew, b. ca 1847 Ala.

14. John Minshew, b. ca 1849 Ala.

Other sources:
1850 Census Pike Co., Ala.

Zacheus Nix patented land Southwest of Clayton in 1829. By 1850, he was living in Pike Co., Ala., and died in Henry Co., Ala. in 1863 at "ad advanced age".

The 1850 Census of Pike Co., Ala. states that he was age 48, born in Ga.. His will names wife Lavicey Verely Nix and the following children:

1. John E. Nix, b. ca 1826 Ala., m. Temperance ----. Known issue:

   a. Zacheus W. Nix.

   b. John G. Nix.

2. William E. Nix, b. ca 1828 Ala.

3. Mary E. Nix, b. ca 1829 Ala., m. ---- Whiddon.

4. Nancy M. Nix, b. ca 1832 Ala., m. ---- Mercer.

5. Lavicey V. Z. Nix, b. ca 1836, m. ---- Williams.

Also in the household of Zacheus and Lavicey Nix in 1850 were:

Hickman, Elizabeth, age 21, born N. C.

Spivey, Elisha, age 24, born N. C.

There is a William S. Nix, b. 1804, d. 1878, buried at Pleasant Plains Baptist Church Cemetery in Barbour Co., Ala.. The relationship, if any, to Zacheus Nix is not known.

Sources of information:

Barbour Co., Ala. Probate Records
Barbour Co., Ala. Cemetery Records
Pike Co., Ala. Census Records
Henry Co., Ala. Probate Records

William Norton, a Revolutionary Soldier, was born 1739 New Hanover Co., N. C., died 1806 Horry Co., S. C., married Mrs. Patience Minsey, a widow. She died by 1833 in Barbour Co., Ala. Issue:

1. Lewis Norton

2. Mary Norton m. Isaac Lewis.

3. William Norton, Jr. (see later).

4. James Norton (Rev.), died Columbia, S. C. in 1828.

5. Ruth Norton m. Joel Lewis (son of William Lewis and Mourning Vamplet of Horry Co., S. C.), moved to Miss..

6. John W. Norton (see later).

William Norton, Jr., b. ca 1784 Horry Co., S. C., died before 1836 Barbour Co., Ala., m. Lucretia (Creasy) Harralson, daughter of Josiah Harralson (who died 1822 Horry Co., S. C.) and Mary Vick. Lucretia (Harralson) Norton was born ca 1788, died ca 1837 Barbour Co., Ala.. William Norton, Jr., along with Stephen Johnson and others, came to Pike Co., Ala. about 1826, settling in the section from which Barbour Co. was formed in 1832. Issue:

1. Anna Jane Norton, died by 1837, married Benjamin Sellers. He may have been related to the Benjamin Sellers who was associated with William Norton in Horry Co., S. C.. Issue:

   a. Eliza Sellers m. ---- Crawford.

   b. Aida Sellers

   c. Losson (Lawson?) Sellers

2. James Russell Norton, b. 21 Dec. 1804 S. C., d. 24 Sept. 1886, m. Margaret C. Johnston, daughter of John Johnston (see JOHNSTON). She was born 4 Oct. 1808 S. C., died 30 July 1864. They are buried at Pleasant Plains Baptist Church

Cem. Issue:

a. John Johnston Norton, b. 2 Nov. 1824 S. C., d. 9 Aug.
    1887, m. Nancy J. Floyd 29 July 1841, daughter of Theo-
    philus Floyd (see FLOYD). She was born 31 July 1823 S.
    C., died 5 June 1879. They are buried at Pleasant Plains
    Baptist Church Cem.. He married (2) Josephine ---- by
    1880.[2]

b. Mary Ann Norton, b. 15 June 1826 S. C., d. 26 Sept. 1906,
    m. Thomas Ventress 21 March 1854 (see VENTRESS).

c. William James Norton, b. 19 Oct. 1827 S. C., d. 9 May
    1886, m. Sarah T. Hart, b. 4 Dec. 1829, d. 30 Dec. 1877.
    Both are buried in Judson Baptist Church Cem., Henry Co.,
    Ala..

d. Elizabeth Jane Norton, b. 22 Jan. 1829, d. 9 March 1851.

e. Norman Asbury Norton, b. 21 March 1830 Ala., d. 1 Sept.
    1898, m. Mary A. Beasley 4 Nov. 1858. She was born 24
    Sept. 1831, died 22 April 1910 (see BEASLEY). They are
    buried in Louisville Cem..

f. Catherine Margaret Norton, b. 3 Feb. 1831 Ala., d. 20
    Feb. 1871, never married. She is buried in Pleasant
    Plains Baptist Church Cem..

g. Lewis Volentine Norton, b. 8 Feb. 1833 Ala., d. 27 Nov.
    1867, m. Rosanna Cox 23 Dec. 1852, daughter of Jimpsey
    Cox and Rachel Johnson (see JOHNSON). She was born 6
    Oct. 1834, died 8 Feb. 1912. They are buried in Bethle-
    hem Cem..

h. Russell Norton, b. 2 Nov. 1834 Ala., d. 1895, m. Julia
    Ann Herring 13 Nov. 1856, daughter of John Herring. She
    was born ca 1842 Ala., died after 1880. They are buried
    in Bethlehem Cem., but the graves are not marked.

i. Martha A. Norton, b. 20 Jan. 1836 Ala., d. 12 July 1912,

m. (1) Calvin L. McCraney 15 May 1862 (2) John G. Martin
6 Jan. 1869. He was born 15 June 1830, died 13 April
1902. Martha A. and John G. Martin are buried in Old
Scott Cem..

j. an infant (twin of Martha A. Norton), b. 20 Jan. 1836,
died Aug. 1836.

k. Daniel Norton, b. 9 March 1838 Ala., d. 27 June 1898, m.
Barbara Ella Beverly 6 April 1871 (see BEASLEY). They
are buried in Pleasant Plains Baptist Ch. Cem..

l. James Norton, b. 6 June 1839 Ala., d. 4 Sept. 1888, m.
Angie T. Gravitt 27 Jan. 1876. He is buried in Pleasant
Plains Baptist Church Cem..

m. George Westley Norton, b. 17 Jan. 1841 Ala., d. 17 March
1926, m. Mary Ann Farrior 26 March 1865.

n. Fletcher Johnston Norton, b. 20 May 1842 Ala., d. in
1862 in the Civil War.

o. Patience C. Norton, b. 6 April 1844 Ala., d. 26 Jan.
1905, m. John S. Nix 15 Nov. 1860.

p. Harriett H. Norton, b. 26 May 1845 Ala., d. 9 Aug. 1869,
m. William A. Hughes 4 Feb. 1868.

q. a son, born 20 June 1846, died young.

r. a son, born 1 June 1848, died young.

s. Ann Eliza Norton, b. 20 Sept. 1849, d. 1850.

t. Cornelia Norton, b. 24 March 1852 Ala., d. 19 Oct. 1908,
m. John L. Stewart 13 Feb. 1868. He was born 1840 Newberry Dist., S. C. and died 14 Aug. 1913. They are buried in Mt. Serene Cem..

3. William Vick Norton, b. ca 1807 S. C., d. 12 June 1849 (buried Tabernacle Church Cem.), m. Isabella Floyd, b. ca 1810
S. C., d. after 1880 (see FLOYD). Issue:

a. Lucinda K. Norton, b. ca 1832 Ala., d. by 1851.

b. Delilah Amanda Norton, b. 31 Jan. 1835, d. after 1902,
    never married.

c. Caroline Elizabeth Norton, b. ca 1836 Ala., d. by 1902,
    m. Daniel B. Snead 31 Aug. 1852. He was born ca 1829
    N. C., probably died Aug. 1881.[1]

d. Nancy Ann Norton, b. ca 1838 Ala., d. June 1891, m. N.
    Allen Petty 13 Feb. 1854. He was born ca 1827 in New
    York, died 29 Aug. 1884.

e. Franklin W. Norton, b. ca 1839 Ala., d. before 1902, m.
    Sarah Hunter 23 Nov. 1869.

f. Thomas C. Norton, b. ca 1840 Ala., d. May 1902, m. Sarah
    J. McCraney 26 Feb. 1880, daughter of Norman McCraney.
    She was born ca 1856 Ala., probably died March 1885.

g. Tolbert W. M. Norton, b. ca 1841 Ala., died before 1902,
    may have married Roxie Smith 16 July 1869. She was born
    29 Dec. 1849, died 21 Feb. 1873, buried in Center Ridge
    Church Cem..

h. Erban Watson Norton, b. ca 1842 Ala., d. after 1870.

4. Mary C. Norton m. ---- Coleman.

5. Daniel Asbury Norton, b. ca 1813 S. C., moved to La. by 1891,
    died 1897. He married Lucinda Johnson 30 Nov. 1834, b. 30
    April 1811 S. C., d. by 1892, daughter of Stephen Johnson
    and Rosanna Williams (see JOHNSON). Known issue:

    a. William Asbury Norton, b. 8 March 1836 Ala., d. 10 July
        1865 in Texas.

    b. James Norton, b. 11 May 1837 Ala., d. 2 April 1864 in
        the Civil War.

    c. Mary Alizar Norton, b. 16 May 1839 Ala., d. 6 Nov. 1851.

    d. Julia Ann Norton, b. 22 May 1840 Ala., d. 26 Jan. 1908,
        probably never married.

    e. Lewis Fletcher Norton, b. 26 Oct. 1843 Ala., d. Nov.

1862 in the Civil War.

    f. Ann Elizabeth Norton, b. 28 May 1846 Ala., d. Arcadia, La., probably never married.

    g. Josephine Palestine Norton, b. 4 Aug. 1848 Ala., d. 17 Oct. 1908, m. John Burt.

    h. Frances C. Norton, b. 16 Dec. 1850 Ala., d. 15 Jan. 1915, m. Langdon Perrett.

6. John Kennedy Norton, b. ca 1816, probably left Barbour Co. between 1860 and 1870, m. Christian McLeod. Issue:

    a. John D. Norton, b. ca 1837 Ala., m. C. F. Bradberry 17 Oct. 1863.

    b. Andrew J. Norton, b. ca 1838 Ala.

    c. William C. Norton, b. ca 1840 Ala.

    d. Nancy A. Norton, b. ca 1840 Ala. (twin to William C. Norton), m. James R. Eidson 20 Dec. 1860.

    e. Sarah J. Norton, b. ca 1842 Ala.

    f. Mary E. Norton, b. ca 1844 Ala.

    g. Viney M. Norton, b. ca 1847 Ala.

    h. Laura Norton, b. ca 1854 Ala.

    i. Franklin Pierce Norton, b. 17 March 1857 Ala., died 8 Oct. 1860, buried Providence Cem..

7. Patience Elizabeth Norton, b. ca 1818/22 S. C., d. 10 May 1863, m. Lewis A. T. Johnson 3 Dec. 1837. He was born 23 March 1817 S. C., died 7 Aug. 1891 La.. He m. (2) Eliza Jane Burleson 8 Oct. 1865. Lewis A. T. Johnson was a son of Stephen and Rosanna (Williams) Johnson (see JOHNSON). Issue: By 1st wife:

    a. Nancy Ann Johnson, b. 28 July 1838 Ala., d. 29 July 1892, m. William McLeod 30 Sept. 1856. She is buried in Fairview Cem., Eufaula, Ala.. He was born 10 Aug. 1830 Kershaw Dist., S. C., died 15 Sept. 1910, m. (2) Julia Cade.

(see McLEOD).

b.   Felder Johnson, b. ca 1842 Ala., died in the Civil War.

c.   Elizabeth Johnson, b. 10 May 1845 Ala., d. 11 Sept. 1913,
     m. John W. Blair 31 Aug. 1865. He was born 25 Oct. 1836,
     died 19 June 1900. She is buried in Fairview Cem., he
     in the Bishop-Blair Cem..

d.   Rosanna Johnson, b. ca 1847 Ala., died in La..

e.   Thomas Johnson, b. 15 June 1850 Ala., d. 10 April 1909
     La., m. Julia A. Perrett in La. (Claiborne Par.?)

f.   William Ardis Johnson, b. 21 Dec. 1853 Ala., d. 28 July
     1925 La..

g.   Mary Johnson, b. ca 1856 Ala.

h.   Emma Leola Johnson, b. 5 Nov. 1858 Ala., m. William Berry
     Madden in La..

By 2nd wife:

i.   Louis Nathaniel David Johnson, b. ca 1867 Ala.

j.   Lily Johnson, b. ca 1870 Ala.

k.   Stephen Richard Johnson, b. ca 1871 Ala.

l.   Ella Elizabeth Johnson, b. ca 1873 Ala.

m.   Lucinda S. Johnson, b. ca 1875 Ala.

n.   Joseph Francis Johnson, b. ca 1878 Ala.

o.   Rastus Fouts Johnson, b. ca 1880 Ala..

John W. Norton, a Methodist minister and brother of William
Norton, Jr., entered land adjoining that of William and Lucretia
Norton by 1834. He was born 22 Jan. 1794 S. C., died 15 March
1862, m. Nancy A. Phillips. She was born 8 July 1802 N. C.,
died 8 June 1853. They are buried in Providence Cem.. Issue:

1.   Lewis Fletcher Norton, b. 1820 S. C., d. 1843, n.m.

2.   William Kennedy Norton, a Methodist minister, b. 23 Nov.
     1821 S. C., d. 13 Aug. 1894 Bullock Co., Ala., m. Martha
     Amanda Mason 19 Oct. 1854 Wilcox Co., Ala.. She was born 24

Jan. 1836 Wilcox Co., Ala., died 3 Jan. 1920 Dawson, Ga..
They are buried in Enon Cem., Bullock Co., Ala.. Issue:

a. John Mason Norton, b. 1856, d. 1930, m. Willie Narcissa
    Petty 14 Nov. 1880.

b. Willie Amanda Norton, b. 1858, d. 1859.

c. Charles Thomas Norton, b. 1861, d. 21 June 1941, m.
    Annie Belmont Petty in 1888.

d. Anna Marcella Norton, b. 1863, d. 1952, m. Uriah Cin-
    cinnatus Vinson 5 June 1902.

e. Ida Pauline Norton, b. 1865, m. Arthur Laymon Beach in
    1913.

f. Addie Lavonia Norton, b. 1867, m. Richard Edwin Pruett
    in 1891.

g. William Roccers Norton, b. 1 March 1871, d. 9 Sept. 1885,
    buried Enon Cem., Bullock Co., Ala..

h. James Tarver Norton, born and died 1874, buried Enon
    Cem., Bullock Co., Ala.

i. Paul Wesley Norton, b. 1877, d. 1905, never married.

j. Lewis K. Norton, b. 19 Aug. 1889, d. 25 July 1890.

3. Mary Ann Norton, b. 7 Dec. 1823, d. Aug. 1863, m. John E.
    Lowman 21 Sept. 1843. She is buried in Providence Cem..
    Issue:

a. Robert Franklin Lowman, b. ca 1844 Ala.

b. Adolphus W. Lowman, b. ca 1846 Ala.

c. Mariah Levonia Lowman, b. ca 1848 Ala.

4. Charity P. Norton, b. ca 1826 S. C., d. 1889, m. Dr. Charles
    Pickett 25 April 1850. He was born ca 1823 in S. C. Known
    issue:

a. John M. Pickett, b. 21 Jan. 1851, d. 29 Oct. 1852, bur-
    ied in Providence Cem..

b. William Pickett, born & died 12 Oct. 1852, buried in

Providence Cem..

c. James Pickett, b. ca 1853 Ala.

d. Mary Pickett, b. ca 1856 Ala.

e. Sally Pickett, b. ca 1858 Ala.

f. Charles Pickett, Jr., b. 20 Nov. 1859, d. 23 Nov. 1859, buried Providence Cem..

5. James Wesley Norton, b. ca 1827 S. C., d. 1902, m. Mrs. Ruth (Neally) Maxwell 28 March 1854. He was a Methodist minister.

6. Jane Ruth Norton, b. ca 1829 Ala., d. 1866, never married.

7. Lucy Catherine Norton, b. 18 Oct. 1830 Ala., d. 24 May 1902, buried in Louisville Cem.. She never married.

8. Eliza Amanda Norton, b. 1832, d. 1833.

9. Martha Juliet Norton, b. ca 1834 Ala., d. 1917 Pike Co., Ala., m. Rev. John Frederick Dickinson 18 Nov. 1852. He was born 8 Aug. 1828 Henry Co., Ala., died 31 March 1870 Pike Co., Ala., son of Rev. John Phillips Dickinson and Elvira Eliza Legg. They are buried in Little Oak Cem., Pike Co., Ala.. Issue:

a. Mary Eliza Dickinson, b. 1853, d. 1914, m. James V. Bradley.

b. James Norton Dickinson, b. 5 Oct. 1855, d. 12 Dec. 1918, m. Regina Cowart who was born 27 Feb. 1853 and died 14 Feb. 1921. They are buried in Little Oak Cem., Pike Co., Ala.

c. Sarah Elizabeth Dickinson, b. 1858, d. 1871.

d. Ella Levonia Dickinson, b. 1861, d. 1922.

e. John Phillips Dickinson (Rev.), b. 9 Dec. 1863, d. 24 June 1925, m. Emily Frances Rogers 14 June 1889.

f. Lula Cornelia Dickinson, b. 1866, d. 9 July 1904, m. James Franklin Paul.

g. George Frederick Dickinson, b. 21 May 1869, d. 24 Dec.

1952 Houston Co., Ala., m. Addie Beulah Worthington of Lumpkin, Ga. on 16 Jan. 1894. They are buried in Little Oak Cem., Pike Co., Ala..

10. Ethelbert Brinkley Norton (Rev.), b. 15 March 1836 Ala., d. 14 May 1872 Oxford, Ala., m. (1) Lucinda B. Storey 9 Aug. 1859 Macon Co., Ala.. She was born 21 Sept. 1837 Fayette Co., Ga., died 7 Nov. 1861 and is buried in Providence Cem.. She was a daughter of Rev. Elias Wells Storey and Anna Hill. He married (2) Rebecca Frances Slaughter 11 Nov. 1862 Chambers Co., Ala.. She was born 30 March 1841 Putnam Co., Ga., died 25 Oct. 1902 Athens, Ala., daughter of William Allen Slaughter and Mary Susan Mathis. She is buried at Oxford, Ala.. Issue:

By 1st wife:

a. John Wells Norton (Rev.), b. 2 Sept. 1860, d. 20 June 1940, m. Martha Ann Maddux 30 July 1882.

b. Charles Edward Norton, b. 3 Nov. 1861, d. 11 April 1879 White Plains, Ala., never married.

By 2nd wife:

c. Eugene Harwell Norton, b. 14 Aug. 1863, d. 26 April 1933 in Texas, m. Delilah Estelle Elrod 24 Dec. 1883 of Geraldine, Ala..

d. Ethelbert Brinkley Norton (Rev.), Jr., b. 9 Oct. 1865, d. 8 June 1938, m. Betty Grace Myatt 28 May 1895.

e. William Rutledge Norton, b. 6 Aug. 1868, d. 1949, m. Mary Elizabeth Glass in 1895.

f. Thomas Watkins Norton, b. 22 April 1870, d. 11 April 1888, never married.

g. Susan Cunningham Norton, b. 27 Dec. 1871, d. 14 April 1917, never married - buried Elmwood Cem., B'ham, Ala..

11. Edward Arnold Norton, b. 1838 Ala., d. 1879, m. Bettie

Ellen Smith.

12. Wilbur Fisk Norton (Rev.), b. 22 July 1840 Ala., d. 14 Sept.
    1906 Bronson, Fla., m. Sarah Elizabeth Cassady 7 Dec. 1865,
    daughter of Alexander and Temperance Cassady. She was born
    17 Sept. 1844 Henry Co., Ala., died 10 Oct. 1913 Bronson,
    Fla. where both are buried. Issue:

    a. Stella Ellen Norton, b. 22 May 1868 Bullock Co., Ala.,
        d. 28 Feb. 1945, m. Edward Kirby Whiddon 31 Dec. 1890.

    b. William Clarence Norton (Rev.), b. 20 Feb. 1870, d. 17
        July 1954, m. Eva May Watts.

    c. Minnie Lee Norton, b. 2 April 1872, m. Samuel Leonidas
        Bean 25 April 1901.

    d. Wilbur Fisk Norton, Jr., b. 2 Jan. 1875, m. Bessie Lee
        Thatcher 31 July 1903.

    e. Marvin Hendricks Norton (Rev.), b. 20 July 1877, d. 3
        Aug. 1945, m. Maud McKenzie 9 June 1910.

    f. Annie Lore Norton, b. 1 June 1879, d. 10 Oct. 1920, m.
        John Reddick Willis 1902.

13. Georgiana Dickinson Norton, b. 2 Oct. 1842 Ala., d. 8 May
    1902, m. John Robert Allen Passmore 20 May 1867.

14. Thomas Coke Norton, b. 1845 Ala., d. 1867, never married.
    He was also a Methodist minister.

15. Cornelia Adrena Caroline Norton, b. 18 Aug. 1848 Ala., d. 25
    June 1876 at Lawrenceville (Henry Co.), Ala., m. Alexander
    A. Cassady 29 Dec. 1874, possibly in Bullock Co., Ala..

Other sources:
Methodist Conference Historical Records
Horry Co., S. C. Court records
William R. Johnson Bible
CSA records
Henry Co., Ala. Cemetery records
Pike Co., Ala. Cemetery records

1. She married (2) D. E. Nix 13 Sept. 1896.

2. John J. Norton m. (2) Joe (Josephine) Raley 24 June 1880.

PARMER

Three Parmer's (Benjamin, Jacob and George W.) were very early settlers of this area. They were probably closely related, as they patented land in the same general neighborhood.

Benjamin Parmer was born ca 1781 Maryland, according to the 1850 Census, and died 28 Jan. 1857. The name of his first wife is not known - he married (2) Nancy ---- ca 1836. She was born ca 1822 S. C., died by 1856 and he married (3) Mary (Grubbs) Sloan, widow of John Sloan, Sr., on 1 Oct. 1856. She was born ca 1803 Ga.....she married (4) Mathew Laseter 24 Sept. 1857 (see GRUBBS). Benjamin Parmer served in the War of 1812 in the Jones Co., Ga. Militia. Issue (by 1st wife):

1. Jefferson Parmer, b. ca 1806 Ga., d. after 1860, probably never married. He was living with Benjamin Parmer in 1850 and with Jacob Parmer in 1860.

2. Saleta Parmer, b. ca 1807 Ga., m. Richard Sikes. Issue (from 1850 and 1860 Census):

    a. Mary Ann Mahala Sikes, b. ca 1838 Ala., m. (1)Charles Stewart ca 1858 (2) Newton M. B. Scrimshire 14 March 1867 Clarke Co., Miss.

    b. John R. Sikes, b. ca 1842 Ala., in Clarke Co., Miss. by 1880.

    c. Martha C. Sikes, b. ca 1843 Ala..

    d. Hetty E. Sikes, b. ca 1845 Ala., m. Jordon Welch ca 1873 in Clarke Co., Miss. in 1880.

    d. Nancy Jane Sikes, b. ca 1847 Ala., m. ---- Brazier ca 1867, in Clarke Co., Miss. in 1880.

3. Nancy Parmer, b. ca 1812 Ga., d. 7 July 1879, m. William Grubbs (see GRUBBS).

4. Hettie Parmer, b. 16 Aug. 1810 Ga., d. 20 July 1885, m. Lewis Miller, b. 8 May 1803 N. C., d. 10 May 1895. Both are

239

buried in Rocky Mount Cem.. Probable issue:

a. James Miller, b. ca 1830 Ala., d. July 1895 (?), may have married Mary Kent 21 Dec. 1853.

b. Catherine Miller, b. ca 1834 Ala., possibly married William Winslett 26 Dec. 1850.

c. Mary Miller, b. ca 1836 Ala.

d. Cinthia Miller, b. ca 1838 Ala.

e. Nancy J. Miller, b. ca 1840, not married in 1880.

f. Amanda Miller, b. ca 1841 Ala., not married 1870.

g. Joanna (Savannah?) Miller, b. ca 1842 Ala., not married in 1880.

h. Emeline Miller, b. ca 1844 Ala.

i. Jinsey A. Miller, b. ca 1845 Ala., not married in 1880.

j. Jefferson Miller, b. ca 1848 Ala., m. Dolly Vann 13 Oct. 1870.

k. Lewis William Miller, b. ca 1856 Ala., m. Alabama ---- by 1880.

5. Zachariah Wesley Parmer, b. ca 1820 Ala., m. Mary (Jane?) Tindall 16 June 1842. In 1857, they were living in Texas. Issue (from 1850 Census):

a. James Parmer, b. ca 1846 Ala.

b. Henrietta Parmer, b. ca 1849 Ala.

6. Jacob H. Parmer, b. ca 1824 Ala., m. Lydia F. Pendol and moved to Henderson Co., Texas. Issue:

a. Mary P. Parmer, b. ca 1849 Ala., m. ---- Bragg.

b. Sarah E. Parmer, b. ca 1856 Ala.

c. Ann R. Parmer, b. ca 1857 Ala.

d. male, born ca 1860 Ala.

e. Ida Parmer, b. 17 March 1868 Upshure Co., Texas, d. 16 March 1942 Garvin Co., Okla. (from death certificate), m. William Theodore Williams. He was born 13 April 1865

Texas, died 15 Nov. 1931 Garvin Co., Okla..

7. Cynthia Parmer, died by 1856, m. ---- Williams. Issue:

   a. Stephen Williams, living in Henry Co., Ala. and of age
      in 1857.

   Issue (by 2nd wife):

8. George W. Parmer, b. ca 1839 Ala., living with John P.
   DuBose in 1860.

9. Sarah A. E. Parmer, b. ca 1841 Ala., m. John P. DuBose 28
   Jan. 1858. Issue (from 1860 & 1870 Census):

   a. Leonora DuBose, b. ca 1859 Ala.

   b. Eugene DuBose, b. ca 1862 Ala.

   c. Eulalia DuBose, b. ca 1865 Ala.

   d. Ewel DuBose (female?), b. ca 1866 Ala.

   e. John DuBose, b. ca 1868 Ala.

   f. Sarah DuBose, b. March 1870 Ala.

10. Amanda P. Parmer, b. ca 1844 Ala., m. Goodwin Streator 19
    Dec. 1867. He died 15 June 1872. Issue:

    a. Wallace Streator, b. ca 1869 Ala.

    b. Mary Streator

11. Andrew J. Parmer, b. ca 1846 Ala., may have married Minerva
    Reaves 24 Dec. 1868.

12. James Lafayette Parmer, b. ca 1846 (twin to Andrew J.
    Parmer).

13. John F. (or H.) Parmer, b. ca 1848 Ala.

14. William B. Parmer, minor in 1857.

15. Green Beauchamp Parmer, minor in 1857.

Jacob Parmer, b. ca 1794 Ga., d. 2 Oct. 1866, m. Martha
Stripling 30 Dec. 1812 Jones Co., Ga.. She was born ca 1795 and
died ca June 1883. Jacob Parmer was in the War of 1812 in the
Georgia Militia and later received bounty land in Barbour Co.,
Ala. for his service. Issue:

241

1. Elizabeth Parmer, b. ca 1816 Ga., d. by 1884, m. William Gilmore. He was born ca 1807 Ga., died by 1884. In 1869, they were living in Green Co., Ala.. Known issue:

   a. Martha Gilmore, b. ca 1838 Ala., m. William L. Rigdon 17 Jan. 1867.

   b. Rebecca A. Gilmore, b. ca 1840 Ala., probably died young.

   c. George Gilmore, b. ca 1843 Ala., probably died young.

   d. Aaron W. Gilmore, b. ca 1848 Ala., living Green Co., Ala. in 1884.

   e. Joseph Gilmore, living Green Co., Ala. in 1884.

   f. Mary Gilmore, living Green Co., Ala. in 1884.

2. Ellender (Nelly) C. Parmer, b. ca 1818 Ga., d. by 1887, m. Asher Reaves 17 Dec. 1845 (she was his second wife). He was born ca 1799 N. C., died Jan. 1887. Issue (by 1st wife):

   a. Elizabeth Reaves m. John Jones 31 July 1842.

   b. Mary Ann Reaves m. John A. Rogers 23 Sept. 1845, living in Texas in 1887.

   c. David S. Reaves, b. ca 1821 Ga., d. 6 Dec. 1900, buried Mt. Serene Cem. (grave not marked), m. (1) Mahala Evans 13 Nov. 1842 (2) Mrs. Jane Stewart in 1864.

   d. Sarah Reaves, b. ca 1826 Ga., m. Hardy Stephenson 7 Jan. 1842.

   e. Rebecca Ann Reaves, b. ca 1835 Ga., m. William Flowers 13 Feb. 1853, living Henry Co., Ala. 1887.

   f. Lydia Reaves, b. ca 1830 Ga., d. by 1887, m. (James?) Glass in 1850. Their children were in Butler Co., Ala. in 1887.

   g. Wellborn J. Reaves, b. ca 1838 Ala., d. by 1880, m. Mary Amanda Williams 2 Dec. 1857 (see WILLIAMS).

   h. Scitha Reaves, b. ca 1841 Ala., m. (1) Malcolm McGilvray 30 Sept. 1858 (see McGILVRAY). She m. (2) William Woods

242

27 May 1869.

Issue (by 2nd wife):

i. Amanda (Nancy?) Reaves, b. ca 1847 Ala., m. William J.
Fortner 29 Nov. 1865.

j. Martha C. Reaves, b. ca 1849 Ala., d. after 1887, m.
John F. Faulk 31 Dec. 1867. He was born 5 March 1847
Ala., d. 29 Dec. 1938 in Oklahoma. In 1880, they were
living in Navarro Co., Texas (see FAULK).

k. Narcissa Reaves, b. ca 1853 Ala., probably never married.

l. Margaret L. Reaves, b. ca 1855 Ala., m. James Ventress
25 May 1880 (see VENTRESS).

3. Mary Pary Parmer, b. ca 1820 Ga., d. 24 Oct. 1884, m. Robert
B. Lee 15 Dec. 1842. He was born 11 Dec. 1822 S. C., d. 7
June 1903. They are buried in Pond Bethel Cem.. He m. (2)
Ida E. Griffin 27 Sept. 1887 (see LEE). Known issue (by
1st wife):

a. Needham T. Lee, b. 22 Sept. 1843 Ala., d. 7 Jan. 1906,
buried Pond Bethel Cem .. He may have married Annie E.
Bryan 11 July 1872.

b. Elmira P. Lee, b. ca 1846 Ala., m. James T. (or F.)
Creel 28 Aug. 1867. In 1884, they were living in Georgia
and in 1903 they were living in Bluffton, Ga..

c. Matilda A. Lee, b. 24 Nov. 1847 Ala., d. 18 Dec. 1925,
m. Joseph Searcy. He was born 8 Feb. 1846, died 11 Aug.
1925. In 1884, they were living in Henry Co., Ala. but
they are buried in Pond Bethel Cem..

d. Mary A. E. Lee, b. 10 July 1850 Ala., d. 10 Sept. 1917,
m. George W. Zorn 11 Feb. 1869. He was b. 9 April 1846,
d. 22 Dec. 1922 - both are buried in Pond Bethel Cem..

Issue (by 2nd wife):

e. Jeffie E. Lee, b. ca 1888, m. Onie E. Green 20 Dec. 1908.

f. Edna I. Lee, b. 8 Feb. 1894, m. T. C. Green 29 Jan. 1911. He was born 13 Nov. 1891 and died 26 Jan. 1948. They are buried in Pond Bethel Cem..

g. Robert E. Lee m. Mayme Delle Bruner 24 Dec. 1919.

4. Rebecca Parmer, b. 8 Dec. 1822 Ga., m. Abner Wilkerson 1 Nov. 1881. He was born 16 May 1818 Ga., died 24 March 1889. She was his third wife - he married (1) Matilda Taylor 1 Feb. 1842 (2) Rosaline J. Kent 15 Dec. 1863. Probable issue:

a. Frances Wilkerson, b. 9 Feb. 1843.

b. Lewis Wilkerson, b. 15 Nov. 1844.

c. Daniel Wilkerson, b. 23 Oct. 1845.

d. Nora Wilkerson, b. 16 June 1846.

e. J. P. D. Wilkerson, b. 7 Oct. 1850.

f. Sarah Wilkerson, b. 4 June 1853.

g. Matilda R. Wilkerson, b. 14 Sept. 1855.

h. Edmond A. Wilkerson, b. 21 Nov. 1857 Ga.

i. Neil T. Wilkerson, b. 24 Jan. 1861 Ga., d. 2 Oct. 1940, m. Vickie Caroline Baker 27 Dec. 1884. She was born 21 Feb. 1865 and died 5 July 1921. They are buried in Rocky Mount Cem..

5. Matilda (Cynthia?) Parmer, b. ca 1827 Ala., d. by 1884, m. William D. Cooper 17 Jan. 1850. He was born ca 1828 Ala.. In 1869, they were living in Titus Co., Texas. Issue:

a. James Cooper, b. ca 1851 Ala.

b. John Cooper, b. ca 1853 Ala.

c. Cynthia Cooper, b. ca 1855 Ala.

d. William Cooper, b. ca 1856 Ala.

e. Thomas J. Cooper, b. ca 1858 Ala.

f. Charles Cooper

g. Jacob Cooper

h. Amanda Cooper

6. Nancy Parmer, b. ca 1828 Ala., d. after 1884, m. Timothy Lee 14 Nov. 1845 (see LEE).

7. Eliza Parmer m. Jackson Moore - they lived in Butler Co., Ala..

8. Benjamin Ephriam George Parmer, b. 22 Dec. 1830 Ala., d. 11 Oct. 1918, m. Mary A. Holly 23 Jan. 1851. She was born 30 Aug. 1825, died 18 March 1900. They are buried in Rocky Mount Cem.. Issue:

   a. Aaron Parmer, b. 1851 Ala., d. 1948, m. Elizabeth Holly 2 Jan. 1896. She was born 22 Sept. 1857, died 17 Oct. 1901. They are buried in Rocky Mount Cem..

   b. Moses E. Parmer, b. 1853 Ala., d. 1934, m. Lydia A. Parmer (daughter of Jacob Parmer and Adaline Baker) on 28 Feb. 1877. She was born 1851 Ala., d. 1935 - both buried Rocky Mount Cem..

   c. Martha J. Parmer, b. 24 Feb. 1857 Ala., d. 27 Jan. 1936, m. Quinn Lewis 19 Jan. 1879. He was born 22 May 1852 and died 5 Feb. 1906.

   d. John Parmer, b. ca 1868 Ala.

9. Joseph L. Parmer, b. ca 1834 Ala., d. after 1884, m. Roxanna Bush 2 Nov. 1854 (see BUSH). In 1884, they were living in Lauderdale Springs, Miss. Known issue:

   a. Gordon Parmer, b. ca 1855 Ala.

   b. Edward Parmer, b. ca 1859 Ala.

   c. Dora Parmer, b. ca 1862 Ala.

   d. Tyson Pitt Parmer, b. ca 1868 Ala.

10. John W. Parmer, b. ca 1840 Ala., d. by 1866, m. Angeline Thomas 14 July 1859. She m. (2) Riley Morris 10 June 1866. Issue:

    a. John W. Parmer

    b. Martha Parmer, b. ca 1862

245

c. Camilla Jane Parmer m. John Preston (or James Preston).

11. William W. Parmer, b. ca 1838 Ala., d. by 1884, m. Sarah DuBose 28 Oct. 1861.

George W. Parmer, b. ca 1797 Ga., d. by May 1864, m. (1) Rightly Kent 6 June 1815 Jones Co., Ga. (2) Nancy DuBose 20 Oct. 1850. Issue (all by 1st wife):

1. Martha Parmer m. William R. Tomlin 14 Nov. 1843. They were living in Dale Co., Ala. in 1866, later in Butler Co., Ala.

2. Benjamin C. Parmer, b. 22 July 1818 Ga., d. 7 Oct. 1885, m. Sarah Ann (Spurlock?). She was born 27 April 1820 Ga., died 28 June 1905. They are buried in Bethel Cem.. Probable issue:

    a. Sarah Jane Parmer, b. ca 1841 Ala.

    b. Lucinda Parmer, b. ca 1844 Ala.

    c. Mary C. Parmer, b. ca 1847 Ala., not married 1880.

    d. George W. Parmer, Jr., b. 13 Sept. 1849 Ala., d. 27 Nov. 1937, m. Mary J. Helms 8 Jan. 1873. She was born 3 March 1844, died 29 June 1910. They are buried in Bethel Baptist Cem..

    e. Eliza Parmer, b. ca 1859 Ala., not married 1880.

    f. Emaline Parmer, b. ca 1861 Ala., not married 1880.

    g. William Benjamin Parmer, b. 3 Jan. 1855 Ala., d. 8 April 1891, m. Margaret Horn 17 Dec. 1874. She was born 3 April 1856 and died 22 July 1938. They are buried in Bethel Baptist Cem..

    h. John Berry Parmer, b. 15 June 1853, d. 25 Nov. 1921, m. Sarah Jane Miller 19 Dec. 1877. She was born 1860, died 1944 Bethel Baptist Cem..

3. L. B. (Littleberry) J. Parmer, b. ca 1820 Ga., d. ca March 1883, buried Edwin Cem., Henry Co., Ala.. He married Mrs. Elizabeth (Horn?) Winslett. They were living in Dale Co.,

Ala. in 1868 and in Henry Co., Ala. in 1870. Known issue:

a. Amanda Parmer, b. ca 1839 Ala., no record after 1850.

b. George C. Parmer, b. ca 1839 Ala.

c. Parazade Parmer, b. ca 1841 Ala.

d. Rosanna Parmer, b. ca 1846 Ala.

e. Jacob J. Parmer, b. ca 1849 Ala.

f. Georgeann A. Parmer, b. ca 1852 Ala.

g. Mary Ann Parmer, b. 3 July 1856 Ala., m. Wesley Solon Wright 1 Jan. 1874. He was born 6 April 1854, died 11 Nov. 1902.

Also in the L. B. J. Parmer household in 1850 was Judy Horne, age ·102, born Virginia.

4. Jacob Parmer, b. ca 1826 Ga., d. by 1868, m. Adeline Baker 4 Oct. 1849 (daughter of James Baker, Jr.). Issue:

a. James Berry Parmer, b. 1850 Ala., probably married Annie Valentine 22 Jan. 1879.

b. William W. Parmer, b. ca 1854 Ala.

c. Lydia Ann Parmer, b. ca 1852 Ala., m. Moses E. Parmer 28 Feb. 1877 (son of B. E. G. Parmer).

d. Enos H. (or A.) Parmer, b. ca 1856 Ala., living in Taylor, Texas in 1897.

e. Margaret E. Parmer, b. ca 1857 Ala., not married in 1897 and living in Taylor, Texas.

f. John T. Parmer, b. ca 1858 Ala., m. Sallie J. Sims 8 March 1887, living Granger, Texas 1897.

g. Mary V. Parmer, b. ca 1861 Ala., m. ---- Cummings, probably living Taylor, Texas in 1897.

h. Emma A. Parmer, b. ca 1866 Ala., m. ---- Lee, living Taylor, Texas in 1897.

i. Ida Parmer, probably died by 1897.

5. Eliza Parmer, b. ca 1832 Ga., m. William R. Smith 29 Nov.

1849. They went to Texas in 1870 with Elijah Ray. A daughter, Lydia, married Willis House Ray, son of Elijah Ray.

6. Elizabeth Parmer m. Green Miller 12 Oct. 1848. He died by 1868.

7. Caroline Parmer, b. ca 1836 Ala., d. by 1868 m. (1) John Thomas Carter 27 June 1855 (2) ---- Eason by 1866, lived Dale Co., Ala.. Issue:

   a. Marion Carter

   b. Isaac Carter

8. William Wellborn Parmer, b. ca 1839 Ala.

9. Mary Parmer m. John Bullock.

Other sources:

Jones Co., Ga. Marriage records
Wilkerson family Bible
Pension Application of Martha Stripling Parmer
Information from descendants

PAYNE

Elijah Payne entered land east of Louisville in 1829, but probably never lived on it. He died in Dale Co., Ala. in October 1885. John Payne and Benjamin Payne entered land in Barbour Co. in 1836, but there is no indication that any of them were kin. Benjamin Payne sold his land in 1837.

Williamson Payne died in Barbour Co. ca June 1849. His wife, Sarah ----, was born ca 1804 S. C., and was living with Joseph Payne in 1850. His estate was left to his wife and the following brothers and sisters:

1. Joseph Payne, b. ca 1808 S. C., d. 12 Nov. 1880, m. Lydia ----, b. ca 1815 S. C., d. after 1880. Issue:

   a. Frankey Payne, b. ca 1834 Ala., m. Thompson Howell. In 1880, they were living in Union Co., Ark.

   b. Rhoda Payne, b. 9 Aug. 1836 Ala., d. 27 Feb. 1898, m. S. K. Shirah, b. 1 Oct. 1818, d. 27 Feb. 1898. They are buried in Bethel Baptist Church Cemetery.

   c. Sarah Payne, b. ca 1838 Ala.

   d. Absalom Payne, b. ca 1841 Ala.

   e. Nancy Payne, b. ca 1843 Ala., m. John Dykes 11 Jan. 1866. In 1880, they were living in Dale Co., Ala.

   f. Judge S. Payne, b. ca 1845 Ala.

   g. Elizabeth Payne, b. ca 1848 Ala., m. Franklin Leroy Medley 11 Jan. 1866.

   h. Joseph Payne, b. ca 1856 Ala., living in Dale Co., Ala. 1880.

   i. Lydia E. Payne, b. ca 1858 Ala., m. John Medley. They were living in Dale Co., Ala. in 1880.

2. Martha Payne, m. Odin Martin. In 1852, they were living in Georgia.

3. Mary Payne m. Williamson Collier. In 1852, they were living

in Dale Co., Ala.

4. A. Jackson Payne, living in Dale Co., Ala. in 1852.

5. John Payne, living in Georgia in 1852.

6. L. C. Davis Payne, living in Georgia in 1852.

7. A. E. Payne, d. ca 1881 in Dale Co., Ala.

8. Elisha Payne, residence unknown in 1852.

Sources of information:

Barbour Co., Ala. Probate records
Barbour Co., Ala. Census records
Barbour Co., Ala. Cemetery records

PETERSON

Thomas B. Peterson entered land West of Louisville in 1827 and 1829. He was not enumerated in any early Barbour Co. census, so he probably never lived on his land. There was a Thomas B. Peterson who was enumerated in the 1830 Census of Early Co., Ga., who could have been the same man. In 1830, Early Co., Ga. extended much further North, and part of it lay directly across the line from Barbour Co., Ala..

Sources of information:

Barbour Co., Ala. Probate Records
Early Co., Ga. Census Records

PITTS

Obadiah Pitts patented land West of Louisville in 1827. There is no further record of him in Barbour Co. He was a county commissioner of Pike Co., Ala. in 1822.

Source of information:

Barbour Co., Ala. Probate Records

PRUETT
(Pruitt)

John Pruett first entered land Northwest of Louisville in 1829, and continued to enter land in this area until 1836. In 1836 and 1837, Robert B. Pruett and James M. Pruett entered land adjoining him. In 1847, James M. Pruett entered land in what is now Bullock Co., Ala., and he was living there by 1860. Although there is nothing in the probate records to prove it, John Pruett was probably the father of Robert B. and James M. Pruett.

In 1840, John Pruett and wife, Mary, sold their land to John Douglass. In 1850, Mary Pruett, b. ca 1790 in Ga., was enumerated next to James M. Pruett. John Pruett, b. 3 Jan. 1785, d. 11 July 1842 and Mary Pruett, d. 29 Oct. 1855, age 62 years, are buried in Fellowship Cemetery, Bullock Co., Ala. Probable issue of John and Mary Pruett:

1. Robert Pruett - may have married Ann Augusta Coleman, daughter of William and Kiziah Coleman.

2. James Madison Pruett, b. 1815 Ga., d. 17 Nov. 1878 Bullock Co., Ala., m. Louisa, daughter of Samuel Feagin on 17 May 1836. She was born 28 March 1818 Ga., died 8 Dec. 1895 Bullock Co., Ala.. Both are buried in Fellowship Cemetery, Bullock Co., Ala.. Issue:

   a. Martha Pruett, b. ca 1839, m. James Turman 3 June 1857.

   b. Sarah Pruett, b. ca 1840 Ala., m. ---- Griffin.

   c. William H. Pruett, b. 20 May 1841 Ala., d. 9 Jan. 1910, m. (1) Ann E. Browder 9 Dec. 1867. She was born 18 Jan. 1843, died 10 Nov. 1880. Both are buried in Fairview Cemetery, Eufaula, Ala.. He married (2) Ann Roberts, b. 4 June 1847, died 26 Jan. 1891, also buried in Fairview Cemetery.

   d. John E. Pruett, b. ca 1843 Ala., killed in Civil War.

e. Samuel T. Pruett, b. ca 1846 Ala.

f. James W. Pruett, b. ca 1847 Ala.

g. Lee Pruett, b. ca 1849 Ala.

h. Seth G. Pruett, b. ca 1850 Ala., d. Feb. 1901 in Mont-
    gomery (Ala.).

i. George Pruett, b. ca 1852 Ala.

j. Louisa Pruett, b. ca 1855 Ala., d. June 1893, m. E. H.
    Fitzpatrick.

"Memorial Record of Alabama" states that John Pruett, son of
a Revolutionary Soldier who died in the Revolution, came to what
is now Barbour Co., Ala. about 1819 and settled near Louisville.

Sources of information:

Barbour Co., Ala. Probate Records
Barbour Co., Ala. Census Records
Barbour Co., Ala. Cemetery Records
Bullock Co., Ala. Cemetery Records
"Memorial Record of Alabama"

Robert Pugh, b. ca 1784, d. 5 Aug. 1831 (buried Fairview Cemetery, Eufaula, Ala.), m. Anne Silvia Tilman.* They lived in Burke Co., Ga. until about 1824, and she probably died there. Possible issue:

1. Alfred Pugh, b. by 1812, probably in Ga., entered land in the Southwest part of Barbour Co. in 1829 and 1834. He is listed in the 1838 Census of Barbour Co., living alone. In 1840, he deeded his land in Pike Co., Ala. to his brother, Robert Pugh, Jr..

2. Ann S. Pugh, b. ca 1812 Ga., d. 1869 Bullock Co., Ala., m. Dr. William L. Cowan 21 Feb. 1834. He was born ca 1807 Tenn., died 2 May 1859 at Eufaula, Ala.. Known issue:

   a. Maldonetta Cowan, b. ca 1837 Ala., m. (1) Samuel W. Wallace 22 March 1854, (2) James M. Buford 14 June 1859.

   b. Laura J. Cowan, b. ca 1839 Ala., m. Robert A. Fleming 22 Sept. 1858.

   c. James Cowan, b. ca 1840 Ala.

   d. Mary Cowan, b. ca 1842 Ala., may have married William A. Bishop 20 Oct. 1875.

   e. Ann Cowan, b. ca 1844 Ala.

   f. Emily Cowan, b. ca 1846 Ala.

   g. Rosa Cowan, b. ca 1848 Ala.

   h. Willie Cowan, b. ca 1857 Ala., d. 25 Dec. 1885 Atlanta, Ga., m. Robert G. Jelks 18 Jan. 1883.

3. Mary Pugh m. William J. Bush 16 Nov. 1846.

4. Theophilis Pugh - in 1834, he was a minor, living in Pike Co., Ala.. His guardian was Benjamin D. Sellars.

5. Robert Pugh, Jr. was a minor in 1833. The bond of his guardian, Alfred Pugh, was recorded in Pike Co., Ala. on 5 June 1833. On 27 Jan. 1840, Alfred Pugh deeded land in

Pike Co., Ala. to him.

6. James Lawrence Pugh, b. 12 Dec. 1820 Ga., d. 9 March 1907 in
    Washington, D. C., m. Sarah Serena Hunter 1 Nov. 1846. She
    was born 10 Aug. 1830 S. C., died 22 Nov. 1911. Both are
    buried in Fairview Cemetery, Eufaula, Ala.. Issue:

    a. Laura Teresa Pugh, b. 19 Oct. 1849, d. 19 April 1935, m.
        Alfred Wellborn Cochran 22 Oct. 1869. He was born 29
        July 1845, died 1935. They are buried in Fairview Ceme-
        tery, Eufaula, Ala..

    b. Jefferson Buford Pugh, b. 17 Dec. 1851, d. 18 Dec. 1851,
        buried in Fairview Cemetery, Eufaula, Ala.

    c. James Pugh

    d. Edward Pugh

    e. John Pugh m. Inez Powell

    f. Sarah Pugh, b. 10 March 1864, d. 18 Oct. 1949, m. Albert
        Elliott. She is buried in Fairview Cemetery, Eufaula,
        Ala..

    g. Robert Pugh, b. ca 1871, d. 15 Dec. 1879, buried in
        Fairview Cemetery, Eufaula, Ala.

James Pugh, a nephew or brother of Robert Pugh, patented
land near Louisville between 1829 and 1833. He was sheriff of
Pike Co., Ala. in 1829, and is listed in the 1830 Census there,
as are Francis W. Pugh, Thomas Pugh, John M. Pugh, Jesse M. Pugh,
Levi (Lewis?) Pugh and Alfred Pugh. James Pugh married Elizabeth ----, died by July 1835. The names of his children, if any,
are not given in the county records.

Jesse Pugh, b. ca 1776 Va., d. by March 1852 in Pike Co.,
Ala., probably never lived in Barbour Co.. However, as he is
evidently related to the Pugh family of Barbour Co., his family
is included here. His wife was Lydia ----, b. ca 1777 Va., d.

by 1870 in Pike Co., Ala.. Known issue:

1. Martin (or Mastin) B. Pugh, b. ca 1795 S. C., m. Charlotte
   ----. She was born ca 1815 N. C.. They were living in Butler Co., Ala. in 1870. Known issue:
   a. Margaret Pugh, b. ca 1835 Ala.
   b. Lydia Pugh, b. ca 1837 Ala.
   c. Adaline Pugh, b. ca 1839 Ala.
   d. Mary Pugh, b. ca 1841 Ala.
   e. Oliver Pugh, b. ca 1843 Ala.
   f. Rhody Pugh, b. ca 1845 Ala.
   g. Louisa Pugh, b. ca 1846 Ala.
   h. William Pugh, b. ca 1848 Ala.
   i. Lucinda Pugh, b. ca 1849 Ala.

2. Malinda Pugh m. ---- Stinson. She was a widow by 1852.

3. Burrell B. Pugh, b. ca 1799 S. C., d. 20 Sept. 1855 Pike Co.,
   Ala., m. Barbara ----. Known issue:
   a. Willoughby Pugh, b. ca 1827 Ala.
   b. Sarah Pugh, b. ca 1831 Ala., m. ---- Wingard.
   c. Hannah Pugh, b. ca 1833 Ala., m. ---- Smart.
   d. Adaline Pugh, b. ca 1835 Ala.
   e. Alexander Pugh, b. ca 1838 Ala.
   f. Jesse Pugh, b. ca 1840 Ala.
   g. Lydia Pugh, b. ca 1842 Ala.
   h. Mary Pugh, b. ca 1844 Ala.
   i. David Pugh, b. ca 1846 Ala.
   j. (possibly) Wade Pugh, b. ca 1826 Ala.

4. Mary (Polly) Ann Pugh, died by 1852, m. (Edmond M.?) Wiggins.
   Known issue:
   a. Lydia Wiggins
   b. Jane Wiggins
   c. Rhoda Wiggins

d. Margaret Wiggins

e. Martha Wiggins

f. Jesse Wiggins

g. Harrison Wiggins

h. Mastin Wiggins

5. Elizabeth Pugh, died by 1852. The records are not clear as
    to whether she was a daughter or daughter-in-law. Her chil-
    dren were:

    a. Jesse Pugh

    b. Louis Pugh

    c. John Pugh

    d. Emeline Pugh

    e. Rebecca Pugh

    f. Lydia Pugh

    g. Albert D. Pugh

    h. Betsey Pugh

6. Ira Pugh, living in Lowndes Co., Ala. in 1870.

7. Albert B. Pugh, living in Butler Co., Ala. in 1870.

8. Lewis Pugh, living in Montgomery Co., Ala. in 1870.

9. Adaline Pugh m. Stephen Blackburn. He died by 1870, and at
    that time she was living in Butler Co., Ala.

There was another Lewis Pugh, who died between 1836 and 1838
in either Barbour or Pike Co.. His wife, Rebecca ----. Known
issue:

1. Jesse N. Pugh

2. Emaline B. Pugh m. Simon Stinson by 1836.

Thomas Pugh was the first Clerk of Circuit Court of Barbour
Co.. He entered land near Louisville in 1833 and 1835. There
was also a Dr. Thomas F. Pugh who married Nancy McSwean 26 Feb.
1850, daughter of Roderick C. McSwean (see McSwean family). They

258

moved to Jefferson Co., Texas by 1852.

Finally, there was a Francis W. Pugh, who was involved in many land transactions in Barbour Co.. He is listed in the 1830 Census of Pike Co., Ala., and in the 1838 Census of Barbour Co., Ala., at which time there were 2 males under 21, 1 male over 21, 2 females under 21 and 1 female over 21 in his household. He is not included in any other census of Barbour Co., although he was still called "of Barbour Co." in deeds after 1840. In the deed records, his wife signed as Mary Pugh. In 1834, Francis W. Pugh and Churchwell Gorman patented land together, which they sold to Seth Lore in 1835. Also in 1835, James Gorman, Churchwell Gorman, William Gorman and Nancy Pugh gave a power-of-attorney to John Gorman to sell land in Houston Co., Ga. which was drawn by them. There is nothing more in the early records of Barbour Co. that tells where Francis W. Pugh came from, where he went, or the names of his children.

Sources of information:

Barbour Co., Ala. Probate Records
Barbour Co., Ala. Census Records
Barbour Co., Ala. Cemetery Records
Pike Co., Ala. Probate Records
Pike Co., Ala. Census Records
"Alabama Series" Vol. II by Helen S. Foley
"Dictionary of Alabama Biography"
"History of Barbour Co., Ala." by Thompson

*ADDITIONS & CORRECTIONS AS OF JUNE 1, 1979:

Anne Silvia Tilman (Tillman) who married Robert Pugh was a sister of Robert Tillman (b. ca 1806 Washington Co., Ga., d. 1860 Barbour Co., Ala.). Their father was Littleberry Tillman, a Rev. Soldier (b. ca 1754 Brunswick Co., Va., d. Henry Co., Ala.).

PURIFOY (PUREFOY)

John Purifoy was born 21 Sept. 1787 Craven Co., N. C., died
25 Aug. 1839 while on a visit to Shelby Springs, Ala. and is
buried there, married Nancy Williams 21 Dec. 1809 in Hancock Co.,
Ga., daughter of William Williams (see WILLIAMS). He was a son
of Thomas Purifoy of Craven Co., N. C.. Nancy Williams was born
23 March 1792 Ga., died 9 May 1875 Wilcox Co., Ala.. She is
buried in Old Snow Hill Cem. in Wilcox Co., Ala.. John and
Nancy (Williams) Purifoy moved to Pike Co., Ala. (now Barbour
Co.) about Jan. 1824, then to Dallas Co., Ala. a few years
later.
Issue:
1. William Madison Purifoy, b. 29 Nov. 1810, d. 7 July 1863,
   m. Mary Harrod 3 April 1831. She was born 22 May 1817 Ga.,
   died 18 June 1860. Issue:
   a. Sarah Jane Purifoy, b. 26 May 1832, d. 13 Oct. 1847,
      buried in family cemetery near Old Snow Hill, Ala..
   b. Eliza Matilda Purifoy, b. 30 July 1834, d. 15 Aug. 1835,
      buried in family cemetery.
   c. Dr. John Harrod Purifoy, b. 9 Sept. 1837 Snow Hill,
      Ala., d. 22 Nov. 1908, m. (1) Janie Elizabeth Spiers
      (2) Mary Alabama Peeples. He is buried in the family
      cemetery.
   d. Judge Williams Purifoy, b. 29 Oct. 1839 Snow Hill, Ala.,
      d. 14 Aug. 1864 (CSA), buried near Forsyth, Ga. in
      Greenwood Cem..
   e. Mary Purifoy, b. ca 1842 Ala.
   f. Nancy Purifoy, b. ca 1844 Ala.
   g. William Madison Purifoy, Jr., b. 27 Oct. 1848 Snow Hill,
      Ala., d. 1915 (buried in family cemetery), married (1)
      Sarah Frances Jones (2) Alberta Brazille.

h. Buckner Purifoy - no further record on him.

i. Patience Caroline Purifoy, b. 11 May 1859, d. 2 Nov. 1860, buried in family cemetery.

2. Henry Marshall Purifoy, b. 10 Nov. 1812, d. 8 Sept. 1882, buried Nevada Co., Ark., m. (1) Frances Ann Griffin 1 June 1834 (2) unknown (3) Martha Handley 1851. She was born 1830, died 1890. Known issue:

a. William I. Purifoy, b. 16 June 1839

b. Henry Harrison Purifoy, b. 28 Aug. 1841 Snow Hill, Ala., moved to Camden, Ark..

c. Nancy C. Purifoy, b. 10 March 1844

d. John Griffin Purifoy, b. 4 Feb. 1847

e. Albert Francis Purifoy, b. 19 May 1848

f. James W. Purifoy, b. 27 Feb. 1851

g. J. C. L. Purifoy, b. 23 Oct. 1852

h. C. W. Purifoy, b. 2 Jan. 1854

i. M. H. Purifoy, b. 30 July 1856

j. M. E. Purifoy, b. 2 Jan. 1860.

3. Martha Williams Purifoy, b. 6 Sept. 1814, d. 25 Dec. 1911, m. Edmond Hobdy 5 Jan. 1829 Pike Co., Ala.. He was born 14 July 1805 N. C., d. 6 Dec. 1861. They are buried in Old Snow Hill Cem.. (See HOBDY). Issue:

a. William Madison Hobdy, b. 11 July 1830 Pike Co., Ala., m. Adeline Carter.

b. Emily Hobdy, b. 16 Oct. 1836, d. 3 Jan. 1916, m. Leonard Moore, b. 1 April 1832, d. 3 Feb. 1895. They are buried in Old Snow Hill Cem..

c. J. N. Hobdy, b. 16 Feb. 1849, d. 18 Jan. 1851, buried in Old Snow Hill Cem..

d. Frances Hobdy, may have married Lewis Fitch.

e. Lavinia Hobdy m. John Simpson.

f.   (possibly) John H. Hobdy, b. 31 Dec. 1854, d. 26 July
     1887, married Annie Bragg, buried Old Snow Hill Cem..

g.   Eliza Hobdy m. Edmund Hunter. He was born 21 March 1829
     Dallas Co., Ala., d. 29 April 1878, buried in Old Snow
     Hill Cem..

h.   Edmund P. Hobdy m. Lou Scott.

4. Leroy Purifoy, b. 2 Dec. 1816, m. Elizabeth Gulley 23 Aug.
    1835. Known issue:

a.   John Gulley Purifoy, b. 14 Dec. 1837 Wilcox Co., Ala.,
     lived in Ark.

b.   William Leroy Purifoy, b. 10 July 1842 Conecuh Co.,
     Ala., killed in CSA, buried Corinth, Miss.

c.   Thomas Henry Purifoy, b. 9 Sept. 1844 Conecuh Co., Ala.,
     d. CSA, buried Alton, Ill.

5. Francis Marion Purifoy, b. 4 Oct. 1818 Ga., d. 31 May 1858
    Wilcox Co., Ala., m. (1) Nancy Lucinda Thigpen 22 Aug. 1841.
    She was born 23 Nov. 1821, died 20 July 1846. They are bur-
    ied in Old Snow Hill Cem.. He married (2) Penelope Ann
    Synthiana Moore, born 1831, died 1879. She married (2) Al-
    len Kendrick Albritton 9 Aug. 1860 Wilcox Co., Ala., moved
    to Texas. Issue:

a.   John Purifoy, b. 21 March 1842 Dallas Co., Ala.

b.   James Wesley Purifoy, b. 7 Sept. 1843 Old Snow Hill, d.
     29 Aug. 1864 (CSA), buried Greenwood Cem., near Forsyth,
     Ga..

c.   William Scott Purifoy, b. 16 Nov. 1844 Wilcox Co., Ala.,
     d. 14 Dec. 1907 (buried Old Snow Hill Cem.), lived Fur-
     man, Ala., married Mary Leah Watson.

d.   Edmund Hobdy Purifoy, b. 5 Jan. 1846 Snow Hill, Ala.,
     d. 8 Dec. 1932 Selma, Ala., m. Mary Harville 17 Feb.
     1871. She was born 15 June 1851, died 21 Oct. 1928.

Both are buried in Live Oak Cem., Selma, Ala..

By 2nd wife:

e. Nancy L. Purifoy, b. ca 1847 Ala..

f. Eustasia Purifoy, b. ca 1849 Ala., m. James Allen Stuart
    6 Aug. 1868 Wilcox Co., Ala.. He was born 7 May 1850,
    died 21 Feb. 1905, buried Camden, Ala..

g. Francis Allen Purifoy, b. 22 Oct. 1851, d. 12 May 1852,
    buried Old Snow Hill Cem..

6. Mary Ellen Purifoy, b. 28 June 1820, d. 11 Nov. 1857, buried
Friendship Cem., Union Parish, La., m. James Heywood Gulley
28 Feb. 1836. Issue:

a. Nancy L. Gulley, b. 21 April 1837 Ala., m. Washington J.
    Pickel 28 March 1855, lived Union Parish, La..

b. Caroline Elizabeth Gulley, b. 21 Aug. 1839, d. y.

c. Mary Magdaline Gulley, b. 28 July 1841 Ala., d. 1 July
    1849.

d. Henry Calhoun Gulley, b. 22 Sept. 1843 Ala., d. April
    1864 (CSA), buried Washington, Ark..

e. Martha Williams Gulley, b. 28 Feb. 1846 Ala., d. 8 Dec.
    1919 Natchitoches Parish, La., m. Robert Calvert Murphy
    17 Aug. 1865. He was born 16 Nov. 1842 Ark., d. 16
    Feb. 1936. They are buried in Cane River Cem., Natchi-
    toches Parish, La..

f. John Purifoy Gulley, b. 1 Feb. 1850, m. Henrietta P.
    Murphy (sister of Robert Calvert Murphy). He is buried
    in Spring Hill Cem., Oakland, La..

g. Patience Emma Gulley, b. 22 Dec. 1855, m. Starling Lee.

7. John Wesley Purifoy, b. 22 July 1823 Hancock Co., Ga., d.
1897, m. Nancy Warren Carter 29 March 1862. She was born
1827 Conecuh Co., Ala., d. 1919. They are buried in Old
Snow Hill Cem.. Known issue:

a. Effie Purifoy, b. 1865, d. 1888, buried Old Snow Hill Cem..

b. Frances Warren Purifoy, b. 11 Nov. 1869, d. 16 July 1961, m. Eli Lawrence Cunningham 4 May 1898. He was born 24 Nov. 1866, died 28 Sept. 1946.

8. Patience Caroline Purifoy, b. 3 Jan. 1827, d. 9 Nov. 1904 in Pine Bluff, Ark. where she had gone to live with her sons, Andrew and Lloyd Lee. She married John Allen Lee 16 Jan. 1845. He was born 16 July 1824, died 18 Aug. 1863 and is buried in Old Snow Hill Cem.. Issue:

a. Martha Jane Lee, b. 6 Oct. 1845, d. 31 July 1846, buried Old Snow Hill Cem..

b. William Eaton Lee, b. 23 June 1847, d. 31 July 1852.

c. John Francis Lee, b. 8 March 1849, d. 15 Feb. 1906 m. Ora Ulrica Scarborough 20 Dec. 1876 Lowndes Co., Ala..

d. Henry Marshall Lee, b. 6 Feb. 1851, m. Emma Octavia Lee.

e. Clarence Leroy Lee, b. 17 Feb. 1853, d. 19 April 1853.

f. Julius Jefferson Lee, b. 6 May 1854, d. 31 Jan. 1904.

g. Julia Dorcas Lee, b. 6 May 1854, d. 25 Oct. 1881, m. Dr. D. D. Jones 1875. She is buried Old Snow Hill Cem.

h. Andrew Millard Lee, b. 16 July 1856, lived Pine Bluff, Ark..

i. Judge Martin Lee, b. 28 June 1858.

j. Joseph Lloyd Lee, b. 13 April 1860, lived Pine Bluff, Ark..

k. Wesley Cato Lee, b. 1 May 1862.

9. Robert A. Purifoy, d. y.

10. Emily Purifoy, d. y.

Much of the information for the Purifoy family was furnished by Mrs. H. T. Ellison of Hurtsboro, Ala..

Other sources:

Old Snow Hill Cem., Wilcox Co., Ala.
"Descendants of John Purifoy" by Francis Marion Purifoy
Dallas Co., Ala., Will Book D, page 512
1850 Census Wilcox Co., Ala..

PYNES

Rutha Pynes was born ca 1780 S. C. and died by 1859 in Henry Co., Ala.. She was probably the widow of Daniel Pynes who died by 1831, also in Henry Co.. His estate was not settled until after the death of Rutha Pynes. Issue (all but Fair Pynes lived in Henry Co., Ala.):

1. Benjamin Pynes, b. ca 1802 S. C., died after 1859, m. Louisa L. Evans 1 Dec. 1855 in Henry Co., Ala..

2. James Pynes, b. ca 1802 S. C., died by 1876, m. Winefred ----, b. ca 1811 (she may have been his second wife). Known issue:

    a. Penelope C. Pynes, b. ca 1821 Ala., died by 1876, m. William H. Smith 29 July 1852 Henry Co., Ala..

    b. Missouri Pynes, b. ca 1843 Ala., m. William Wood.

    c. Virginia Pynes, b. ca 1845 Ala., m. William P. Leslie 24 Dec. 1867.

3. Fair Pynes, b. ca 1804 S. C., died by 1854, m. Maryanna Creech 10 Jan. 1828 in Henry Co., Ala.. She was born ca 1810 Ga., died after 1860. Issue:

    a. Lupina Pynes, b. ca 1829 Ala., m. Jesse Clements 27 Dec. 1846. In 1860, they were living in Choctaw Co., Ala..

    b. Francis Marion Pynes, b. ca 1832 Ala. - no record after 1860.

    c. Jasper Pynes, b. ca 1834 Ala. - no record after 1860.

    d. Daniel N. Pynes, b. ca 1837 Ala., possibly married Martha P. Hightower 23 Aug. 1866. This family may have been in Mt. Vernon, Texas in 1891.

    e. Lydia Elizabeth Pynes, b. ca 1839 Ala., m. Simon S. J. Cawthon of Henry Co., Ala. on 27 Jan. 1859. In 1891, they were living in Andalusia, Ala..

    f. Calista Pynes, b. ca 1841 Ala., m. Augustus Robson

28 Nov. 1869.

g. Rutha Jane Pynes, b. ca 1843 Ala., m. Wade Bell, probably lived in Mt. Vernon, Texas.

h. Mary Ann Pynes, b. ca 1846 Ala., m. Derrell H. Blair 28 Nov. 1869. They are buried in Clayton Cem. but no dates are given.

i. Christopher Columbus Pynes, b. ca 1848 Ala., died after 1891, m. Sarah E. Jones 18 July 1867. She died in 1888 at Mt. Vernon, Texas.

j. Thaddeus S. Pynes, b. after 1850, was living in Mt. Vernon, Texas in 1891.

k. Malissa Pynes, b. ca 1852 Ala..

4. Nancy Pynes, died by 1858, m. ---- Dees. Issue:

a. James F. Dees, living Hinds Co., Miss. in 1858.

b. Sarah J. Dees m. William Black, living in Hinds Co., Miss. in 1858.

c. Daniel W. Dees, living Hinds Co., Miss. in 1858.

5. Mary Pynes, died by 1858, m. Alexander Johnson 26 Sept. 1832 Henry Co., Ala.. They lived in Jackson Co., Fla.. Issue:

a. Daniel Johnson - of Coffee Co., Ala. in 1858.

b. John Johnson - of Fla. in 1858.

c. Dallas Johnson - minor in 1858, living in Fla..

d. Rutha Johnson - minor in 1858, living in Fla..

e. William Johnson - minor in 1858, living in Fla..

6. White Pynes, b. ca 1811 Ga., died after 1880, m. Sarah G. Lewis 26 Aug. 1836 in Henry Co., Ala.. Known issue:

a. Hamilton Pynes, b. ca 1837 Ala.

b. James J. Pynes, b. ca 1838 Ala., m. M. D. Martin 8 Feb. 1867 in Henry Co., Ala..

c. Mary J. Pynes, b. ca 1841 Ala.

d. Rutha E. Pynes, b. ca 1844 Ala.

e. Lewis W. Pynes, b. ca 1846 Ala..

f. Louisianna Pynes, b. ca 1848 Ala., not married in 1880 and living with her father in Henry Co., Ala..

Wheaton Pynes, Jr. was enumerated in the 1830 Census of Pike Co., Ala. and in the 1832 Census of Barbour Co., Ala.. He was still in Barbour Co. in 1840, age 50/60 (b. ca 1780/1790) with a female age 50/60 and 2 males age 15/20. In 1835, he witnessed a deed from Rutha Pynes in Henry Co. and in 1839 he was administrator of Green B. Pynes, deceased, of Barbour Co.. His relationship to Daniel Pynes is not clear - possibly he was a brother.

Other sources:

Henry Co., Ala. Probate records
1850 Census Henry Co., Ala..

Robert Richards was a commissioner of Henry Co., Ala. by 1827. At that time, he lived in the part of Henry Co. that was later cut into Barbour Co. when it was formed, in the settlement still known as Richards Cross Roads. He was born ca 1776 in Ireland, died 18 July 1851. He married Eleanor (Black?), who was born ca 1770/80 S. C., died 28 Sept. 1848. They are buried in County Line Cemetery, but their graves are not marked.
Issue:

1. Thomas W. Richards, b. 14 Sept. 1798 Pendleton Dist., S. C., d. 23 June 1879, m. Lucy Carter 22 Aug. 1826 in Henry Co., Ala., daughter of Giles Carter of Henry Co.. She was born 10 May 1806 in Ga., died 14 Sept. 1890. They are buried in unmarked graves in the family cemetery in the yard of the Richards' home place at Richards Cross Roads. Issue:

   a. Andrew Jackson Richards, b. 7 Aug. 1827 Ala., may have been killed 15 Sept. 1863 in the Civil War.

   b. Sonia Jane Richards, b. 16 Aug. 1828 Ala., d. 2 Sept. 1857 (buried in the family cemetery), m. William Mack Hardwick 5 Jan. 1854. He was born 10 Feb. 1834, died 16 May 1919 and is buried in Adaniron Cem., Henry Co., Ala..

   c. Benjamin Franklin Richards, b. 7 June 1830 Ala., d. 15 Sept. 1863 (CSA), m. Emily Byrd 8 Nov. 1852 Henry Co., Ala.. She m. (2) Moses W. Helms 26 March 1864 Henry Co., Ala. He died in 1883 in Vernon, Fla., age 72 years.

   d. Robert Emmet Richards, b. 18 Nov. 1831 Ala., d. 5 Jan. 1863 (CSA), m. Roann Craddock 13 Dec. 1855. She was born ca 1838, died 16 Sept. 1857.

   e. Giles Washington Richards, b. 1 June 1833 Ala., died after 1880, m. Sarah Ann Byrd 18 Sept. 1854 Henry Co.,

Ala.. She was born 3 Oct. 1833 N. C., died 8 Feb. 1895 and is buried in County Line Cem.. He is probably buried there also, but his grave is not marked.

f. Thomas Benton Richards, b. 31 July 1836 Ala., d. after 1880, m. Cleopatra Rebecca Wheeler 27 Jan. 1865 in Henry Co., Ala.. She was born 9 April 1843 Ga., died 13 Oct. 1900 and is buried in East Side Cem., Headland, (Henry Co.), Ala.. She was a daughter of Isiah Wheeler and Delila Searcy who married 16 Feb. 1840 Baldwin Co., Ga.. Delila Searcy Wheeler later married James Searcy, a cousin, of Henry Co., Ala..

g. Seaborn Lafayette Richards, b. 6 Jan. 1839 Ala., d. 1 May 1840.

h. William Wesley Richards, b. 28 Feb. 1841 Ala., d. after 1880, m. Sophia Frances Wood (see WOOD). She was born ca 1843 Ala., died after 1880.

i. Lucy Ann Richards, b. 19 Jan. 1845 Ala., d. 14 Feb. 1915, m. (1) Marion C. J. Searcy 24 Sept. 1863. He was a son of James Searcy of Henry Co., Ala. and his first wife, Achsah Norwood. Marion C. J. Searcy died 9 Dec. 1863 (buried Adaniron Cem., Henry Co., Ala.) and she m. (2) William Mack Hardwick 5 Jan. 1868 (his first wife was her sister, Sonia Jane Richards).

j. Joseph Lafayette Richards, b. 28 March 1847 Ala., d. 22 Feb. 1857. He is buried in the family cemetery.

k. Alonzo Locratous Richards, b. 28 April 1849 Ala., d. 26 Aug. 1929, m. Abigail R. Wood 15 Dec. 1881. She was born 20 July 1850, died 8 June 1938 (see WOOD). They are buried in County Line Cem..

1. Frances Richards, b. 11 July 1851, d. 7 Aug. 1851.

2. William Richards, b. ca 1802 S. C., d. by 1855, m. Matilda

McVay 19 Jan. 1826 Henry Co., Ala.. She was born ca 1807
S. C., died after 1870. They are buried in unmarked graves
in County Line Cem.. Probable issue:

a. Eleanor Richards m. Monroe Stanford 1 Feb. 1850.

b. Malinda Richards, b. ca 1830 Ala., m. Lewis K. (H.?)
    Holmes of Henry Co., Ala. on 28 April 1852. He was born
    5 July 1829, died 28 May 1887 and is buried in County
    Line Cem..

c. Mary M. Richards, b. 1 Jan. 1832 Ala., d. 2 June 1901,
    m. Robert Hardy Dawkins 4 Nov. 1851. He was born 14
    March 1829 and died 8 Dec. 1890. They are buried in
    Lawrenceville Cem., Henry Co., Ala..

d. James M. Richards, b. ca 1839 Ala..

e. Martha Louisa Richards, b. ca 1841 Ala., m. B. J. Drig-
    gars 18 Dec. 1873.

f. Thomas Dallas Richards, b. ca 1843 Ala., m. Virginia A.
    Manley 29 Oct. 1868 in Henry Co., Ala.. She was born
    16 Nov. 1847, died 17 Oct. 1890 and is buried in Mt.
    Pleasant Cem.

g. Robert Jesse Richards, b. 19 July 1847, d. 27 March
    1882, m. Caroline L. Hardwick 28 Nov. 1867. She was
    born 20 June 1849 Ala., died 11 Dec. 1876. He married
    (2) Lucy Jane Richards 19 Dec. 1878. She was born 10
    April 1860 Ala., died 1 Feb. 1903, daughter of Giles
    Washington Richards and Sarah Ann Byrd. She married
    (2) John W. Rollins. Robert J. and Carrie L. Richards
    are buried in County Line Cem.. John W. Rollins had
    married (1) Fanny Richards, also a daughter of Giles
    Washington Richards and Sarah Ann Byrd. She died 2 Feb.
    1891 and he married Lucy Jane, widow of Robert Jesse
    Richards.

h. Elizabeth Caldonia Richards, b. ca 1850 Ala., may have
married Charles A. Hardwick.

i. William Jefferson Richards, born before 1835, died
before 1850.

3. Elouisa Richards, b. 1808 S. C., d. 2 April 1895, m. James
M. Richards by 1835. He was born ca 1811 S. C., died ca
Oct. 1893. They are buried in County Line Cem., but his
grave is not marked. He was a son of William Richards of
Coosa Co., Ala., who was a half-brother of Robert Richards
(b. ca 1776 Ireland). This line will be discussed later in
this chapter. Issue:

a. Harriet J. Richards, b. 9 June 1836 Ala., d. 7 Nov.
1886· (or 1896), m. Sherod J. Belcher 30 Sept. 1856. He
was born 18 Sept. 1829 Ga., died Aug. 1921. They are
buried in County Line Cem..

b. Nancy E. Richards, b. 22 Dec. 1838 Ala., d. 7 April
1904, m. Rev. Julius W. Malone after 1880 - she was his
second wife. He was born 1832, died 1918. She is buried
in County Line Cem. and he is buried in Judson Baptist
Church Cem., Henry Co., Ala..

c. Matilda Richards, b. 25 Dec. 1840 Ala., d. 8 Nov. 1893,
buried County Line Cem.. She never married.

d. William Augustus Richards, b. 23 March 1843 Ala., d. 18
Jan. 1926, m. Emma Lucie Tyler in Jan. 1868. She was
born 24 Sept. 1841, died 17 Nov. 1924. They are buried
in Christian Grove Cem..

e. James L. Richards, b. 29 March 1845 Ala., d. 24 March
1914, m. Cynthia E. Ray 12 Nov. 1867. She was born 4
March 1846 and died 20 March 1927 - buried in County
Line Cem..

f. Robert Decatur Richards, b. 22 Feb. 1847 Ala., d. 26

April 1906, m. Ursula Angelina Tyler 22 Oct. 1866. She
was born 25 March 1848 S. C., died 3 Sept. 1825. They
are buried in County Line Cem..

g. Andrew Jackson Richards, b. 19 Aug. 1849 Ala., d. 29
    Oct. 1908, m. Lydia Jerusa Baker 24 Oct. 1889. She was
    born 22 July 1867, died 2 Feb. 1932. They are buried in
    County Line Cem..

Robert Richards (b. ca 1776 Ireland) had an older half-brother, William Richards, who lived in Coosa Co., Ala.. He married (1) Nancy Warren (2) Susannah Waters Edwards ca 1839.
Issue:
By 1st wife:
1. James E. Richards (see Elouisa Richards).
2. Mary A. Richards, b. ca 1822 Ala., never married. She died
    in 1882 and is buried in County Line Cem..
3. Thomas William Richards, b. ca 1824 Ala., d. ca 1869 Barbour
    Co., Ala., m. Temperance Smith 14 Sept. 1843, daughter of
    Isiah Smith. Issue:
    a. James M. Richards, b. ca 1844 Ala., m. Ann R. Lee 15
        Jan. 1865.
    b. William H. Richards, b. ca 1846 Ala.
    c. Thomas J. Richards, b. ca 1849 Ala.
    d. John Q. Richards, b. ca 1853 Ala.
    e. Mary J. Richards, b. ca 1855 Ala.
    f. Sarah R. Richards, b. ca 1857 Ala.
    g. Robert J. Richards, b. ca 1860 Ala.
    h. Lucinda E. Richards, b. ca 1861 Ala.
    i. Susan P. Richards, b. ca 1863 Ala.
4. George W. Richards, b. ca 1826 Ala., d. by Dec. 1862, m.
    Mary Ann Grubbs 11 Nov. 1847 (see GRUBBS). She was born ca
    1830 Ala., d. 18 July 1892. Issue:

a. William Richards, b. ca 1849 Ala., m. Sarah A. Walker 7 April 1870. She was born ca 1852 Ala..

b. Nancy Jane Richards, b. ca 1851 Ala., m. Jeff Spurlock 20 Feb. 1887.

c. Sarah E. Richards, b. ca 1853 Ala., m. W. Henry Vinson 30 Dec. 1880.

d. Robert W. Richards, b. ca 1855 Ala..

e. John T. (or F.) Richards, b. ca 1859 Ala., m. Amanda E. ----.

f. Green W. Richards, b. 11 Oct. 1861 Ala., d. 15 April 1902, buried Mt. Aerial Cem..

5. Robert J. Richards, b. Feb. 1827 Ala., d. 17 March 1895, m. Nancy L. Cox 6 Jan. 1861, daughter of Jimpsey Cox. She was born 16 Oct. 1836, died 30 June 1920. They are buried in Bethlehem Cem.. Issue:

a. Nancy Louisa Richards, b. ca 1862 Ala.

b. Robert Jimpsey Richards, b. 29 Jan. 1863 Ala., d. 8 June 1927, m. Callie Beverly 18 Jan. 1885. She was born 7 Feb. 1861, died 21 May 1943. They are buried in Clayton Cem..

c. William H. Richards, b. ca 1866 Ala.

d. Rachael Ann Richards, b. ca 1867 Ala.

e. Julia E. Richards, b. ca 1868 Ala.

f. Mary J. Richards, b. ca 1871 Ala.

g. Rosa M. Richards, b. ca 1873 Ala.

h. James A. Richards, b. ca 1875 Ala.

6. Margaret Richards married Gabriel Jones and moved to Texas.

7. Elizabeth Richards married ---- Corbitt and moved to Texas.

8. Julia Richards married (1) ---- Turlington (2) David McRee.

All of the children of William Richards and his first wife came to Barbour Co., Ala. except Margaret, Elizabeth and possibly

274

Julia.

Issue:

By 2nd wife:

9. John Allen Richards, killed in Civil War.

10. Henry Taylor Richards, m. Margaret Jane Thornell.

Other sources:

Henry Co., Ala. Marriage Records
Henry Co., Ala. Cemetery Records
Richards Bibles
Information from descendants

James Shipman patented land West of Louisville from 1829 through 1848. He was born ca 1789 N. C., died by Aug. 1853. His wife was Elizabeth ----, b. ca 1796 N. C., died after 1860. Issue:

1. Catharine A. Shipman, b. ca 1817 N. C., m. Jonathan Lampley. Issue:

    a. Linton (Hinton?) Lampley, b. ca 1846 Ala.

    b. Laura Lampley m. James A. Baxter 27 Dec. 1866.

    c. John Lampley, b. ca 1850 Ala.

    d. Caleb Lampley, b. ca 1852 Ala.

    e. Edward Lampley, b. ca 1856 Ala.

2. Alexander Shipman, b. 27 Sept. 1818 N. C., d. 23 July 1867, m. Mary W. Westbrook 23 Jan. 1841. She was born 3 March 1816 in N. C., died 20 June 1898. Both are buried in Pea River Cemetery. Issue:

    a. Sarah E. Shipman, b. 20 Jan. 1842 Ala., d. 22 Oct 1917, never married. She is buried in Pea River Cemetery.

    b. Ann E. Shipman, b. ca 1843 Ala., m. R. C. McBride 11 Dec. 1867.

    c. John W. Shipman, b. 6 Nov. 1844 Ala., d. 13 Sept. 1922, m. Jennie Wallace, b. 27 June 1842, d. 27 Jan. 1916. Both are buried in Pea River Cemetery.

    d. James H. Shipman, b. 11 Oct. 1846 Ala., d. 18 March 1893, m. Mary L. ----, b. 11 July 1848, d. 11 Sept. 1880. Both are buried in Pea River Cemetery.

    e. Alexander Harvey Shipman, b. 29 Nov. 1848 Ala., d. 6 March 1926, m. Sarah Julia Capps, b. 9 Feb. 1858, d. 21 Nov. 1920. Both are buried in Pea River Cemetery.

    f. Lewis C. Shipman, b. 14 Aug. 1850 Ala., d. 24 Aug. 1895, never married. He is buried in Pea River Cemetery.

g. Mary Jane Shipman, b. 21 June 1852 Ala., d. 28 April
    1871, never married. She is buried in Pea River Ceme-
    tery.

h. Amanda Shipman, b. ca 1854 Ala., d. after 1880 - not
    married in 1880.

i. Lucy Shipman, b. ca 1856 Ala.

3. Apaline Shipman, b. ca 1821 N. C., m. Benjamin Lampley. They
    were living in Pike Co., Ala. in 1853.

4. James L. Shipman, b. 11 June 1822 N. C., d. 18 March 1893,
    m. Adelina A. Wynn 4 May 1869. Known issue:

a. James A. Shipman, b. ca 1870 Ala.

b. John H. Shipman, b. ca 1870 Ala.

c. Rosa L. Shipman, b. ca 1873 Ala.

d. Elizabeth M. Shipman, b. ca 1875 Ala.

e. Lena B. Shipman, b. ca 1877 Ala.

5. Eliza Shipman, b. ca 1825 N. C., d. after 1880 - not married
    in 1880.

6. Lucy Shipman, b. 17 July 1828 Ala., d. 1 April 1877, m. Har-
    vey A. McRae 25 March 1849 (see McRae family).

7. George L. Shipman, b. ca 1832 Ala., d. before 1880, m. Eliza
    A. F. McBride 15 July 1858. She was born 22 May 1834, died
    9 Aug. 1914. Both are buried in Pea River Cemetery. Issue:

a. William Franklin Shipman, b. 11 July 1859 Ala., d. 10
    Sept. 1923.

b. Clinton J. Shipman, b. 20 Nov. 1860 Ala., d. 9 March
    1939, m. Minnie C. ----.

c. Ada A. Shipman, b. ca 1863 Ala.

d. George L. Shipman, b. 31 Dec. 1864 Ala., d. 27 Dec.
    1927, buried in Pea River Cemetery.

8. Lewis Shipman, b. ca 1834 Ala.

9. Jesse Shipman, b. ca 1836 Ala.

10. Benjamin Franklin Shipman, b. ca 1838 Ala.

Sources of information:

Barbour Co., Ala. Probate Records
Barbour Co., Ala. Census Records
Barbour Co., Ala. Cemetery Records
Pike Co., Ala. Census Records

SILER

Although Solomon Siler patented land in (now) Barbour Co., Ala. in 1827 and 1829, his home was at Orion, Pike Co., Ala.. In 1818, Solomon Siler and Andrew Siler were listed on the tax list of Conecuh Co., Ala., from which Pike Co. was formed in 1821.

Solomon Siler was born ca 1789 N. C., died by Feb. 1854 in Orion, Pike Co., Ala.. His wife was Jane Owen Glenn Park, born Ga., died after 1854. They were married 8 Feb. 1843 in Pike Co., Ala.. Jane O. G. Park was the daughter of John Park, b. 26 Dec. 1786 Prince Edward Co., Va., and his wife, Sara Owen Musgrove,* b. 29 Jan. 1788 in Oglethorpe Co., Ga.. They both died in Pike Co., Ala.. Issue of Solomon Siler and Jane O. G. Park:

1. Laurentina Narcissa Siler, b. ca 1844 Ala.

2. Leonora America Siler, b. ca 1845 Ala.

3. Mary Augustus Crabtree Siler, b. ca 1848 Ala.

4. Quintus Cincinnatus Park Siler, b. ca 1849 Ala.

5. Orlando Littlejohn Siler, b. after 1850.

The will of Solomon Siler mentions his niece, Comfort Siler, and his nephews, John R. and Denham Siler.

Sources of information:

Barbour Co., Ala. Probate Records
Barbour Co., Ala. Census Records
Pike Co., Ala. Probate Records
Pike Co., Ala. Census Records
"Alabama Historical Quarterly", Spring 1957

*ADDITIONS & CORRECTIONS AS OF JUNE 1, 1979:

John Park, b. 26 Dec. 1786 Prince Edward Co., Va., m. Sarah Owen Musgrove (b. 29 Jan. 1788 Oglethorpe Co., Ga.) in Georgia and came to Pike Co., Ala. by 1840. Issue:

1. J. T. Sankey Park

2. Frank Park

3. Jane Owen Glenn Park m. Solomon Siler

4. Joseph Harrison Park, b. 3 March 1815 Green Co., Ga., d. 24
    April 1887 Pike Co., Ala., m. Apsey Kolb, b. 20 Oct. 1824
    Conecuh Co., Ala., d. 24 Oct. 1879 Pike Co., Ala.

5. James M. Park

In 1827, Charles Sutton patented land West of Clio, Ala..
In 1832 and 1836, Jesse Sutton also patented land in this area.
They may have been brothers.

Charles Sutton was born ca 1787 S. C., died after 1850, married Charity ----. She was born ca 1800 Ga., died after 1850.
Probable issue:

1. Benjamin Sutton, b. ca 1824 Ala.

2. Joshua Sutton, b. ca 1827 Ala., m. Elizabeth Hutchinson 25 May 1848.

3. Susan Sutton, b. ca 1830 Ala., m. John Mingo 5 Dec. 1850.

4. Mahala Sutton, b. ca 1831 Ala.

5. Francis Sutton, b. ca 1838 Ala.

6. Jackson Sutton, b. ca 1843 Ala.

In 1850, Mary Bryant, b. ca 1754 Va., was living in this household.

Jesse Sutton was born 12 Dec. 1793 S. C., died 3 June 1860.
He is buried in the family cemetery near Louisville. His wife,
Elizabeth, is buried next to him, but no dates are given. She
was born ca 1796 Ga., died after 1870. Issue:

1. Needham B. Sutton, b. ca 1821 Ga., d. after 1875, m. (1)
   Amanda Caroline E. Campbell 12 March 1846. She died before
   Nov. 1859, as he married (2) Sarah Hall 6 Nov. 1859. They
   were living in Polk Co., Fla. by 1875. Known issue:

   a. Elizabeth Sutton, b. ca 1848 Ala.

   b. William J. Sutton, b. ca 1848 Ala.

   c. Jacob Sutton, b. ca 1850 Ala.

2. Caroline S. Sutton, b. 30 March 1823 Ga., d. 10 April 1905,
   m. (1) Henry H. Phillips, who died 21 Oct. 1844 (2) Arrington H. H. Phillips 18 Nov. 1860, whose first wife was her

sister, Martha Sutton.   Known issue:

By 1st husband:

a.   Nancy E. K. Phillips, b. 23 Nov. 1844 Ala., d. 29 Feb.
     1916, m. B. F. Ketcham 28 Oct. 1869. He was born 9 Sept.
     1841, died 20 Feb. 1931. Both are buried in Pea River
     Cemetery.

b.   Elizabeth R. Phillips

By 2nd husband:

c.   Benjamin H. Phillips, b. ca 1863 Ala., m. Mary J. Casey
     9 Jan. 1881.

d.   Susanna Phillips, b. ca 1864 Ala.

3.   Susan N. Sutton, b. ca 1825 Ga., m. Aladdin Thompson ca 1840.
     He was born ca 1818 S. C., son of Robert and Rhoda (Grubbs)
     Thompson. Known issue:*

     a.   Henry Thompson, b. ca 1841 Ala., may have married Miss
          E. C. Powell 12 Oct. 1865.

     b.   Jesse Thompson, b. ca 1845 Ala.

     c.   *Robert Thompson, b. ca 1849 Ala., m. Jane L. (Faulk)
          Miles 7 Feb. 1867. She was the daughter of Andrew Shep-
          pard Faulk. Her first husband was Andrew Miles.

4.   *Mary D. Sutton, b. ca 1825 Ga., d. after 1876, m. Henry H.
     Moreland 20 Dec. 1849. He was born ca 1825 Ga.. By 1876,
     they were living in Carthage, Texas.

5.   Huldy Sutton, b. 27 Aug. 1831 Ala., d. 5 Jan. 1905, m.
     Thomas P. C. Phillips 7 March 1851. They are buried in Elam
     Cemetery. Known issue:

     a.   Martha Analisabeth Phillips, b. 19 Aug. 1852 Ala., d. 21
          May 1900, never married. She is buried in Elam Cemetery.

     b.   Joseph Phillips, b. ca 1865 Ala.

6.   Dijah Sutton, b. 11 Oct. 1836 Ala., d. Nov. 1872, buried in
     the Sutton family cemetery. She married Christopher C. Teal

20 Aug. 1857 - he died by March 1863. Known issue:

a. James Benjamin Teal, b. 9 June 1857 Ala., d. 21 Nov. 1936, m. Susanna ----. She was born 3 July 1864, died 6 June 1951. Both are buried in Elam Cemetery.

b. Jesse C. Teal, b. ca 1860 Ala.

c. Nancy Isabella Teal, b. 19 June 1863, died 10 Sept. 1938, m. Rev. James Alfred Phillips. He was born 25 April 1856, died 19 Feb. 1932. Both are buried in Elam Cemetery.

d. Christopher Columbus Teal, b. ca 1864 Ala.

7. Matilda Sutton, b. ca 1839 Ala., d. after 1880, m. Parcebee Byrd 1 Nov. 1860. He was born 8 April 1831 Ala., died 4 Nov. 1875, is buried in the Sutton family cemetery. Known issue:

a. Gracy Byrd, b. ca 1861 Ala., died 15 April 1933, buried in Elam Cemetery.

b. Bright Byrd, b. 26 May 1863 Ala., d. 8 Sept. 1925, m. Lena Burke. She was born 17 Nov. 1869, died 29 July 1918. Both are buried in Elam Cemetery.

c. Joseph Byrd, b. ca 1865 Ala.

d. Zada Ann Byrd, b. 1867 Ala., d. 1924, m. ---- Garner. She is buried in Elam Cemetery.

e. Needham Byrd, b. 8 Feb. 1869 Ala., d. 16 Feb. 1919, buried in Elam Cemetery.

f. Mary Jane Byrd, b. ca 1872 Ala.

g. Lula J. Byrd, b. 18 June 1876 Ala., d. 6 March 1921, m. John T. Bell. He was born 31 March 1862, died 25 Nov. 1921. Both are buried in Clayton Cemetery.

8. Louisa Sutton m. Edward Byrd. They were living in Dale Co., Ala. in 1860.

9. Benjamin H. Sutton, b. 12 Feb. 1842 Ala., d. 9 Jan. 1921, m.

Margaret Teal 7 Dec. 1865. She was born 6 Dec. 1848, died 31 Oct. 1902. Both are buried in the Sutton family cemetery. Known issue:

a. Jesse Sutton, b. ca 1867 Ala.

b. Mary Isebel Sutton, b. ca 1868, d. 12 Sept. 1871, buried in the Sutton family cemetery.

c. Elizabeth Sutton, b. 5 Sept. 1870 Ala.

d. Sarah Jane Sutton, b. ca 1872 Ala.

e. Dijah Sutton, b. ca 1874 Ala.

f. William N. Sutton, b. ca 1875 Ala.

g. Charles E. Sutton, b. ca 1878 Aal.

h. Daniel A. Sutton, b. July 1880 Ala.

i. Ida Mae Sutton, b. 1 Feb. 1887, d. 24 July 1903, buried in the Sutton family cemetery.

10. Martha A. Sutton, b. ca 1829 Ala., d. 1852, buried in the Sutton family cemetery. She married Arrington H. H. Phillips 16 April 1846. He was born 8 March 1823 Ga., died 28 April 1906, buried in Elam Cemetery. He married (2) Martha B. Porter 24 Nov. 1853. She was born 1837, died March 1857, is buried near Elamville. He married (3) Caroline S. (Sutton) Phillips. Known issue:

By 1st wife:

a. Jesse Phillips, b. ca 1848 Ala.

b. Thomas C. Phillips, b. 1850 Ala., m. Epsey D. ---- ca 1880.

c. Needham B. Phillips

By 2nd wife:

d. Anne E. Phillips, b. ca 1855 Ala.

e. James Phillips, b. ca 1857 Ala.

Sources of information:
Barbour Co., Ala. Probate Records
Barbour Co., Ala. Census Records
Barbour Co., Ala. Cemetery Records

*ADDITIONS & CORRECTIONS AS OF JUNE 1, 1979:

Additional issue of Susan N. Sutton and Alladin Thompson:

d. Sarah J. Thompson

e. C. D. Thompson

f. William P. Thompson

g. C. Thompson

This Robert Thompson did not marry rs. Jane Lucretia (Faulk) Miles - she married his uncle, Robert Thompson, who was born ca 1835.

Mary Drew Sutton, b. 5 Aug. 1825 Ga., d. 19 Jan. 1916, m. Henry Haywood Moreland 20 Dec. 1849. He was born 10 Dec. 1825 Ga., d. 11 Jan. 1900. They moved to Panola Co., Texas ca 1876 and are buried in Bethel Baptist Church Cem., Clayton, Texas.
Issue:

a. Jane Moreland, b. ca 1849 Ala., m. Ike Dillard in Texas.

b. Tabitha Ann Moreland, b. 8 April 1852 Ala., d. 10 Nov. 1917, m. Ichabod B. Gillis ca 1870 in Ala.. He was born 9 March 1850 in Ala., d. 21 May 1921. Both are buried in Mt. Mariah Cem., Shady Grove, Nacogdoches Co., Texas.

c. Elizabeth Moreland, b. ca 1855 Ala., m. (1) Charles Draggers ca 1876 (2) Grain Harris after 1880 in Texas.

d. Pocahontas Moreland, b. ca 1859, m. William Ballou in Texas.

e. Susan Ann Moreland, b. 12 Feb. 1859 Ala., d. 31 May 1945 Texas, m. Thomas H. Lee 20 Dec. 1883 in Texas. He was born ca 1856 Ga., d. 7 May 1927. Both are buried in Cushing, Tx.

f. James H. Moreland, b. 10 March 1866 Ala., d. 15 March 1883, never married. He may be buried in Bethel Baptist Church Cem., Clayton, Texas.

SWILLEY

Samuel Swilley entered land West of Clio in 1827. In 1831, Jaredo Swilley entered land South of Clayton. They were brothers and Samuel Swilley was made guardian of the minor children of Jaredo Swilley after his death.

Samuel Swilley, b. ca 1797 Ga., d. by Oct. 1864 in Sumter Co., Ala., m. Martha ----, b. ca 1800 Ga.. Probable issue:

1. Mary L. Swilley, b. ca 1829 Ala., m. Henry G. Johnston in Sumter Co., Ala. on 21 Jan. 1847.

2. Sarah Swilley, b. ca 1831 Ala.

3. Martha A. Swilley, b. ca 1833 Ala.

4. Elizabeth C. Swilley, b. ca 1835 Ala., m. ---- Stewart.

5. Emily T. Swilley, b. ca 1839 Ala.

6. William J. Swilley, b. ca 1841 Ala.

Jaredo Swilley died by Nov. 1834 in Barbour Co., Ala.. In 1834, White Pynes was appointed guardian of his minor children; in 1835, their guardian was Watts Mann; and by July 1847, their guardian was their uncle, Samuel Swilley of Sumter Co., Ala.. Issue (all living in Sumter Co., Ala. in 1853):

1. Stephen D. Swilley, m. Susan C. ----.

2. John Swilley m. Harriet ----.

3. Mary Swilley m. Green Boyette 4 Oct. 1842 in Sumter Co., Ala., later lived in Greene Co., Ala.

4. Nicholas Swilley.

There was a Samuel Swilley in Liberty Co., Ga. in 1805 who had a prize draw in the lottery that year. At the same time, John and Nicholas Swilley were in Tattnall Co., Ga.

In the War of 1812, Samuel E. and Reason F. Swilley were in Capt. Robert Quarterman's Co., 2nd Regt., Georgia Militia.

In 1814, a Samuel Swilley was in the Militia of Baldwin Co., Ga. along with Jacinth and Joseph Jackson. Jacinth Jackson was also an early settler of Barbour Co., Ala..

In 1820, there was a Samuel Swilley listed in Appling Co., Ga., also a Reason Swilley.

In 1832, the orphans of Samuel Swilley were living in Houston Co., Ga..

Sources of information:

Barbour Co., Ala. Probate Records
Sumter Co., Ala. Probate Records
Sumter Co., Ala. Census Records
Georgia Land Lottery Records
Georgia Military Records

THOMAS

Elliott Thomas entered land near Oateston between 1829 and
1842. In 1833, he also entered land in the area that is now
Clayton. He was born ca 1789, possibly in Virginia, died by
Feb. 1852. His first wife was Sarah Berry, who died between
1833 and 1850. His second wife was Ann B. (1850 Census says Isabella) Grephill (or Boyleston), b. ca 1820 S. C., d. by Dec.
1851. There were no children by the second marriage. Issue by
first marriage:*

1. Joseph Thomas, died by 1857, m. (1) Jane Taylor (2) Sarah
   Baker Philingam 6 Aug. 1849. Known issue:
   a. Amanda Thomas
   b. Sarah Thomas, b. ca 1839 Ala., m. Dennis C. Condry 14
      Oct. 1858. He was born 16 June 1833, died 28 May 1908,
      is buried in Pond Bethel Cemetery.
   c. Angelina Thomas
   d. Mahala Narcissa Thomas
   e. Charity Thomas

2. Jonathan Thomas, b. 3 May 1815 Ga., d. 3 April 1881, buried
   New Hope Cemetery, m. Maria J. Bush 12 Jan. 1834, daughter
   of Zachariah Bush. She was born 4 Aug. 1819 Ga., died 25
   Sept. 1904, is buried in Clayton Cemetery. Known issue:
   a. Zachariah Thomas, b. 28 Dec. 1834, d. 18 Sept. 1857,
      buried New Hope Cemetery. He may have married Drucilla
      A. DuBose 30 Sept. 1852.
   b. Sarah J. Thomas, b. 5 Feb. 1837 Ala., d. 21 March 1926,
      m. Anderson C. Crews, 18 Jan. 1857. He was born 1 March
      1831, died 27 Jan. 1910, buried Clayton Cemetery.
   c. Elliott James Thomas, b. ca 1839 Ala.
   d. William Hamilton Thomas, b. 30 Nov. 1842 Ala., d. 22
      Jan. 1904, m. Margaret Ann McCraney 29 Nov. 1866. She

was born 10 Feb. 1847, died 3 Sept. 1927. They are buried in Clayton Cemetery.

e. Henry Crowell Thomas, b. ca 1843 Ala.

f. Jonathan Carter Thomas, b. 22 Feb. 1847 Ala., d. 18 May 1914, m. Evaline Virginia Mallard 24 June 1871. She was born 23 March 1850, died 1 March 1920. They are buried in Clayton Cemetery.

g. David K. Thomas, b. 13 April 1849 Ala., d. 26 May 1899, m. Ann Elizabeth Floyd 25 Nov. 1869. She was born 1 Jan. 1851, died 20 Oct. 1937. They are buried in Clayton Cemetery.

h. Jesse G. Thomas, b. 8 March 1839, d. 4 June 1843, buried in New Hope Cemetery.

i. Ida Leonora Thomas, b. 1 Aug. 1857, d. 27 Sept. 1858, buried in New Hope Cemetery.

j. *Alvenia P. Thomas, b. ca 1850 Ala.

k. *Charity C. Thomas, b. ca 1852 Ala.

l. M. Leman Thomas, b. ca 1858 Ala.

m. Adda Leonah Thomas, b. 23 March 1855, died 19 Dec. 1877, buried New Hope Church.

Jonathan Thomas was the guardian of four children of Sarah Jane (Thomas) McGilvray and three children of Charity Waterson. He also had eleven children of his own.

3. William Berry Tomas, b. ca 1816 Ga., m. Catherine McInnis, b. ca 1815 N. C.. She was the daughter of Angus McInnis. Known issue:

a. Eliza J. Thomas, b. ca 1835 Ala., m. Silas Bush of Dale Co., Ala.

b. Nancy Caroline Thomas, b. ca 1837 Ala., m. Wyatt Snow of Dale Co., Ala..

c. Sarah E. Thomas, b. ca 1839 Ala., m. Francis Marion

Pridgen of Dale Co., Ala..

d. William Marion Thomas, b. ca 1841 Ala., m. Mrs. Catherine Chaney Brewer.

e. James D. Thomas, b. ca 1844 Ala.

f. Lewis Bryan Thomas, b. ca 1847 Ala., d. y..

g. Mary Ann Thomas, b. ca 1850 Ala., m. William Carroll and moved to Texas.

4. Sarah Jane Thomas - the records are not clear whether she married James McGilvray or Chester Faulkner. However, most evidence tends to confirm the McGilvray marriage (see McGilvray family).

5. James E. Thomas (deaf and dumb), b. ca 1821 Ga., m. Dorcas Herring (or Heidt), b. ca 1818 N. C.. Known issue:

a. Ann Thomas, b. ca 1842 Ala.

b. Josephine Thomas, b. ca 1848 Ala.

c. Margaret Thomas, b. ca 1850 Ala.

d. John Thomas, b. ca 1852 Ala.

e. Florida P. Thomas, b. ca 1857 Ala.

6. Eli Thomas, b. ca 1824 Ala., d. by March 1852, m. (1) Retencey Emeline Bush 31 Dec. 1840. She died by 1849 and he married (2) Catherine Zorn 20 Dec. 1849. He may have married (3) Sarah Jane Zorn.* Issue, all by first wife:

a. Mary Parnelia Thomas, b. ca 1844 Ala., m. Marion Calhoun.

b. George Hilliard Thomas, b. 16 July 1845 Ala., d. 1 Feb. 1897 Dale Co., Ala., m. Mary Walker ca Feb. 1866, daughter of Lewis and Nancy (McInnis) Walker.

c. Zachariah Taylor Thomas, b. ca 1848 Ala., m. Martha Carter of Henry Co., Ala..

d. John Thomas, d. y..

7. Aaron Thomas, b. ca 1832 Ala., d. 17 Jan. 1871, m. Almira C. (Heidt?), b. ca 1829 Ga.. Known issue:

a. Charles E. Thomas, b. ca 1854 Ala.

b. Augustus C. Thomas, b. ca 1859 Ala..

8. Charity Thomas (deaf and dumb), b. ca 1830 Ala., may have married John Waterson. Possible issue:

a. Robert Waterson, b. ca 1864 Ala.

b. George Waterson, b. ca 1858 Ala.

9. Elliott Thomas, b. 30 Nov. 1833 Ala., d. 18 July 1857 Dale Co., Ala., buried in New Hope Cemetery. He is probably the Elliott Thomas who married Ruth Caroline Bush 16 Sept. 1852. She m. (2) John Q. Wise and was living in Coffee Co., Ala. in 1870. Possible issue:

a. Jonathan E. Thomas

b. Arincey Jane Thomas.

John DeLochiou Thomas, brother of Elliott Thomas, was born ca 1787 in Charleston, S. C., died in 1859. When he was 17 years old, he volunteered for service in the War of 1812. After the war, he joined a group of emigrants who were planning to settle in Florida. This group stopped in Twiggs Co., Ga., and while there, he married Nancy Williams, daughter of the leader of the emigrants, Mark Williams. In 1823, the band of emigrants camped at Eufaula, and liked it so much that they decided to settle there. Known issue of John DeLochiou Thomas and Nancy Williams:

1. Winifred Thomas, b. ca 1824 Twiggs Co., Ga., m. John Barefield. Known issue:

a. John A. J. Barefield, b. ca 1838 Ala. (possibly).

b. George W. Barefield, b. ca 1843 Ala.

c. Charity Barefield, b. ca 1845 Ala.

d. Catherine Barefield, b. ca 1847 Ala.

e. Mary L. Barefield, b. ca 1849 Ala.

f. James M. Barefield, b. ca 1850 Ala.

2. Emeline Thomas, b. ca 1830 Ala., d. 1916, m. Jasper Sawyer.

Known issue:

a. Walter Sawyer, b. ca 1858 Ala.

b. James Sawyer, b. ca 1860 Ala.

c. Cathason Sawyer, b. ca 1862 Ala.

d. Cassidy Sawyer, b. ca 1864 Ala.

3. Elliott Thomas, b. ca 1832 Ala., d. ca 16 June 1872, m. Lucinda ----. She was born ca 1840 Ga., d. 1885. Known issue:

a. Sarah Thomas, b. ca 1859 Ala.

b. Frances Thomas, b. ca 1861 Ala., d. by 1872.

c. John D. Thomas, b. ca 1864 Ala.

d. Elliott Thomas, b. ca 1867 Ala.

e. Mamie (or Mary) Thomas, b. ca 1870 Ala.

f. Hattie Thomas, b. ca 1873 Ala.

4. Henry A. Thomas, b. ca 1837 Ala., d. Dale Co., Ala., m. Pheribee Hunt. No issue, but adopted a son and a daughter.

5. John Curtis Thomas, b. 27 Feb. 1842 Ala., d. 18 Aug. 1891, m. Martha M. Ann Virginia Aldee of Lumpkin, Ga. on 9 June 1863. She was born 23 Feb. 1845, died 28 Oct. 1918. Issue:

a. Mattie Croker Thomas, b. 23 June 1865, d. 11 Feb. 1948, m. Charles M. Thompson 17 Dec. 1902.

b. Annie Virginia Thomas, b. 12 Nov. 1867, d. 21 Dec. 1890, m. Wm. M. Tully 22 April 1885.

c. Edith Curtis Thomas, b. 15 March 1871, d. 2 June 1878.

d. John Cortez Thomas, b. 3 March 1874, died 8 May 1934, m. Eleanor E. Boyleston 25 Dec. 1902.*

e. Arthur Morse Thomas, b. 3 June 1877, d. 31 Dec. 1878.

f. Nelly Thomas, b. 22 Feb. 1879, d. 30 June 1879.

g. Herbert Spencer Thomas, b. 17 Nov. 1882, d. 17 April 1966.

h. Randolph Rush Thomas, b. 12 April 1889, d. 18 Aug. 1941, m. Willie Mae Hinton 1 May 1912.

6. Nancy Thomas, b. ca 1843 Ala., not married in 1880.

7. Christianna Thomas, b. ca 1845 Ala.

Sources of information:

Barbour Co., Ala. Probate Records
Barbour Co., Ala. Census Records
Barbour Co., Ala. Cemetery Records
Thomas family Bible
"History of Barbour Co., Ala." by Thompson

*ADDITIONS & CORRECTIONS AS OF JUNE 1, 1979:

Heirs of Ann (Grephill) Thomas, widow of Elliott Thomas, Sr. on

26 Dec. 1853 were:

Eleanor, wife of Joseph C. Boyleston (sister)

Zachariah Grephill of S. C. (brother)

Wiley Grephill of S. C. (brother)

Margaret Grephill of S. C. (sister)

Also the following heirs of Elliott Thomas:

James E. Thomas

Sarah J., wife of Chestnut (?) Faulkner

William B. Thomas

Joseph Thomas, a minor

Jonathan Thomas, a minor

Aaron Thomas, a minor

Elliott Thomas, a minor

Mrs. A. P. Jones, wife of Harrison Jones of Rocky Mount (Barbour Co.), died 26 July 1892, leaving ten children.

Charity Caroline Thomas m. James Orr, Jr. 18 Dec. 1873. She was his second wife.

Mrs. Sarah Jane (Zorn) Thomas m. D. E. Corbet 26 Nov. 1856. She was the third wife of Eli Thomas.

Mrs. Egletine Boyleston Thomas died April 1905 at Uniontown, Ala. age 30, wife of John C. Thomas. She was born near Clayton, Ala. but raised at Apalachacola, Fla.. She was buried in Eufaula.

UTSEY

Jacob Utsey, b. ca 1790/98 S. C., d. after 1860, m. Mary
----. She was born ca 1800 S. C.. He entered land East of Clio
from 1829 to 1838. In 1838, he owned 15 slaves, and in 1840, he
owned 21 slaves - which was above the average for this area at
that time.

There is no estate settlement for him in Barbour Co., but
census records and deeds indicate the following issue:

1. Absolom F. Utsey, b. ca 1820 S. C., m. Mary E. Warren, daughter of Thomas and Rebecca Warren. She was born ca 1830 Ala.,
   died after 1850. Known issue:

   a. Jacob Utsey, b. ca 1843, d. 13 Nov. 1913, m. Rachael A.
      Johnson, b. 1838, d. 1914. They are buried in Clayton
      Cemetery.

   b. John F. Utsey, b. ca 1846 Ala..

   c. Thomas E. Utsey, b. ca 1849 Ala..

2. Mahala Utsey m. Albert Keils 18 March 1843.

3. J. J. Utsey, b. ca 1826 Ala., m. Martha ----, b. ca 1829
   Ala.. Known issue:

   a. Mary Utsey, b. ca 1848 Ala.

4. Goran Utsey, b. ca 1829 Ala., m. Mary F. Thomas 11 July 1863.

5. LaFayette Utsey, b. ca 1831 Ala..

6. Catherine Utsey, b. ca 1834 Ala., m. Columbus Herring 19 Oct.
   1854.

7. Mary Utsey, b. ca 1836 Ala.

8. R. V. Utsey, b. ca 1838 Ala.

Sources of information:

Barbour Co., Ala. Probate Records
Barbour Co., Ala. Census Records
Barbour Co., Ala. Cemetery Records

Family tradition says that the parents of the Ventress family
of Barbour Co. lived in Monroe and Jones Co., Ga. before moving
to this area. They were probably Stephen Ventress and wife,
Nancy. One Stephen Ventress married Nancy Wilkerson 8 Nov. 1808
in Putnam Co., Ga.. Stephen Ventress was enumerated in the 1830
Census of Pike Co., Ala., and Nancy Ventress was in the 1832 and
1840 Census of Barbour Co.. In 1850, she was living with Jesse
B. and Nancy (Ventress) Coleman, age 60, born Ga..

At least four of their children lived in Barbour Co. as
follows:

1. Sophie Ventress m. O. J. Williams (see WILLIAMS).

2. Thomas Ventress (see later).

3. James Ventress (see later).

4. Nancy Ventress m. Jesse B. Coleman (see later).

Thomas Ventress came to Barbour (then Pike) Co., Ala. about
1826 and entered land between Clayton and Bakerhill in 1839. He
was born 8 Sept. 1813 Jones Co., Ga., died 17 Oct. 1886, married
(1) Mary A. (Loveless?) who was born ca 1818 Ga., died ca 1850.
He married (2) Mary A. Norton (see NORTON) 21 March 1854. She
was born 15 June 1826 Ala., died 26 Sept. 1906. They are buried
in Clayton Cem.. Issue:

By 1st wife:

1. William E. Ventress, b. ca 1837 Ala., d. by 1870 (maybe in
    the Civil War), m. Mary E. Johnson 18 Aug. 1859 (see JOHNSON).
    She was born ca 1836 Ala., died 24 April 1914, daughter of
    Jesse Johnson. She probably married (2) James M. King 27
    Jan. 1876. Known issue:

    a. A. C. Ventress, b. 1860 Ala., d. 1930, buried in Clayton
        Cem..

2. James Ventress, b. ca 1840 Ala., must have died young as he is not in the 1860 Census and they named another son James in 1858.

3. Stephen F. Ventress, b. ca 1843 Ala., living Montgomery, Ala. in 1886, possibly married Matilda P. Heard 15 June 1865.

4. Martha A. Ventress, b. ca 1845 Ala., m. Virgil Taylor. They were living in Miss. in 1886.

5. Thomas H. Ventress, b. 4 Aug. 1847 Ala., d. 30 Oct. 1917, m. (1) Arrena Norton 14 Dec. 1872 (see NORTON). She was born 28 Feb. 1858 Ala., died 12 April 1897. He married (2) Julia Emma Richards 7 Nov. 1897. She was born 9 May 1869, died 30 Jan. 1953. They are buried in Clayton Cem.. Issue (all by 1st wife):

   a. William Volentine Ventress, b. 29 Nov. 1877 Ala., d. 22 Sept. 1886, buried in Bethlehem Cem..

   b. Andrew V. Ventress, b. 18 Nov. 1879, d. 31 July 1881, buried in Bethlehem Cem.

   c. Rosa Arrena Ventress, b. 25 Aug. 1881 (?), d. 23 May 1965, m. Charles C. Tarver 26 Nov. 1901. He died 7 Jan. 1952.

   d. Phelix (Felix?) Hamilton Ventress, b. 24 July 1883, d. 4 May 1966, m. Zenobia Green 24 July 1908.

   e. Earnest Edward Ventress, b. 13 March 1885, m. Annie Bell Munn 26 June 1912. She died 31 July 1967.

   f. Loveless Ventress, b. 2 Feb. 1887, d. 6 Aug. 1966, m. Irene Andrews 26 Dec. 1916.

   g. Stephen Franklin Ventress, b. 24 April 1889, d. 18 Aug. 1950, m. Agnes Bennett 10 Aug. 1920.

   h. Louis Augustus Ventress, b. 24 April 1891, m. (1) Ada Teal 26 July 1916. She died 26 March 1952 and he married (2) Mrs. Onyx (Evans) Clark 17 Oct. 1954.

i. a son, born 26 March 1894, died 3 May 1894, buried in Clayton Cem..

j. Rena Ventress, b. 15 Feb. 1897, d. 9 Aug. 1897, buried in Clayton Cem..

6. Cornelia Ventress, b. ca 1849 Ala.. There is no further record of her unless she is the Mary E. (or C.) Ventress who married John Taylor and lived in Jackson, Tenn.

By 2nd wife:

7. Ann Eliza Ventress, b. ca 1855 Ala., m. George W. Lee 13 May 1875 (see LEE).

8. Addie C. Ventress, b. 6 Jan. 1857 Ala., d. 3 Feb. 1932, never married. She is buried in Clayton Cem..

9. James Clayton Ventress, b. 9 Jan. 1858 Ala., d. 18 July 1939, m. Willie E. Blair 9 Aug. 1888. She was born 6 April 1871, died 4 Aug. 1947. They are buried in Clayton Cem..

James Ventress, b. 15 Oct. 1818 Ga., d. 13 Jan. 1892, m. (1) Mary Jane Dill 4 June 1846. She was born 18 Nov. 1827 Ala., died 24 April 1877, granddaughter of Jesse Rix. He married (2) Margaret L. Reeves 25 May 1880 - born 31 Aug. 1855 Ala., died by 1896. Issue (from 1850 & 1860 Census):

1. Sarah O. Ventress, b. 12 May 1847 Ala., d. 1 Oct. 1886, m. W. H. (or C.) Williams in March 1871 (see WILLIAMS). Issue:
   a. Dolly Williams
   b. Lila Williams
   c. Harris Williams
   d. Joe Williams
   e. Belle Williams
   f. Mamie Williams m. George Hinson, living in Fla. 1896.
   g. Ella Williams m. E. Gilmore

2. Ella V. Ventress, b. 5 Nov. 1848 Ala., m. W. G. Sheehee 19 Dec. 1872. In 1896, they were living in Florida.

298

3. Wallace Ventress, b. 24 Feb. 1850, d. 12 May 1851.

4. John Robert Ventress, b. 6 Oct. 1851 Ala., d. 16 Nov. 1931, m. Clifford Ann Crews 26 Feb. 1879. Issue:

   a. John Robert Ventress, born & died 23 Aug. 1889.

   b. Emma Marshall Ventress, b. 2 Dec. 1891 Clayton, Ala., probably died 28 May 1933, m. B. B. Warren 31 Dec. 1912.

   c. Mary Marshall Ventress, b. 24 Jan. 1894 Clayton Ala., m. Robert Lee Fenn 16 Jan. 1926 in Chattanooga, Tenn..

5. Thomas Ventress, b. 23 March 1853 Ala., married Ida Fields 24 Nov. 1880.

6. Charles P. Ventress, b. 18 Feb. 1855 Ala., residence not known in 1896.

7. William Ventress, b. 23 Dec. 1856 Ala., d. 26 Feb. 1881, probably never married.

8. James Frederick Ventress, b. 20 July 1858 Ala., m. Rebecca A. Warren 18 Dec. 1887.

9. Amos Rist Ventress, b. 11 Feb. 1861 Ala., m. Willie Mae Flowers 27 Nov. 1898.

10. Calvin Rist Ventress, b. 4 Oct. 1862 Ala., d. 21 Aug. 1877.

11. Fannie A. (Minnie) Ventress, b. 1 Aug. 1864 Ala., d. 16 June 1926, m. Robert D. Waterson 2 Dec. 1889.

12. Isla Mae Ventress, b. 10 Dec. 1866 Ala., d. 15 April 1929, m. James A. Davis 24 July 1892. In 1896, they were living in Chattanooga, Tenn..

13. Mary J. Ventress, b. ca 1867 Ala. (not listed in the James Ventress Bible).

14. Hattie Deliah Ventress, b. 10 Sept. 1871 Ala., not married in 1896.

Nancy Ventress, b. ca 1824 Ga., d. after 1880, m. Jesse B. Coleman 16 May 1843, who died by Oct. 1857. Issue:

1. Eugenia Coleman, b. ca 1845 Ala., not married in 1880.

2. Albert Coleman, b. ca 1847 Ala.

3. Ann Coleman, b. ca 1849 Ala., m. Zach. W. Dyches 3 May 1874

Other sources:

Ventress Bibles

WALKER

Solomon Walker (a Revolutionary soldier) was one of the earliest settlers of this area, coming here about 1823 from Cumberland Co., N. C. via Georgia. He was born 1 Aug. 1757, died 11 Aug. 1837, m. Gooden Cox in N. C.. She was born 15 Nov. 1762 N. C., died 5 Nov. 1838. They are buried in a family cemetery on land entered by the Walker family - his grave has a DAR marker in addition to the headstone. Issue:

1. Maisy Walker, b. 21 March 1785 Cumberland Co., N. C., d. 19 Aug. 1820 Washington Co., Ga., never married.

2. Lewis Walker, b. 6 Jan. 1791 Cumberland Co., N. C., d. 23 Nov. 1877, m. Nancy McInnis. She was born 10 March 1810 N. C., died 29 March 1893 (see McINNIS). They are buried in the Walker family cemetery. Issue:

   a. Maisy Catharine Walker, b. 21 Dec. 1832 Barbour Co., Ala., d. 17 Jan. 1889 (buried in the Walker family cemetery), m. Arthur Crews 12 May 1863. She was his second wife.

   b. Nancy Jane Walker, b. 16 March 1835 Barbour Co., Ala., d. 23 Aug. 1929, buried Walker cemetery - never married.

   c. Solomon Miles Walker, b. 14 Aug. 1837 Barbour Co., Ala., d. 10 Nov. 1837, buried in the Walker cemetery.

   d. Mary Walker, b. 6 March 1838 Barbour Co., Ala., d. 18 March 1925, m. George H. Thomas 7 Feb. 1866 (see THOMAS).

   e. John Alexander Walker, b. 14 March 1841 Barbour Co., Ala., d. 9 Nov. 1862 in the Civil War.

   f. Amanda Walker, b. 1 Jan. 1844 Barbour Co., Ala., d. 13 Oct. 1931, m. J. M. Keahey. She is buried in the Walker cemetery.

   g. David Lewis Walker, b. 1 Sept. 1846 Barbour Co., Ala., d. 20 March 1935, buried in the Walker cemetery. He was

301

not married in 1880 .

h.   James Franklin Walker, b. 30 March 1849 Barbour Co.,
     Ala., d. 25 Sept. 1933 Dale Co., Ala., m. (1) Nancy Ann
     Victoria McCraney 25 Jan. 1876. She was born 31 Dec.
     1852, died 22 Nov. 1876. The name of his second wife
     is not known.

i.   Cynthia Caroline Walker, b. 19 Dec. 1851 Barbour Co.,
     Ala., d. 29 Jan. 1945, m. David A. Wilson 25 Jan. 1870.

Other sources:

Ventress Bibles
Crews family letter
Walker Bibles

In 1829 and 1830, Henry R. Ward patented land near Louisville and in Clayton. In Jan. 1833, he and his wife, Luticia T., of Pike Co., Ala., put up part of this land as security on a note. In 1837, they were living in Butler Co., Ala.

Micajah B. Ward, b. Ga., d. between 1834 and 1840, m. Ann Dean, sister of Susan, wife of Jesse Burch. She died by Nov. 1848. In 1829, he patented land near Louisville, which was then in Pike Co., and in the 1830 Census of Pike Co., Ala., he and H. R. Ward were adjoining.

The heirs of Micajah B. and Ann (Dean) Ward were:

1. Lewis D. Ward, b. ca 1826 Ala., d. after 1880, m. (1) Nancy Warren, who died by Oct. 1851 - no issue by this marriage. He m. (2) Julia Ann Warren, sister of Nancy. She was born ca 1838 Ala.. Known issue:

   a. Henry Richard Ward, b. ca 1856 Ala.

   b. Mary Frances Ward, b. ca 1858 Ala.

   c. Lula Ward, b. ca 1863 Ala.

   d. Ulric Ward, b. ca 1865 Ala.

   e. Annie Ward, b. ca 1868 Ala.

   f. Van Ward, b. ca 1871 Ala.

   g. Julia Ward, b. ca 1874 Ala.

2. Henry C. Ward, b. ca 1830 Ala., m. Lucinda A. Warren on 1 Jan. 1854. She was born 19 Oct. 1838, died 6 Feb. 1915. Issue:

   a. Edward D. Ward, b. 5 March 1865, d. 21 June 1933.

   b. Lizzie Frances Ward, b. 25 April 1870, d. 22 Feb. 1892.

   c. Ernest V. Ward, b. 4 April 1874, d. 14 April 1947, m. Minter Bush Cox.

Lucinda A. (Warren) Ward and her three above named children

are buried in Clayton Cemetery.

3. Mary Ann E. Ward, b. ca 1825 Ala., d. after 1864, m. Benjamin
   A. Barron 18 Sept. 1842. He was born ca 1820 Ga., d. by June
   1864. Known issue:

   a. Ann E. Barron, b. ca 1845 Ala.

   b. Leonidas Barron, b. ca 1848 Ala.

   c. Elizabeth Barron, b. 1850, d. 1852, buried Clayton
      cemetery.

   d. Julia F. Barron, b. 1853, d. 1855, buried Clayton ceme-
      tery.

   e. Mary Barron, born and died 1856, buried Clayton cemetery.

   In the 1820 Georgia Census, M. B. Ward is lsited in
Burke Co., Ga..

   In 1833, James B. Holcombe of Monroe Co., Ga. gave a slave
to his step-daughter, Ann Ward, wife of Micajah B. Ward. In
1834, he gave a slave to his step-daughter, Susan Burch, wife of
Jesse Burch. The will of James B. Holcombe was probated in Talbot Co., Ga. on 1 March 1852. He named his wife, Elizabeth,
step-son Seaborn L. Dean, and mentioned Lewis D. Ward, Henry C.
Ward and Mary Ann E. Barron.

Sources of information:

Barbour Co., Ala. Probate Records
Barbour Co., Ala. Census Records
Barbour Co., Ala. Cemetery Records
Talbot Co., Ga. Records

In 1829, Hinchey (Hinchea) Warren entered land in plots scat-
tered over the Southwest area of Barbour Co., but it is doubtful
if he lived on any of them. There was a Hinch Warren living in
Conecuh Co., Ala. in 1818, also Richard, Malakiah, Robert and
Ketral Warren. On 14 Aug. 1837, Hinchey Warren and wife, Mary
H., of Conecuh Co., Ala. sold part of their land in Barbour Co.
to Jared Williams, so it is probable that he stayed in Conecuh
Co.. If he was related to the family of Thomas Warren, it is
not shown in the records.

There was a Hinch Warren living in Burke Co., Ga. at the
time of the 1805 Land Lottery.

Also in 1829, Thomas Warren entered his first land in Barbour Co., due South of Clayton. His brother, Burris Warren,
entered the land on which the family cemeteries are located (due
West of Clayton) in 1835.

Thomas Warren (the elder) wrote his will in Edgefield Dist.,
S. C. on 4 Sept. 1815, and it was probated there by 23 Jan. 1821.
It was rerecorded in Barbour Co., Ala. on 25 June 1842. Elizabeth, his wife, evidently came to Barbour Co. with her children,
as she is listed in the 1840 Census next of Lucy Efurd. Issue
of Thomas and Elizabeth Warren:

1. John Warren - no record of him in Barbour Co. unless he was
   the John Warren of Muscogee Co., Ga. who entered much land
   here in 1835. He was probably a land speculator.

2. James Warren - no record of him in Barbour Co.

3. Thomas Warren, Sr. (so designated in Barbour Co. records)
   died Feb. 1849, m. Rebecca ----. She was born 1790 in N. C.,
   died 26 May 1854. Issue:

   a. Thomas J. Warren, died by July 1850, m. Sarah ----.* She
      m. (2) Thomas C. Helms by 1856.

305

b. Martha Warren, died by 1854, m. William Herring.

c. Nancy Warren, b. ca 1824, m. Franklin Anglin.

d. Joel D. Warren, b. ca 1826 Ala., m. Hannah M. Lampley 4 March 1851.

e. James E. Warren, b. ca 1827 Ala., was living in Texas in 1855.

f. Mary Ann E. Warren, b. ca 1830 Ala., m. Absolom F. Utsey by 1845.

g. Milly (Mildred?) Warren, b. 1832 Ala., d. 1915, m. John M. Lampley 22 June 1847.

h. ---- Warren (a daughter), died before 1840, m. Giles C. Efurd (see Efurd family).

4. (James?) Burris Warren, b. 21 July 1788, d. 21 Nov. 1845 m. Lucinda Efurd, b. 28 Feb. 1811 S. C., d. 10 March 1888. Both are buried in family cemeteries on the old Burris Warren place. Issue:

a. Adeline Warren, b. 25 Aug. 1827 S. C., d. 18 Jan. 1894, m. Gilbert McCall 24 Sept. 1846. He was born 19 March 1821 N. C., died 8 April 1903. Both are buried in the Warren family cemetery.

b. Cleopatra Warren, died after 1888, m. Thomas S. Smart 14 Oct. 1848.

c. Daniel Warren, b. ca 1830 Ala., d. by 1888, m. Amanda J. Dukes 2 Feb. 1854.

d. *Joanna Warren, b. 9 March 1833 Ala., d. 4 Sept. 1853, n.m. She is buried in the Warren family cemetery.

e. Monroe J. Warren (Dr.), b. 11 July 1837 Ala., d. 19 Feb. 1886, m. Mary Frances Lawson. She was born 2 Jan. 1843 Ga., died 5 Dec. 1925. Both are buried in the Warren family cemetery.

f. James Burris Warren, Jr., b. 1 Jan. 1839, d. 28 Jan. 1912

m. Mary Jane Dickert, daughter of James W. and Jane M. Dickert. She was born 27 Oct. 1853, died 17 May 1920. Both are buried in the Warren family cemetery.

g. Georgiana Warren, b. 13 Oct. 1840 Ala., d. 17 Nov. 1919, is buried in the Warren family cemetery, m. Wilson S. Smart 29 Oct. 1857.

h. Bates Warren, b. 19 June 1842, d. 21 Aug. 1860, buried in the Warren family cemetery.

Note: Also buried in the Warren family cemetery is: Elzever Warren, b. 10 Oct. 1795, d. 3 July 1842.

5. Edward Warren, died by Dec. 1850, m. Nancy ----. She m. (2) William Loveless on 9 June 1850. Issue of Nancy and Edward Warren:

a. Thomas E. Warren, b. 4 March 1830, d. 2 Dec. 1895, m. Frances Sophronia Loveless 1 Aug. 1850. She was born 4 March 1835, death date illegible. Both are buried at Center Ridge Church.

b. Nancy Warren, died by 1850, m. Lewis D. Ward (see Ward family).

c. Lucy E. Warren, died by 1851, m. William L. Loveless 18 Jan. 1848.

d. Julia Ann Warren, b. ca 1832 Ala., m. Lewis D. Ward 21 Dec. 1851. She was his second wife - his first wife was her sister, Nancy.

e. America Warren, b. ca 1834 Ala.

f. Mahala Frances Warren, b. ca 1835 Ala., d. by 1852.

g. Jackson L. Warren, b. ca 1837 Ala.

h. Sarah A. E. Warren, b. ca 1839 Ala.

i. Adeline Warren, b. ca 1841 Ala., m. M. K. Shelby 14 Dec. 1858.

j. Lucinda Warren, b. ca 1843 Ala.

k. Edward K. P. Warren, b. ca 1846 Ala.

l. William Warren, b. ca 1849 Ala. He is in the 1850 Census of Barbour Co., but is not mentioned in the estate of Edward Warren, so he probably died young.

6. Gracy Warren m. ---- Martin.

7. Nancy Warren

8. Elizabeth Warren

9. Milly Warren

Sources of information:

Barbour Co., Ala. Probate Records
Barbour Co., Ala. Census Records
Barbour Co., Ala. Cemetery Records

*ADDITIONS & CORRECTIONS AS OF JUNE 1, 1979:

Thomas J. Warren m. Sarah Lightner by 1844. She was a daughter of Michael Lightner.

Joanna Warren m. Duncan McCall and had one child, R. H. H. McCall.

William C. Watson patented land between Louisville and Clio in 1827, in what was then Pike Co., Ala.. He died by March 1833. In Aug. 1837, James C. Watson (guardian of the orphans of William C. Watson) sold the land belonging to their estate - the deed was headed Muscogee Co., Ga..

James C. Watson was a prominent man in Columbus, Ga.. He was president of the Insurance Bank of Columbus and a speculator in Indian lands. He died in 1843, probably in Columbus, Ga.. His executors were John H. Watson and B. W. Walker.

The names of the wife and children of William C. Watson do not appear in the Barbour Co. records, but from a deed, it is apparent that one of his daughters married Benjamin Carne of Early Co., Ga.. Also, in Muscogee Co., Ga. on 5 March 1833, James C. Watson was appointed guardian of James S. Watson and William C. Watson, minor heirs of William C. Watson, deceased.

"Two Centuries With a Willis Family" by D. M. Willis states that Nathan Watson married Susan Zachary, and they were the parents of Thomas and Peter Watson, who entered land in Barbour Co. in 1835. If they were related to William C. and James C. Watson, it is not shown in the county records. Their land lay near Three Notch (now in Bullock Co., Ala.), and they were killed there by Indians during the Creek Indian War in 1836.

Peter Watson, d. by 1836, m. Elizabeth ----, b. ca 1798 in Ga.. He is buried in the family cemetery near Three Notch, Ala.. Issue:

1. Mary Ann Watson, b. ca 1814 Ga., m. Francis M. Moseley, b. ca 1814 Ga.. They may have moved to Tyler, Texas by 1891. Known issue:

    a. James J. Moseley, b. ca 1837 Ala.

b.   William Moseley, b. ca 1840 Ala.

c.   Safrona Moseley, b. ca 1842 Ala.

d.   Francis M. Moseley, b. ca 1845 Ala.

e.   Mary Moseley, b. ca 1846 Ala.

f.   Martha Moseley, b. ca 1849 Ala., m. N. Wynn

g.   Thomas Moseley

2.   Thomas J. Watson, living in La. by 1891.

3.   Jesse Z. Watson, b. ca 1822 Ala.

4.   Susan Ann E. Watson, b. ca 1825, m. John G. Gaines 2 Feb.
     1845. Known issue:

a.   Thomas Gaines

b.   Mary Gaines

5.   Daniel (or David) G. Watson, b. ca 1826 Ala., may have moved
     to La. by 1891.

6.   Rebecca J. Watson, b. ca 1829 Ala., m. Henson K. Paul 21 Nov.
     1851. They were living in Pike Co., Ala. in 1891.

7.   Nathan C. Watson, b. 12 May 1830 Ala., d. 8 Oct. 1902, m.
     Martha C. Sellars. They are buried in Ramah Cemetery, Pike
     Co., Ala.. Known issue:

a.   D. Y. Watson

b.   A. R. Watson (female)

8.   John J. Watson, b. ca 1832 Ala., may have married Ann Re-
     becca Murphy 15 June 1858.

9.   James F. Watson, b. ca 1834 Ala.

10. Peter Watson, b. ca 1836 Ala., may have moved to Texas by
     1891.

Thomas Watson, brother of Peter Watson, was also killed by
Indians about 1836, and is buried in the Watson family cemetery
near Three Notch. He married Elizabeth, daughter of Joshua and
Laura Grace Calloway. She married (2) Zacheus J. Babb by 24
April 1840, and the family may have moved to Conecuh Co., Ala..

Issue (by 1st husband):

1. Emily Watson, m. Joseph D. Gibson 13 Oct. 1842. They were living in Meridian, Miss. in 1891.

2. Stephen D. Watson

3. Anna Eliza Watson, b. 7 June 1832 Ala., d. 14 June 1900, m. (1) William Anon Willis 29 Nov. 1845 (2) William Moore. She was in Snow Hill, Texas in 1891.

4. Narcissa Watson, m. ---- Dukes. They were living in Evergreen, Ala. in 1891.

5. *Thomas C. Watson, may have married Mary R., daughter of Zachariah Bush. He was living at Burnt Corn, Conecuh Co., Ala. in 1891.

Sources of information:

Barbour Co., Ala. Probate Records
Barbour Co., Ala. Census Records
Barbour Co., Ala. Cemetery Records
Pike Co., Ala. Cemetery Records
"Two Centuries With a Willis Family" by D. M. Willis
"Redskins, Ruffleshirts and Rednecks" by Mary E. Young

*ADDITIONS & CORRECTIONS AS OF JUNE 1, 1979:

Thomas C. Watson did not marry Mary R. Bush.

There were at least three families of this name that settled
in Barbour Co. at a very early date. Possibly the earliest was
William Williams who founded Williamston about 1820...one of the
first communities in Barbour Co.

Another was Edward Williams, who came to Eufaula in the
early 1820's. He is believed to be the builder of the Tavern,
one of the oldest structures in Eufaula.

The third group are the children of the William Williams who
died in Hancock Co., Ga. ca 1805. Four of his children migrated
to Barbour Co..

The family of Zachariah Williams was not here as early as
those mentioned above, but is also discussed in this chapter.
There were so many other Williams families in Barbour Co. by
1850 that it is not practical to include them all.

William Williams

William Williams, b. ca 1760/70, d. by Nov. 1846, m. Elizabeth ----, b. ca 1770/80, d. after 1846. They settled the town
of Williamston, one of the earliest in Barbour Co.. Issue:[2]
1. Jarret Williams, b. ca 1790/1800, d. by Jan. 1842, m. Tempy
    (Vinson?), b. ca 1790/1800, d. by 1849. Issue:
    a. Lovett Williams, over 21 and living in Fla. in 1851.
    b. William J. Williams, over 21 and living in La. in 1851,
        probably died by 1857.
    c. Elizabeth Williams, over 21 and living in La. in 1851,
        m. Wright Margalin (Mongalin?) by 1856.
    d. Delila Williams, over 21 and living in La. in 1851
        (possibly Bienville Par.), m. John Brewer.
    e. Jarret O. Williams, under 21 and living in La. in 1851
        (possibly Bienville Par.).

f. Wesley Williams, b. ca 1801 Ga., m. Charity ----.

g. Nancy Williams, over 21 in 1851 and living in Coffee Co., Ala. in 1857, m. James Deal.

h. Wiley Williams, died by 1851, m. Alice ---- who may have married (2) Canady Benton Anderson 7 March 1844.

i. John G. Williams, b. ca 1821 Ala., d. 1 Jan. 1857, m. Christian Margaret Ann McLean 23 March 1845. She m. (2) Wm. J. Martin 12 Nov. 1857.

j. Mary E. Williams, over 21 in 1851, m. William G. Bush 15 Oct. 1845, living Coffee Co., Ala. in 1859.

k. Braddock W. Williams, under 21 in 1851, possibly died by 1857.

1. Sarah Williams, b. ca 1837 Ala., m. David Davis 24 Dec. 1851, living in La. 1857.

2. Braddock Williams m. Sarah Williams 22 Dec. 1822 Henry Co., Ala.. No further record.

3. Sarah Williams m. ---- Bush (William Bush, Sr. who died before 1836?).

4. John L. Williams, b. ca 1804 Ga., d. by April 1875, m. Sarah (Leverett?), b. ca 1813 Ga., d. after 1875. Issue:

a. Stephen L. Williams, b. ca 1832 Ala., not married in 1860.

b. Amanda Williams, b. ca 1836 Ala., d. by 1875, m. Peter Cunningham 11 May 1854. She was his second wife.

c. Josephine Williams, b. ca 1837 Ala., probably died young.

d. Louisianna Jane Williams, b. ca 1839 Ala., m. John C. Reese 21 Feb. 1867.

e. John C. Williams, b. 21 April 1840 Ala., d. 31 Aug. 1902, m. Sarah McDonald 5 Sept. 1860. She was born 5 Jan. 1843 Ala., died 19 March 1933 - both are buried in Clayton Cem..

313

f.　Sarah C. Williams, b. ca 1842 Ala..

g.　George R. Williams, b. ca 1844 Ala., probably died by
1870.

h.　Charles F. Williams, b. ca 1845 Ala., m. Nancy E. Lasse-
ter 2 Feb. 1868.

i.　Susan V. Williams, b. ca 1847 Ala., m. R. Monroe Lasse-
ter 10 Jan. 1867. He was born 1841, died 2 Sept. 1907
and is buried in Clayton Cem..

j.　Mary E. Williams, b. ca 1850 Ala..

k.　Ann E. Williams, b. ca 1856 Ala..

5.　Malinda Williams m. N. W. Turner. She died by Feb. 1849.

6.　Elizabeth Williams m. James Pugh 17 Nov. 1822 Henry Co.,
Ala.. This may have been the James Pugh mentioned on
page 256.[1]

7.　William Williams, Jr., b. ca 1817 Ga., m. Arrensa Bush, b.
ca 1825 Ala., d. by 1852, daughter of Zachariah Bush (see
BUSH). Issue:

a.　Mary Amanda Williams, b. ca 1841 Ala., m. Welborn J.
Reaves 2 Dec. 1857 (see PARMER).

b.　Jane A. Williams, b. ca 1843 Ala..

c.　Columbiana Williams, b. ca 1845 Ala., may have married
Gideon T. Nix 25 Nov. 1868.

d.　Sarah E. Williams, b. 13 Jan. 1848 Ala., d. 6 Nov. 1900,
m. C. H. Houston 20 Dec. 1867. He was born in 1836,
died 1915. Both are buried in Rocky Mount Cem..

e.　Louisianna (Lucy) A. Williams, b. ca 1851, may have
married John Dowel 18 March 1867.

8.　Council B. Williams, b. ca 1820/5.

9.　Lucinda Williams.

10.　Owen G. Williams, d. by 1846, may have married a Parmer.
One daughter, Ellender Caroline Williams...Jacob Parmer was

314

her guardian until 1856 when Thomas S. Kettler became her guardian and asked that the estate be moved to Butler Co., Ala..

George Walker Williams, b. 3 April 1816 or 1818 Ga., d. 10 July 1900, m. (1) Sarah A. Ryan 15 Dec. 1841, daughter of Hampton Ryan. She was born ca 1825 Ga.. Census records indicate that he married a second time, and that wife was also named Sarah. She died after 1900 (age 50 in 1900). "Backtracking in Barbour Co., Ala." by A. K. Walker states that this branch of the family is related to those of the Williamston settlement. Issue:

1. Georgia Ann Williams, b. ca 1842 Ala., d. July 1900, m. John W. Johnston 9 Nov. 1859. He was born 1832 and died 1 June 1862 in the Civil War (see JOHNSTON).

2. Risdin Pitt Williams, b. ca 1844 Ala., died in Civil War.

3. William Williams, b. ca 1846 Ala., probably died young.

4. John Cochran Williams, b. 13 Sept. 1845 Ala., d. 27 Sept. 1895, m. Josie Rollins, daughter of G. W. Rollins. She was born 16 July 1853, died 16 Sept. 1942. They are buried in Rocky Mount Cem..

5. Charles M. Williams, b. ca 1852, d. by 1900, m. Clifford ----. In 1900, she was living in New York state.

6. Sarah Margrette Williams, b. ca 1854 Ala., d. 13 Sept. 1883, m. Daniel J. Grantham 4 March 1869 (see JOHNSTON). Issue:
    a. George Grantham, b. 1870, d. 1933.
    b. Mary Grantham m. ---- Watson.
    c. Horace Grantham.
    d. Charlie Grantham.
    e. John A. Grantham.

7. Rachael A. Williams, b. ca 1856 Ala., m. Wm. Craddock 7 Jan. 1870. In 1900, they were living in Dothan, Ala..

315

8. Lula Williams, b. ca 1860 Ala., m. Daniel J. Grantham ca
   29 Feb. 1884. His first wife was her sister, Sarah Margrette
   Williams (see JOHNSTON).

9. Augusta (Gussie) P. Williams m. Thomas Jefferson McGilvray
   29 Dec. 1879. His second wife was Jennie Lee Smith (see
   McGILVRAY).

Edward Williams

Edward Williams came to Eufaula from Cuthbert, Ga., and is
believed to have built the Tavern. He was born ca 1784 N. C.,
died after 1860, married Sarah ----, who was born 3 May 1788 and
died 10 April 1852. She is buried in Fairview Cem., Eufaula,
Ala.. Of their five children, only four are known:

1. Cynthia F. Williams, b. ca 1826 Ga., m. Dr. Webster M.
   Rains.

2. Lucinda Williams, b. ca 1828 Ga.

3. Sarah Williams, b. ca 1831 Ga.

4. Edward Wesley Williams.

Other sources:

"Backtracking in Barbour Co., Ala." by A. K. Walker

WILLIAM WILLIAMS
(of Hancock Co., Ga.)

William Williams, who died ca 1805 Hancock Co., Ga., m.
Elviney (Mullins?). Of their children, at least four came to
Barbour Co., Ala.. Issue:

1. Nancy Williams m. John Purifoy and came to Barbour Co.,
   Ala. (see PURIFOY).

2. Elizabeth Williams m. ---- Pearce, living Baldwin Co., Ga.
   in 1805.

3. Buckner Williams, b. ca 1795 Ga., died between 1870 and 1880
   Barbour Co., Ala., m. Rhoda (Johnson ? - believed to be a

daughter of Phillip Johnson). She was born ca 1811 S. C., died after 1895. Issue:

a. George W. Williams, b. ca 1831 Ala., d. after 1880, m. Adeline Collins 16 Nov. 1858. She was born 12 Jan. 1841, died 21 March 1885. They are buried in Clayton Cem..

b. Louisa Williams, b. 1 Nov. 1836 Ala., d. 8 Oct. 1865, buried in Clayton Cem.. She married Hartwell Collins 9 May 1854. He was born ca 1829 Ala., died after 1880.

c. Ann L. Williams, b. ca 1837 Ala., d. Sept. 1895, m. ---- McDonald. She died in Enterprise, Ala..

d. Mary A. Williams, b. ca 1839 Ala., probably died by 1895, m. William T. Mullen 11 Sept. 1860.

e. William Harrison Williams, b. ca 1841 Ala., died after 1895, m. Sarah O. Ventress in March 1871 (see VENTRESS).

f. Laona (Leonora?) Williams, b. ca 1846 Ala., probably died by 1895.

g. Laura Williams, b. ca 1850 Ala., probably died by 1895.

h. Thomas J. Williams, b. ca 1853 Ala., not married in 1880.

4. Osborn J. Williams, b. ca 1799 Ga., d. by July 1854, m. Sophia Ventress (see VENTRESS) ca 1830. She was born ca 1810 Ga., died July 1892. Issue:

a. Ann M. Williams, b. ca 1833 Ala., d. after 1880, m. Augustus L. Oliver 16 Jan. 1850. He was born ca 1825 Ga., died after 1892.

b. James M. Williams, b. ca 1845 Ala., died after 1892.

5. Patience Williams - probably stayed in Georgia.

6. Elliott Williams - probably stayed in Georgia.

7. Judge Stith Williams, b. 17 Feb. 1804 Hancock Co., Ga., d. 29 May 1878, m. Euphemia McNeill ca 1826 Pike Co., Ala. She was born 19 Jan. 1808 N. C., died 4 April 1889. They

317

are buried in Clayton Cem.. Issue:

a. William H. Williams (Dr.), b. ca 1827 Ala., d. 11 Nov.
1855, m. Margaret A. Jackson 29 April 1852. He is
buried in Louisville Cem..

b. Jeremiah Norman Williams, b. 29 May 1829 Barbour Co.,
Ala., d. 1915, m. Mary E. Screws 20 Dec. 1864. She was
born 1841, died 1927 - both are buried in Clayton Cem..

c. John Williams, b. 13 Aug. 1831 Ala., d. 5 Feb. 1891,
never married. He is buried in Clayton Cem..

d. Emily Williams, b. 5 Sept. 1837 Ala., d. 22 Nov. 1889,
m. John W. Flournoy, b. ca Feb. 1826 N. C., d. 8 June
1872. They are buried in Louisville Cem..

e. Richard Williams, b. 27 Sept. 1839 Ala., d. 25 March
1891, may have married Mary E. Lane 30 Nov. 1869. He
lived in Birmingham, Ala. but is buried in Fairview
Cem., Eufaula, Ala..

f. Victoria Williams, b. ca 1842 Ala., m. John C. McEachern (see McEACHERN).

Other sources:

"Memorial Record of Ala.", Vol. I, page 470
"History of Barbour Co., Ala." by Mattie Thompson
Hancock Co., Ga. Will Book C, page 188
Mrs. H. T. Ellison, Hurtsboro, Ala..

Zachariah Williams

Zachariah Williams, b. 10 March 1778, d. 15 Sept. 1840, m.
(1) Martha Walton 5 Oct. 1800. She was born 11 April 1780,
died 9 Oct. 1807, probably in Georgia. He married (2) Sarah
----, born 16 March 1774, died 24 Dec. 1849. Zachariah and
Sarah Williams are buried in the family cemetery near Twin
Springs, Russell Co., Ala.. Known issue:

1. Robert Walton Williams (Dr.), b. 30 Sept. 1803 Ga., d. 8
Jan. 1859, buried in the family cemetery near Twin Springs.

He married Geraldine E. Carter 18 May 1853, daughter of Judge William Carter of Stewart Co., Ga.. She was born ca 1828 Ga., died Sept. 1894. She married (2) Dr. Henry M. Hunter 26 May 1862. Issue (by 1st husband):

a. Anna Martha Williams, b. 18 March 1854 Ala., d. 24 June 1935, Mobile, Ala., m. Dr. Robert Hughes Hayes 5 April 1883 Russell Co., Ala.. He was born 13 May 1853 (Tallapoosa Co., Ala.?), died 6 June 1914 Bullock Co., Ala..

b. Zachariah W. Williams (Dr.), b. ca 1856 Ala., living Glennville (now Russell Co.), Ala. in 1894.

c. Blanche Williams m. Wilbur Carter and was living in Del Rio, Tenn. (Texas?) in 1891.

d. Gazaway D. Williams, b. ca 1858 Ala., living Russell Co., Ala. 1894, probably never married.

By 2nd husband:

e. Geraldine Hunter, b. ca 1864, m. Benjamin Franklin, living in Florida in 1894.

f. Henry M. Hunter (Dr.), b. ca 1866, living in Union Springs, Ala. in 1894.

2. ---- Williams m. John S. Dobbins.

3. Zachariah C. Williams (Dr.), b. ca 1812 Ga.. Issue:

a. Robert Walton Williams.

4. Gazaway Davis Williams, b. 1 May 1814 (or 1824) Ga., d. 2 Oct. 1884, m. (1) Sarah E. Abercrombie, b. 21 April 1824 Ala., d. 17 May 1865. Both are buried in the family cemetery near Twin Springs. He married (2) Belle Puryear, b. 15 Sept. 1840, d. 30 Sept. 1896, also buried in the family cemetery. Known issue (by 1st wife):

a. Gazaline Williams (female), b. ca 1845 Ala., d. ca June 1879 Athens, Ga., m. (1) A. A. Hill (2) ---- Raisler.

b. Mary Williams, b. ca 1847 Ala..

c. Anderson Williams, b. ca 1849 Ala., living Austin, Texas in 1891.

d. Eddie Williams (female), b. ca 1852 Ala., m. John R. Hayes 24 July 1878 Russell Co., Ala..

e. Robert Walton Williams, b. ca 1855 Ala.

f. Mattie Williams, b. ca 1857 Ala., not married in 1891.

g. Evaline Williams, b. ca 1859 Ala., may have married ---- Rood, living Stewart Co., Ga. in 1891.

Note: Also buried in the Williams family cemetery near Twin Springs is Matilda ("Cousin Mat") Harris, b. 28 Aug. 1798 Ga., d. 3 April 1858, daughter of Ezekiel Harris. She was living in the Williams household in 1850.

A descendant of this Williams family is Mrs. J. A. Mims of Mobile, Ala..

1. Elizabeth (Williams) Pugh m. (2) Hinton Rivenbark, who died by Feb. 1849. She had a son, Thomas Pugh, who married Nancy McSwean (see McSWEAN) and a daughter, Mary Pugh, who married William Bush (see BUSH).

2. Another child of William and Elizabeth Williams was Matilda, b. ca 1807 Ga., d. 3 July 1851, buried in the Fenn cemetery near Clayton. She married Matthew Fenn (see FENN).

WILLIAMSON

Seth Williamson first patented land West of Louisville in 1827. The certificate for this land was recorded about Jan. 1837, at which time he was living in Pike Co., Ala.. A second patent, dated 1829, was recorded 31 Jan. 1838. There is nothing else in the Barbour Co. records concerning him, so he probably did not actually live in this count.

Source of information:

Barbour Co., Ala. Probate records

WILLIS

In 1829, William C. Willis patented land Southwest of Rocky
Mount Church. On 26 Jan. 1836, he sold this forty acres to Ar-
thur Crews of Barbour Co. - at this time, he was living in Henry
Co., Ala.. The patent book of Henry Co., Ala. shows that
William C. Willis received land there for military services under
the Act of 1847.

There are no further records of William C. Willis in Barbour
Co..

Joel Willis, b. 12 Feb. 1789 N. C., d. 25 Oct. 1874 Dale
Co., Ala., m. Elizabeth R. Head 2 July 1815 in Jasper Co., Ga..
She was the daughter of Richard Head (see Head family). She was
born 29 April 1794, died 29 Aug. 1876 Dale Co., Ala.. They mi-
grated from Jones Co., Ga. to Barbour Co., Ala. about 1822.
Issue:

1. Asa Willis, b. 18 Aug. 1816 Ga., d. 25 May 1860, m. Seymour
   Caroline Stafford 11 Oct. 1838. She was born 12 Oct. 1823,
   died 11 Dec. 1890 in Texas. Issue:

   a. Mary Ann Elizabeth Willis, b. 5 Sept. 1839 Ala., m.
      Peter W. Watson 12 Aug. 1860. She married (2) Jacob
      Lafayette Belott 25 Dec. 1866. She died in 1918, and
      is buried in Clayton Cemetery.

   b. Samantha Elefair Willis, b. 27 Feb. 1841 Ala., d. 29
      Jan. 1922, m. Thomas B. Pickett 27 Feb. 1859.

   c. Sarah Jane Willis, b. 22 Oct. 1843 Ala., d. 23 Jan. 1915
      in Texas, m. John W. Channell 8 Dec. 1864. He was born
      10 May 1829, died 28 Nov. 1911.

   d. Seymour Magdaline Elizabeth Willis, b. 21 Aug. 1845
      Ala., d. 28 March 1928 in Texas, m. W. Thomas Draper
      4 March 1866.

e. James Joel Stafford Willis, b. 25 March 1847 Miss., d. 20 Oct. 1926, m. Frances Amanda Jane Smith 3 Sept. 1868. She was born 21 Feb. 1848, died 1 April 1927. Both are buried in Clayton Cemetery.

f. Robert Richard Winfield Scott Willis, b. 17 May 1849 Ala., d. 3 June 1932 in Texas, m. Margaret Doughlas 11 May 1876 in Houston Co., Texas. She was born 1 July 1857, died 1 Jan. 1910.

g. John Jefferson Willis, b. 16 May 1851, died 22 July 1851.

h. William Asa Willis, b. 29 June 1852, died 30 July 1852.

2. Mary (Polly) Willis, b. 4 April 1818 Ga., d. 3 March 1870, m. Lorenzo Faulk (see Faulk family).

3. Edmond Gwaltney Willis, b. 17 April 1820 Ga., d. 11 June 1888 in Texas, m. (1) Missouri Ann Baker 2 Aug. 1846. She was born 5 Feb. 1828, died 27 May 1880 - daughter of Jeremiah Baker, (2) Lucinda Pickett. Edmond G. Willis migrated to Texas about 1870. Issue (all by 1st wife):

a. Ricahrd Carey Willis, b. 17 May 1848 Ala., d. ca 1925 in Texas, m. Hattie Avery in Texas.

b. Joel Willis, b. 6 Nov. 1849 Ala., died in Texas, m. Sarah Viola Faulk 15 Dec. 1880 in Bullock Co., Ala.

c. James Monroe Willis, b. 31 March 1851 Ala., died in Texas.

d. Mary A. Willis, b. 24 July 1853 Ala., d. 3 Feb. 1883, m. ---- Blakey.

e. Oates Louis Willis, b. 22 June 1855 Ala., d. 23 Feb. 1930 in Texas m. Martha Rosina Blevins.

f. Missouri Elizabeth Willis, b. 29 July 1857 Ala., d. 1896 in Texas, m. Green B. Wallace.

g. Martha Frances Willis, b. 26 June 1859 Ala., m. J. C. Davis.

h. An infant, born 9 July 1861, died 5 Oct. 1861.

i. Nancy Luiza Willis, b. 8 Oct. 1863 Ala., d. 23 July 1893 in Texas, m. William Thomas Skelton 5 Oct. 1881.

j. Thomas Edmund Willis, b. 24 Feb. 1865, d. 4 June 1937 in Texas, m. Della Bullard 24 Dec. 1889.

k. William Asa Willis, b. 17 July 1868, died 26 March 1911 in Texas, m. Maud Dodd 30 Aug. 1899.

1. Samuel Bunion Willis, b. 20 July 1875 in Texas, d. 10 Nov. 1949 in Texas, m. Evalina May Ormand 20 June 1906.

4. Epsey Willis, b. 14 March 1822, d. 20 Nov. 1877, m. Richard Head 20 March 1844. He was born 21 Nov. 1817 in Ga., died in Texas. Issue:

a. Sarah Elizabeth Head, b. 9 Sept. 1846 Ala., m. James W. Stroman 5 Jan. 1868.

b. Mary Emaline Head, b. 30 July 1848 Ala., d. 15 Dec. 1849.

c. George McDuffie Head, b. 19 Oct. 1850 Ala., m. (1) Cynthia Ann Corbet (or Cordle) 18 March 1875, (2) Laura Crier 8 Nov. 1885.

d. Seymour C. Head, b. 29 Oct. 1852 Ala., d. 25 Jan. 1908 in Texas, m. William Jasper White 24 Nov. 1873.

e. Lorenzo Edmund Head, b. 13 Nov. 1854 Ala.

f. Nancy Ann Eliza Head, b. 18 Sept. 1857 Ala., d. ca 1930 in Texas, m. Joseph David Foster 22 Oct. 1885.

5. William Anon Willis, b. 17 April 1824 Ala., d. 6 Nov. 1862 Fla. (CSA), m. Ana Liza Watson 29 Nov. 1845. She was born 7 June 1832, died 14 June 1900 in Texas. She married (2) Wm. Moore. Issue (by 1st husband):

a. Thomas Joel Willis, b. 29 Sept. 1847 Ala., d. 22 Oct. 1931 in Texas, m. Mary Ann Elizabeth Ogburn 14 April 1867.

b. Epsey Ann Willis, b. 13 Sept. 1849 Ala., d. Feb. 1920 in
    Texas, m. William Henry Ogburn.

c. Archibald Anon Willis, b. 10 June 1853 Ala., d. 17 July
    1935 in Texas, m. Lucy Elizabeth Yancey 5 April 1876.

d. Zenobia Caroline Willis, b. 29 Oct. 1855 Ala., d. 4
    July 1881, m. Lou Hendrick.

e. Edmund Whitfield Willis, b. 23 Aug. 1859 Ala., d. 1 Feb.
    1884 in Texas, m. Ella Johnson.

6. Nancy Willis, b. 14 Feb. 1827 Ala., d. 25 May 1916 Dale Co.,
    Ala., m. Dr. James J. Bottoms 11 Feb. 1845. He was born ca
    1818, died 10 July 1904 Dale Co., Ala.. Issue:

a. John Jefferson Bottoms, b. 29 Nov. 1847 Ala., d. 27
    Sept. 1880 Dale Co., Ala., m. Margaret Victoria Dowling.

b. James M. Bottoms, b. ca 1849 Ala., d. ca 1853 Dale Co.,
    Ala..

c. George McDuffie Bottoms, b. 12 May 1855 Ala., d. ca 1868
    in Dale Co., Ala.

d. William C. Bottoms, b. 18 Oct. 1858 Ala., d. 26 May 1936
    in Coffee Co., Ala., m. Callie Garner.

e. James A. Bottoms, b. 11 June 1861 Ala., d. 21 Nov. 1925
    in Geneva Co., Ala., m. Smithie Agnes Howell.

7. James R. Willis, b. 17 March 1830 Ala., d. 3 May 1863 Va.
    (CSA), m. Martha Ann Elizabeth Knight 9 Feb. 1856. She was
    born 23 Sept. 1838, died 1901. Issue:

a. Mary Ann Missouri Willis, b. 17 Oct. 1858 Ala., d. 20
    Feb. 1945 in La., m. Jackson Parish.

b. Nancy Ann Elizabeth Willis, b. 7 Aug. 1860 Ala., d. 6
    May 1929 Dale Co., Ala., m. Warren Garner.

8. Elizabeth Willis, b. 12 Dec. 1832 Ala., m. Ichabod Stuckey
    3 Dec. 1851. Issue:

a. William Stuckey, b. ca 1855 - living with Richard and

325

Epsey (Willis) Head in Crenshaw Co., Ala. in 1870.

b. Sarah Stuckey, b. ca 1858 - living with Richard and Epsey (Willis) Head in Crenshaw Co., Ala. in 1870.

9. Sarah Willis, b. 8 May 1840 Ala., d. 14 Nov. 1916 in Geneva Co., Ala., m. John Thomas Williams 13 April 1856. He was born 4 July 1838, died Nov. 1862 in Tennessee (CSA). Issue:

a. James Joel Williams, b. 6 Jan. 1857 Ala., d. 12 Jan. 1911 in Kentucky, m. Maude Johnson.

b. John Thomas Williams, b. 24 Dec. 1858 Ala., d. 28 April 1919 in Geneva Co., Ala., m. Sarah J. Marley.

c. Epsey Ann Elizabeth Williams, b. 18 June 1861 Ala., d. 6 May 1933 in Geneva Co., Ala., m. Benjamin Franklin Smith (she was his second wife).

Sources of information:

"Two Centuries With a Willis Family" by D. M. Willis
Barbour Co., Ala. Probate Records
Henry Co., Ala. Probate Records

WINDHAM

In 1828, Levi B. Windham bought a town lot in Monticello, Pike Co., Ala., and in 1829, John R. Windham sold land in Pike Co., Ala. to P. J. Weaver. John R. and Levi B. Windham patented land South of Clayton from 1829 through 1836. In 1833, John R. Windham sold his land in Barbour Co. - his wife, Eliza, signed this deed. In 1834, Levi B. Windham of Pickens Co., Ala. sold land in Barbour Co. He and John R. Windham must have left Barbour Co. about the time these deeds were made.

There was an Anthony Windham who patented land in the Southwest corner of Barbour Co. in 1830, 1836 and 1843. He was probably some relation to John R. and Levi B. Windham. He was also probably related to the Windham family of Henry Co., Ala. and Darlington Dist., S. C..

Anthony Windham was born ca 1808 S. C., died after 1860. His first wife was Hepsey, daughter of Abner Flowers. He married (2) Martha A. McMurray. Probable issue (all by first wife):

1. Edward Windham, b. ca 1837 Ala.
2. Thomas Windham, b. ca 1838 Ala.
3. William (or Abner) Windham, b. ca 1840 Ala.
4. Rebecca Windham, b. ca 1842 Ala.
5. Wright Windham, b. ca 1844 Ala.
6. Julia A. Windham, b. ca 1846 Ala.
7. Mary Windham, b. ca 1848 Ala.
8. Sophronia Windham, b. ca 1851 Ala.
9. Martha Windham, b. ca 1852 Ala.
10. John Windham, b. ca 1854 Ala.
11. Shorter Windham, b. ca 1856 Ala.

Sources of information:

Barbour Co., Ala. Probate Records
Barbour Co., Ala. Census Records
Pike Co., Ala. Probate Records

Between 1834 and 1839, Elizabeth, Gibson M., Jacob, Joel and John C. Winslett patented land between White Oak Station and Batesville. Elizabeth Winslett may have had some connection to Green Norris, as on 11 Sept. 1835, they sold adjoining land separately and one piece of land jointly.

John Carson Winslett, Sr. was one of the earliest settlers of Eufaula. The name of his first wife is not known but he is believed to have had four sons and two daughters by her. After her death, he married a Creek Indian. Known issue (by 1st wife):

1. John Carson Winslett, Jr.

2. Joel Winslett, b. 19 Dec. 1802 Ga., d. 8 April 1860, m. Mary McLeod, sister of Catharine (McLeod) Gillis (see GILLIS). She was born 14 Oct. 1814 S. C., died 8 Feb. 1902. He is buried in Beulah Cem. in Pike Co., Ala.. Known issue:

   a. John G. Winslett, b. 21 June 1835 Ala., d. 23 Sept. 1907, m. Eugenia A. Boyer in 1861. She was born 31 May 1834 and died 2 Sept. 1897. They are buried in Little Oak Cem., Pike Co., Ala..

   b. Sarah Jane Winslett, b. 15 Sept. 1837 Ala., d. 7 April 1922, never married. She is buried in Little Oak Cem., Pike Co., Ala..

   c. William N. Winslett, b. ca 1840 Ala., d. by 1880.

   d. Francis Asberry Winslett, b. ca 1842 Ala., probably died by 1880.

   e. Mary C. Winslett, b. 21 May 1844, d. 17 Feb. 1908, never married. She is buried in Little Oak Cem..

   f. Joel Andrew Winslett, b. 14 Aug. 1845 Ala., d. 13 Dec. 1907, buried Little Oak Cem.. He probably never married.

   g. Wesley Alexander Winslett (Rev.), b. 27 April 1847 Ala.,

d. 3 Dec. 1928, m. Louisa Elmira Lewis 5 Oct. 1875 Pike
Co., Ala., daughter of Elisha Lewis of Pike Co.. She
was born 23 Dec. 1846, died 27 Feb. 1929. They are
buried in Little Oak Cem..

h. Nancy A. Winslett, b. 18 April 1849 Ala., d. 25 June
1922, buried Little Oak Cem., never married.

i. Margaret Alice Winslett, b. ca 1851 Ala.

j. Samuel Pierce Winslett, b. ca 1854 Ala., probably died
by 1880.

Also buried in Little Oak Cem., Pike Co., Ala. are M. A.
Winslett, b. 25 Aug. 1857, d. 1 Dec. 1915 and J. B. Winslett,
b. 2 Aug. 1862, d. 2 Dec. 1918.

3. Gibson Martin Winslett m. Susannah Coleman 4 Nov. 1823 in
Henry Co., Ala.

4. Samuel Winslett.

Other sources:

"Backtracking in Barbour Co., Ala." by A. K. Walker
"The Ala. Historical Quarterly", Vol. XXXV
1860 Census Pike Co., Ala.
Pike Co., Ala. Probate Records
Pike Co., Ala. Newspaper Obits.

Ezekiel Wise patented land near Rocky Mount Church from 1835 through 1845. In the 1830 Census, he was enumerated in Pike Co., Ala. and probably lived in the part that was cut into Barbour Co. in 1832. He was born ca 1797 N. C., died 1874. His wife, Winneford ----, was born ca 1805 Ga., died after 1880. (Note: the 1860 Census says he was born ca 1797 Ga., she was born ca 1808 Ala.). Known issue:

1. Lovie J. Wise, b. ca 1827 Ala.

2. Elizabeth Wise, b. ca 1832 Ala., probably died by 1860, married Andrew S. Williamson 19 Oct. 1852. Known issue:

   a. Narcissa E. Williamson, b. ca 1854 Ala., living with Ezekiel Wise in 1860 and 1870.

3. James H. Wise, b. ca 1835 Ala., probably died by 1874, m. Ann E. Stewart 11 Jan. 1859.

4. Lemuel L. Wise, b. 17 Aug. 1836 Ala., d. 22 Oct. 1896 (?), m. Mary J. Grantham 29 Nov. 1860 at Mary Johnston's. She was born 10 Nov. 1843 S. C., died 6 Oct. 1918 - they are buried in Rocky Mount Cem.. She was a daughter of Edward Grantham and Prudence Johnston (see JOHNSTON). Known issue:

   a. Mary Wise, b. ca 1863 Ala.

   b. Edward L. Wise, b. 30 May 1864, d. 21 July 1939, buried in Rocky Mount Cem..

   c. Patience Wise, b. ca 1866 Ala., m. John T. Baker 19 Dec. 1901. They are buried in Rocky Mount Cem. but no dates are given.

   d. George E. Wise, b. 5 Feb. 1868, d. 8 Dec. 1945, m. Clifford C. Clark 1 March 1894. She was born 1 May 1879, died 20 Nov. 1907. Both buried Rocky Mt. Cem..

   e. John W. Wise, b. 1870 Ala., d. 1 Jan. 1957, married Beulah J. Orr 10 March 1897. She was born 1875, died

1939. They are buried in Rocky Mt. Cem..

    f. James Daniel Wise, b. 1873, d. 1954, buried Rocky Mount Cem..

    g. Adolphus J. Wise, b. 6 July 1876, d. Nov. 1941, buried Rocky Mount Cem..

    h. William Gaino Wise, b. 1878, d. 1960, buried in Rocky Mount Cem..

5. Mary Jane Wise, b. ca 1838 Ala., d. after 1874, m. Turner Howell 4 Aug. 1854. They are buried in Rocky Mount Cem. but no dates are given. Issue:

    a. George Howell, b. ca 1856 Ala.

    b. John Howell, b. ca 1858 Ala.

    c. Mary Jane Howell, b. ca 1859 Ala.

    d. Leonie Howell, b. ca 1868 Ala.

    e. Robert L. Howell, b. ca 1871 Ala., m. Lettie Price 20 Feb. 1896.

    f. Alice V. Howell, b. 1875 Ala., d. 1913, m. Archibald P. McLeod 14 Sept. 1897. She was his second wife.

    g. Ella Howell, b. ca 1875 Ala.

6. Thomas Wise, b. ca 1840 Ala., probably died by 1874.

7. (John?) Edward Wise, b. 1846 Ala., d. 1913, m. Frances Victoria Watson 26 Oct. 1870. She was born 1854 Ala., died 1920. They are buried in Rocky Mount Cem.. Issue:

    a. George M. Wise, b. 1871 Ala., d. 1935, buried Rocky Mount Cem., m. Cora L. Harrison 13 Nov. 1898. She was born 1877, died 1949, buried Rocky Mt. Cem..

    b. Ella Wise, b. ca 1875 Ala.

    c. John L. Wise, b. ca 1877 Ala.

    d. James O. (or D.) Wise, b. ca 1879 Ala.

8. (Susan?) Amanda Wise, b. ca 1847 Ala., may have married Thomas DuBose after 1870.

Also in the household of Ezekiel Wise in 1850 was Isabella Bullock, b. ca 1774 Md..

Ephriam S. Wise patented land a few miles South of Rocky
Mount Church in 1849. He was probably kin to Ezekiel Wise but
the relationship is not shown in the records. He was born ca
1800 N. C., died 21 Nov. 1882. His wife, Martha Ann (Milligan?)
was born ca 1815/20, died after 1880. Known issue:

1. Nancy Wise, b. ca 1833 Ala., m. Harvey Lee 1 Aug. 1853
   (see LEE).

2. William L. Wise, b. ca 1834 Ala., probably married Frances
   J. Purswell 6 Jan. 1853. Issue (from 1860 Census):
   a. Greenberry Wise, b. ca 1853 Ala.
   b. Frederick Wise, b. ca 1855 Ala.
   c. Henry Wise, b. ca 1857 Ala.
   d. Mary Wise, b. ca 1859 Ala.

3. Martha Wise, b. ca 1837 Ala., m. James W. Watson (or Watkins)
   23 Nov. 1856. They may have had a son, A. C. Watson.

4. Ezekiel Wise, b. ca 1840 Ala., d. by 1865, m. Barbara A.
   Vinson 28 July 1861. She m. (2) William H. Snead on 16 Nov.
   1865.

5. John Wise, b. ca 1845 Ala.

6. Sarah Maria Wise, b. 7 Oct. 1847 Ala., d. 29 July 1926, m.
   John G. Snead 9 Feb. 1866. He was born 11 May 1842, died
   28 July 187-. They are buried in Belcher Bethel Cem..

7. Leroy Wise, b. 7 May 1850 Ala., d. 27 Dec. 1928, m. "Daught"
   Ann Flowers 23 Dec. 1873. She was born 3 Aug. 1851, died
   21 April 1927. Both are buried in Rocky Mt. Cem.. Issue:
   a. Ida W. Wise, b. 30 Oct. 1874, d. 5 March 1900, m. W. S.
      Houston 12 Oct. 1893. He married (2) Josephone Wise,
      her sister.
   b. Lizzie J. Wise, b. 27 Feb. 1876, d. 18 Jan. 1964, m.

William E. Houston 20 Dec. 1894. He was born 12 June 1871, died 23 Nov. 1910. They are buried in Clayton Cem..

c. Josephine Wise, b. ca 1878 Ala., m. W. S. Houston 1 Aug. 1900.

d. Calvin Wise, b. 5 Nov. 1879, d. 21 Feb. 1902, never married. He is buried in Rocky Mount Cem..

e. Harry Lee Wise, b. 1 Dec. 1880 (?), d. 15 Feb. 1900, buried in Rocky Mount Cem..

f. Walter H. Wise, b. 10 Oct. 1882, d. 5 Jan. 1957, m. Helen A. Richards 25 Dec. 1904, daughter of Alonzo and Abigail (Wood) Richards (see RICHARDS). She was born 18 June 1887, died 1 Oct. 1926. Both are buried in County Line Cem..

g. Cullis E. Wise, b. ca 1890, d. Alexandria, La., m. Mamie I. Snead 14 Oct. 1913. At one time, they lived in Texas.

h. (H.?) Grady Wise, b. ca 1892, d. ca 1942/3, m. (1) Eulalie Turner 25 Dec. 1912 (2) ----. They lived in Florida.

i. Bunyan Wise, b. ca 1894, m. Thelma Journegan. In 1929, they were living in Albany, Ga..

j. Bowen Wise, b. ca 1894, d. Dec. 1971 Weatherford, Texas. He changed his name to Dink Mowrey.

8. Frances A. Wise, b. ca 1852 Ala., m. Sam J. Snead 28 Dec. 1880. He was born 15 Feb. 1852, died 15 June 1914, buried Belcher Bethel Cem.. Issue:

a. Clarence Snead.

9. Margy A. Wise, b. ca 1854 Ala., may have married William Anderson Lee 21 Jan. 1877 (see LEE).

This chapter on WOOD is included for two reasons - first because many readers of Vol. I has asked about my line, and second because of their close relationship (by marriages) to the RICHARDS family.

The Wood's came to Barbour Co. from Sampson Co., N. C. about 1832/5. Before then, they lived in Wayne and Bertie Cos., N. C. The progenitors of the line in N. C. were Furnifold Wood and his wife, Abigail ----. All but two of their known children migrated to Barbour and Henry Cos.. Issue:

1. Young Wood, b. 22 Sept. 1794 Sampson Co., N. C., d. by April 1862, m. Rosanna Byrd 22 Dec. 1825 in Wayne Co., N. C. She was born 27 Sept. 1802 Lenoir Co., N. C. and died ca Dec. 1884 Henry Co., Ala.. She was a daughter of Richard Byrd (wife Jean) who died in Johnston Co., N. C. Young Wood and Rosanna (Byrd) Wood are buried in unmarked graves in County Line Cem.. Issue:

    a. John R. Wood, b. 9 Nov. 1827 Wayne Co., N. C., - no record of him after 1860, when he was still unmarried and living with his parents. He may have been killed in the Civil War.

    b. Nancy Ann Wood, b. 5 Jan. 1829 Wayne Co., N. C., d. 4 July 1905 Henry Co., Ala., m. George W. Searcy ca 1845 in Georgetown, Ga.. He was born ca 1816 in Ga., died 26 April 1880 Henry Co., Ala.. They are buried in County Line Cem..

    c. Green Wood, b. 22 April 1830 Wayne Co., N. C., d. 23 Nov. 1909, m. Mary Elizabeth Hardwick 17 July 1859, daughter of Robert M. Hardwick. She was born 16 Feb. 1836 Ga., died 1 Oct. 1908. They are buried in County Line Cem..

335

d. William D. Wood, b. 22 Sept. 1835 Barbour Co., Ala. - no record after 1860, when he was practicing law with H. D. Clayton.

2. William Wood, b. 1800 N. C., d. 9 June 1875, never married. He is buried in Mt. Pleasant Cem..

3. James Wood, b. ca 1801 N. C., d. ca 1850/1, m. Nancy Byrd, sister of Rosanna Byrd who married Young Wood. She was born ca 1801 N. C., died between 1860 and 1870. Issue:

   a. Abigail J. Wood, b. ca 1831 N. C., m. Dr. Daniel C. Campbell 18 March 1851.

   b. Furnifold Manley Wood, b. 14 Jan. 1835 Sampson Co., N. C., d. 15 March 1877 Opelika, Ala., m. Sarah Roquemore 21 Dec. 1858, daughter of Zachariah Roquemore and Julia A. F. McGibboney. Sarah Roquemore was born 22 Nov. 1837 Ala., died 29 Oct. 1905. Both are buried in Fairview Cem., Eufaula, Ala..

   c. Zilpha C. Wood, b. ca 1837 Ala., m. Benjamin W. Searcy. They lived in Butler Co., Ala..

   d. Rose Ann Wood, b. ca 1839 Ala., m. Elias D. Stinson 17 May 1860.

   e. Amanda Wood, b. ca 1841 Ala., m. A. D. Fielder after 1880. She was his second wife - his first wife was her sister, Leonora Wood.

   f. Josephine Wood, b. ca 1843 Ala., m. Joel H. Rainer - she was his third wife. In 1880, they were living in Bullock Co., Ala..

   g. James S. (P.?) Wood, b. ca 1845 Ala. - no record after 1860.

   h. Leonora J. Wood, b. ca 1847 Ala., m. A. D. Fielder.

   i. Richard R. Wood, b. ca 1849 Ala., died before 1860.

4. Ollin M. P. Wood, b. ca 1803 N. C., d. July 1871, never

married.

5. Annie Wood, b. ca 1807 N. C., m. Lemuel Searcy ca 1828 in
   N. C.. Issue:

   a. Ollin McKinney Searcy, b. ca 1829 N. C., m. Martha S.
      Vinson 20 March 1868.

   b. James W. Searcy, b. ca 1832 N. C., m. Mahala ---- ca
      1856.

   c. John G. Searcy, b. 17 April 1834 N. C., d. 16 Oct. 1908,
      m. Catherine Pinkerton ca 1858. She was born 6 April
      1838 Ala., died 22 March 1914. They are buried in Mt.
      Pleasant Cem..

   d. Eliza Searcy, b. ca 1839 Ala.

   e. Narcissa Searcy, b. ca 1841 Ala.

   f. L. Dallas Searcy, b. 19 July 1844 Ala., d. 12 Feb. 1919,
      m. Margaret E. ---- ca 1866. She was born 29 June 1850
      Ala. and died 11 Jan. 1902. They are buried in County
      Line Cem..

   g. Emmett M. C. Searcy, b. ca 1846 Ala.

6. McKinney (Quinn) Wood, b. 17 Jan. 1811 N. C., d. 12 Aug.
   1884, m. Frances Landrum 30 Aug. 1837, daughter of George
   Landrum. She was born 28 Dec. 1820 Ga., died 25 Jan. 1905.
   They are buried in Mt. Pleasant Cem.. Issue:

   a. Pauline A. Wood, b. ca 1839 Ala., m. Eldridge G. Murphy
      11 Dec. 1866. They were living in Lorena, Texas in 1905.

   b. America Helen Wood, b. 15 Feb. 1840 Ala., d. 19 Feb.
      1881, never married. She is buried in Mt. Pleasant Cem.

   c. Frances Sophia Wood m. William Wesley Richards 3 Dec.
      1867 (see RICHARDS).

   d. James Carlton Wood, b. 25 Dec. 1845 Ala., d. 24 March
      1923, m. Minerva J. Ennis 23 Dec. 1870 Henry Co., Ala.
      She was born 11 Sept. 1848 and died 9 July 1905. They

are buried in Mt. Pleasant Cem..

e. George McKinney Wood, b. 3 Sept. 1847 Ala., d. 6 April
    1864, probably never married. He is buried in Mt.
    Pleasant Cem..

f. Abigail R. Wood m. Alonzo L. Richards 15 Dec. 1881
    (see RICHARDS).

g. William M. Wood, b. 20 July 1852 Ala., d. 25 Oct. 1926,
    m. Margaret J. Richards 15 Dec. 1881 Henry Co., Ala.
    She was born 14 Aug. 1854, died 25 Oct. 1904. They are
    buried in County Line Cem..

h. Samuel Butler Wood, b. 6 June 1857 Ala., d. 25 May 1932,
    m. Lonie Crawford 16 Dec. 1880. She was born 17 March
    1857, died 19 Oct. 1935 - both are buried in County
    Line Cem..

i. Benjamin L. Wood, b. 13 Dec. 1862 Ala., d. 1 April 1941,
    m. Willie Worrell. She was born 1 Jan. 1882 and died
    18 June 1964. They are buried in White Oak Methodist
    Church Cem..

There is no record in Barbour or Henry Co. of the parentage
of the following, but they were always considered "kin" to the
above Wood family. One source suggests that they are descendants
of Henry Wood, b. 1753 Orange Co., N. C., died after 1832 Burke
Co., Ga., m. Nancy Butler.

1. Green Washington (Wash) Wood, b. 23 Oct. 1812 N. C., d. 15
    Jan. 1905, m. (2) Elizabeth Crawford. She was born 29 Dec.
    1821 N. C., died 27 Dec. 1888. They are buried in Pond
    Bethel Cem.. Issue:
    By 1st wife:
    a. John Wood - no further record.
    b. Mary Wood - no further record.
    By 2nd wife:

339

c. Eleanor Adeline Wood, b. 29 Jan. 1842 Ala., d. 31 Aug. 1895, never married, buried Pond Bethel Cem..

d. John A. Wood, b. ca 1845 Ala., may have died in the Civil War.

e. Minerva Angeline Wood, b. 23 Dec. 1847 Ala., d. 28 Jan. 1920, never married, buried Pond Bethel Cem..

f. George F. (Furnifold?) Wood, b. 13 Jan. 1849 Ala., d. 16 Feb. 1937, m. Jane McGilvray. She was born 21 May 1852 and died 29 June 1940. They are buried in Pond Bethel Cem..

g. Lemuel Huey (Boss) Wood, b. ca 1854 Ala., m. Nancy Griffin. They are buried in Pond Bethel Cem. but there are no dates on their graves.

h. Abigail Wood, b. 1859 Ala., m. Asa C. Adams 19 Feb. 1880.

i. William W. (or Barlow D.) Wood, b. ca 1864 Ala., d. 1926, m. Margaret P. Lee 5 Nov. 1904. She died 1957 - both are buried in Pond Bethel Cem..

2. Epsey Suwanee Wood, b. 17 Feb. 1817 N. C., d. 6 Jan. 1886, m. John Lewis 12 Jan. 1837 in N. C...she was his second wife. He was born 1 March 1810 N. C., died 8 July 1873. Issue: By 1st wife:

a. Martha Jane Lewis, b. 16 Nov. 1827 N. C., d. 15 Aug. 1901, m. Nathan Williams 16 April 1859. He was born ca 1830 S. C., died July 1905. She is buried in Pond Bethel Cem..

b. John Wright Lewis, b. 12 Aug. 1831 N. C., d. 4 Jan. 1901 Texas, m. Alice West 23 June 1857.

c. Stephen Bright Lewis, b. 12 June 1833 N. C., d. 26 Jan. 1922, m. Polly Beasley 30 July 1857. They are buried in Pond Bethel Cem. but their graves may not be marked.

By 2nd wife:

d. George Washington Lewis, b. 2 Jan. 1838 N. C., d. 8 Oct. 1905, m. Mary A. McLain 7 Nov. 1861.

e. William Rufus Lewis, b. 19 July 1839 Ala., died in the Civil War, never married.

f. Lydia Ann Lewis, b. 9 Jan. 1841 Ala., d. 9 Dec. 1909, m. James Jernigan 14 Dec. 1865.

g. James Allen Lewis, b. 5 Nov. 1842 Ala., d. 11 Nov. 1912, buried CSA Cemetery, Mountain Creek, Ala., m. Laura A. Hubbard 3 Oct. 1884.

h. Nancy Texas Lewis, b. 12 Oct. 1844 Ala., d. 15 March 1912, m. H. J. Marley 30 Dec. 1869.

i. Rosa Etta Lewis, b. 29 Jan. 1847 Ala., d. 20 Dec. 1892, never married.

j. Green Angus Lewis, b. 30 March 1849 Ala., d. 13 Jan. 1886, m. Frances Penn 19 Dec. 1872.

k. Quincy Lewis, b. 22 May 1852 Ala., d. 5 Feb. 1906, m. Martha J. Parmer 19 Jan. 1879. She was born 24 Feb. 1857, died 27 Jan. 1936. They are buried in Pond Bethel Cem..

l. Piercy Eveline Lewis, b. 27 Aug. 1854 Ala., d. 22 Oct. 1931, m. E. Preston Adams 11 Nov. 1875.

m. Mary C. Lewis, b. 10 June 1856 Ala., d. 28 July 1913, m. J. W. (Pete) Floyd 3 Feb. 1895.

n. Frances Josephine Lewis, b. 3 May 1858 Ala., d. 2 Feb. 1899, m. James Abner Flowers 6 Nov. 1884. He was born 16 Oct. 1856, died 26 April 1929. He m. (2) Fannie Parish, b. 25 Sept. 1876, d. 15 April 1934. They are all buried in County Line Cem..

o. Marion Dixon Lewis, b. ca 1864 Ala., d. age 17 years.

3. Furnifold (F. F.) Wood, b. ca 1818 N. C., m. Mary ----, b.

ca 1818 N. C.. They may have moved to Biloxi, Miss.. Known issue:

a. Elizabeth Wood, b. ca 1840 Ala.

b. C. G. Wood (female), b. ca 1842 Ala.

c. Arthur C. Wood, b. ca 1845 Ala.

d. Annie E. Wood, b. ca 1847 Ala.

e. Marion Wood, b. ca 1848 Ala.

f. Sarah C. Wood, b. ca 1850 Ala.

g. William McD. Wood, b. ca 1852 Ala.

h. Mary J. Wood, b. ca 1855 Ala.

i. Lindsay Wood (female), b. ca 1858 Ala.

j. a son born 1860 Ala..

Other members of this family were probably Piercy Wood who married David Strickland and William R. Wood, b. ca 1822 N. C., m. Hannah E. Wood 3 Sept. 1840 Henry Co., Ala..

There was another Furnifold Wood (wife Ann) who sold land in Henry Co., Ala. in 1843. Mrs. C. T. Wilson of Florissant, Mo. believes he was the Furnifold Wood (wife Ann) who moved to Choctaw (now Webster) Co., Miss. by 1850. He was born ca 1797 N. C., probably died Webster Co., Miss. after 1860. Issue (from 1850 Census Choctaw Co., Miss.):

1. Anna W. Wood, b. ca 1825 N. C.

2. James B. Wood, b. ca 1826 N. C.

3. William J. Wood, b. ca 1830 N. C.

4. Furnifold Wood, Jr., b. 11 July 1834 N. C., d. 20 Oct. 1909 Webster Co., Miss., m. Mary E. Daniels.

5. Allen C. Wood, b. ca 1837 Ala.

6. Abigail Wood, b. ca 1839 Ala.

7. Young M. Wood, b. ca 1844 Ala.

8. William Henderson Wood, b. ca 1848 Miss.

Other sources:

CSA Pension application of Frances (Landrum) Wood
1850 Census Henry Co., Ala.
Henry Co., Ala. Probate Records
Lewis family data from Norma Lock Montgomery, Eufaula, Ala.
Wood Bible

Nicholas Zorn settled in Pike (now Barbour) Co. about
1829/30. There is also a Mrs. Anne Zorn in the 1830 Pike Co.
census, but no record of her in Barbour Co.. Nicholas Zorn
entered land between Bakerhill and Texasville from 1836 through
1852.

David Zorn (Sr.) also entered land there in 1836. He died
by May 1836, leaving minor heirs David Zorn, Jr. and Rebecca
Zorn....Nicholas Zorn was their guardian. Rebecca Zorn married
Francis Hartzog by Oct. 1844 (see HARTZOG).

There was a David Zorn in Henry Co., Ala. in 1850 and in
Barbour Co. in 1860 who may have been the son of David Zorn,
Sr.. He was born ca 1820 S. C., m. Sarah A. ----, b. ca 1823
S. C.. Their children (from 1850 & 1860 Census) were:

1. Nancy C. Zorn, b. ca 1842 Ala.
2. William H. Zorn, b. ca 1844 Ala., married Georgia Ann Powers
    8 April 1868 Henry Co., Ala.
3. Mary Zorn, b. ca 1846 Ala.
4. Nicholas Zorn, b. ca 1848 Ala.
5. Elizabeth (Esther?) Zorn, b. ca 1849 Ala.
6. Abigail Zorn, b. ca 1856 Ala.
7. Anderson C. Zorn, b. ca 1858 Ala.

David Zorn may have married (2) Caroline Zorn 16 Jan. 1868 in
Henry Co., Ala..

Nicholas Zorn was born ca 1808 S. C., died between 1870 and
1880. His wife, Sarah (Condrey?) was born ca 1808 S. C., died
after 1880. There is no estate record for either of them.
Issue (mostly from census records):

1. Catherine Zorn, b. ca 1830 Ala., m. Eli Thomas 20 Dec. 1849
    (see THOMAS).
2. Mary E. Zorn, b. ca 1832 Ala., m. Thomas L. Holley 24 Dec.

1857. He was born 22 Feb. 1834 Ga., died 12 Feb. 1865, buried New Hope Cem.. (see GRUBBS). Known issue:

    a. Samantha Jane Holley, b. 25 Feb. 1859, d. 26 Sept. 1861, buried New Hope Cem..

    b. Jasper K. Holley, b. 31 Aug. 1860, d. 24 March 1887, buried New Hope Cem..

    c. John Quincy Holley, b. 2 Jan. 1863, d. 30 Sept. 1898, buried New Hope Cem..

    d. Mary Holley, b. ca 1864 Ala..

3. Jane Zorn, b. ca 1834 Ala., may have married (1) ---- Thomas (2) D. E. Corbitt 26 Nov. 1856.

4. James D. Zorn, b. ca 1837 Ala., m. Josephine R. ---- ca 1860. He died by 1867 and she m. (2) Samuel M. Duffell 27 Nov. 1867. Issue (by James D. Zorn):

    a. Mary C. Zorn, b. ca 1860 Ala.

    b. Larkin J. Zorn, b. ca 1861 Ala.

    c. James D. Zorn, b. ca 1865 Ala..

5. Dennis H. Zorn, b. ca 1843 Ala., d. 1899 (buried Pond Bethel Cem.), m. Nancy Caroline Zorn 16 Jan. 1868 Henry Co., Ala. Known issue:

    a. Albert Zorn, b. ca 1870 Ala.

    b. Walter Zorn, b. ca 1872 Ala.

    c. Oscar Zorn, b. ca 1874 Ala.

    d. Alexander Zorn, b. ca 1879 Ala.

6. George W. Zorn, b. 9 April 1846 Ala., d. 25 Dec. 1922, m. Mary Ann Lee 11 Feb. 1869, daughter of Robert Lee (see LEE). She was born 10 July 1850, died 10 Sept. 1917 - both are buried in Pond Bethel Cem.. Known issue (maybe more):

    a. Mary Frances Zorn, b. Oct. 1869 Ala.

    b. James N. Zorn, b. 10 Oct. 1871 Ala., d. Dec. 1966, m. Sallie McLean 22 March 1896, who was born 8 July 1875 and died 22 May 1964. They are buried in Pond Bethel Cem..

c. Ida F. Zorn, b. 18 Oct. 1873, d. 24 Dec. 1873, buried Pond Bethel Cem..

d. Robert W. Zorn, b. 17 Oct. 1874 Ala., d. 25 May 1963, m. Ella V. Fillingim 10 Feb. 1898. She was born 27 Sept. 1873, died 12 Jan. 1952. They are buried Adams Chapel Cem.

e. George Austin Zorn, b. 2 Aug. 1877 Ala., d. 29 Nov. 1953, m. Sarah Addie Hartzog 9 Nov. 1899. She was born 11 May 1879, living in 1964. He is buried Adams Chapel Cem..

f. Emma Matilda Zorn, b. 2 Aug. 1877 Ala., d. 5 Sept. 1884, twin to George Austin Zorn - buried Pond Bethel Cem..

7. Zachary Taylor Zorn, b. ca 1849 Ala., d. Dec. 1887, never married.

In 1870, Harriet Shirah, age 16, was in the household of Nicholas Zorn.

Other sources:

Henry Co., Ala. Probate Records
Henry Co., Ala. Census Records

INDEX

BARBOUR COUNTY, ALABAMA

Prepared by
Eileene Sandlin
Fort Worth, Texas